Variegated Neoliberalism

'Huw Macartney's outstanding book represents a major step forward in our understanding of how neoliberalism has played out in contemporary Europe. It is also a very significant contribution to the growing literature on the role of ideas in political economy.'

Ben Rosamond, Professor, University of Warwick, UK

'Not since Kees van der Pijl's *The Making of an Atlantic Ruling Class* have we had such a fine-grained exploration of how exactly transnationally oriented classes engage with states and economies in order to cement a genuinely hegemonic order. Huw Macartney has done the research, and we are the wiser for it. His argument is one that every student of the contemporary global order will need to consult.'

Randall Germain, Professor, Department of Political Science,
Carleton University, Canada

We know from the cost of the 2007–09 crisis that transnational finance does not operate in a realm removed from our everyday lives.

Variegated Neoliberalism explains why its inequalities persist and how they undermine more social-minded policies towards finance in the EU.

The book suggests that large financial groups capitalize on broader changes in capitalism and emerging assumptions about what benefits society at large. Those pushing these political-economic projects present policy change to cope with financial globalization as a new common sense. Macartney's argument then contests these assumptions through an analysis of the spatial relations of transnational actors, and the political claims made within finance and research communities.

Rather than relying on umbrella concepts like 'transnational capitalist class', *Variegated Neoliberalism* emphasises the national-domestic foundations for transnationalization and what we commonly understand as neoliberalism. The book provides comparative analyses of global and European banking communities, and economic research centres, in the UK, France, and Germany. It explains the constellations underpinning the current neoliberal order in global finance, and the realms of possibility for challenges to it.

Variegated Neoliberalism will be of interest to students and scholars of International Political Economy, and the theories of Marx and Gramsci.

Huw Macartney is Hallsworth Fellow in Political Economy at the University of Manchester, UK.

RIPE series in Global Political Economy

Series Editors: Louise Amoore (*University of Durham, UK*), Jacqueline Best (*University of Ottawa, Canada*), Paul Langley (*Northumbria University, UK*) and Leonard Seabrooke (*Copenhagen Business School, Denmark)*

Formerly edited by Randall Germain (*Carleton University, Canada*), Rorden Wilkinson (*University of Manchester, UK*), Otto Holman (*University of Amsterdam, the Netherlands*), Marianne Marchand (*Universidad de las Américas-Puebla, Mexico)*, Henk Overbeek (*Free University, Amsterdam*) and Marianne Franklin (*Goldsmiths, University of London, UK*)

The RIPE series editorial board are:

Mathias Albert (*Bielefeld University, Germany*), Mark Beeson (*University of Birmingham, UK*), A. Claire Cutler (*University of Victoria, Canada*), Marianne Franklin (*Goldsmiths, University of London, UK*), Randall Germain (*Carleton University, Canada*) Stephen Gill (*York University, Canada*), Jeffrey Hart (*Indiana University, USA*), Eric Helleiner (*Trent University, Canada*), Otto Holman (*University of Amsterdam, the Netherlands*), Marianne H. Marchand *(Universidad de las Américas-Puebla, Mexico)*, Craig N. Murphy (*Wellesley College, USA*), Robert O'Brien (*McMaster University, Canada*), Henk Overbeek (*Vrije Universiteit, the Netherlands*), Anthony Payne (*University of Sheffield, UK*), V. Spike Peterson (*University of Arizona, USA*) and Rorden Wilkinson (*University of Manchester, UK*).

This series, published in association with the *Review of International Political Economy*, provides a forum for current and interdisciplinary debates in international political economy. The series aims to advance understanding of the key issues in the global political economy, and to present innovative analyses of emerging topics. The titles in the series focus on three broad themes:

- the structures, processes and actors of contemporary global transformations
- the changing forms taken by governance, at scales from the local and everyday to the global and systemic
- the inseparability of economic from political, social and cultural questions, including resistance, dissent and social movements.

The series comprises two strands:

The *RIPE Series in Global Political Economy* aims to address the needs of students and teachers, and the titles will be published in hardback and paperback. Titles include:

Transnational Classes and International Relations
Kees van der Pijl

Gender and Global Restructuring
Sightings, sites and resistances
Edited by Marianne H Marchand and Anne Sisson Runyan

Global Political Economy
Contemporary theories
Edited by Ronen Palan

Ideologies of Globalization
Contending visions of a new world order
Mark Rupert

The Clash within Civilisations
Coming to terms with cultural conflicts
Dieter Senghaas

Global Unions?
Theory and strategies of organized labour in the global political economy
Edited by Jeffrey Harrod and Robert O'Brien

Political Economy of a Plural World
Critical reflections on power, morals and civilizations
Robert Cox with Michael Schechter

A Critical Rewriting of Global Political Economy
Integrating reproductive, productive and virtual economies
V. Spike Peterson

Contesting Globalization
Space and place in the world economy
André C. Drainville

Global Institutions and Development
Framing the world?
Edited by Morten Bøås and Desmond McNeill

Global Institutions, Marginalization, and Development
Craig N. Murphy

Critical Theories, International Relations and 'the Anti-Globalisation Movement'
The politics of global resistance
Edited by Catherine Eschle and Bice Maiguashca

Globalization, Governmentality, and Global Politics
Regulation for the rest of us?
Ronnie D. Lipschutz, with James K. Rowe

Critical Perspectives on Global Governance
Rights and regulation in governing regimes
Jean Grugel and Nicola Piper

Beyond States and Markets
The challenges of social reproduction
Edited by Isabella Bakker and Rachel Silvey

The Industrial Vagina
The political economy of the
global sex trade
Sheila Jeffreys

Capital as Power
A study of order and creorder
Jonathan Nitzan and Shimshon Bichler

**The Global Political Economy of
Intellectual Property Rights,
Second Edition**
The new enclosures
Christopher May

**Corporate Power and Ownership in
Contemporary Capitalism**
The politics of resistance and
domination
Susanne Soederberg

Savage Economics
Wealth, poverty and the temporal
walls of capitalism
*David L. Blaney and
Naeem Inayatullah*

Cultural Political Economy
*Edited by Jacqueline Best and
Matthew Paterson*

**Gender and Global Restructuring,
Second Edition**
Sightings, sites and resistances
*Edited by Marianne H. Marchand and
Anne Sisson Runyan*

Routledge/RIPE Studies in Global Political Economy is a forum for innovative new research intended for a high-level specialist readership, and the titles will be available in hardback only. Titles include:

Variegated Neoliberalism

EU varieties of capitalism and international political economy

Huw Macartney

Routledge
Taylor & Francis Group

LONDON AND NEW YORK

First published 2011 by Routledge
2 Park Square Milton Park Abingdon Oxon OX14 4RN
52 Vanderbilt Avenue, New York, NY 10017

Routledge is an imprint of the Taylor & Francis Group, an informa business.

Typeset in Times New Roman
by Keystroke, Station Road, Codsall, Wolverhampton

British Library Cataloguing in Publication Data
A catalogue record for this book is available from the British Library

Library of Congress Cataloging in Publication Data
    Macartney, Huw.
    Variegated neoliberalism : EU varieties of capitalism and international
    political economy / Huw Macartney.
    p. cm. – (RIPE series in global political economy)
    Includes bibliographical references and index.
    1. Finance–European Union countries. 2. Neoliberalism–European
    Union countries. 3. Capitalism–European Union countries.
    4. International economic integration–European Union countries.
    5. European Union. I. Title.
    HG186.A2M33 2011
    330.94–dc22
                                                              2010022702

ISBN: 978–0–415–60150–4 (hbk)

Sa tatlong pinakamamahal ko – Ang Maykapal, and asawa ko, Raquel, at ang aking anak, Asia.

Contents

Figures

Acknowledgements

My interest in financial markets began as an undergraduate at the University of Manchester and I would like to thank Jill Lovecy, Gareth Api Richards and Claire Annesley for their exposition of European varieties of capitalism. I spent some time living in continental Europe, and their module provided an intellectual framework for the real-life experiences I witnessed in the run-up to EMU. Their teaching only served to compound my concerns, however, at what appeared to be the gradual departure from more socially equitable models. Later, these reflections were fleshed out whilst handling insurance products and financial instruments. In particular, it was these experiences that gave me a sense of the 'lottery' that is financial investment. Even then it seemed to me – albeit less explicitly – that the two elements (the relative demise of social equity and the rise of financial markets) were connected. This book is the product of these early musings.

In turn, I owe an incredible intellectual debt to Mick Moran and Stuart Shields. In essence, Mick's pragmatism, wisdom, support, and knowledge of financial markets gave me hope during the wilderness years that are the PhD. Stuart, on the other hand, introduced me to the 'dark side' (*sic*) through his repeated calls to critically examine my earlier – somewhat naive – assumptions; his frequent quips about Anakin Skywalker would have been amusing had they not had more than an element of truth to them. In turn, I am also very grateful to both Andreas Bieler and Adam Morton, both for their earlier efforts to re-engage with Gramsci's writings and for their friendship and support during the postdoctoral fellowship I spent in Nottingham. In terms of circulating earlier drafts of the manuscript for comments, I should add Ian Bruff to this list of acknowledgements; as a fivesome they have been simply invaluable. In addition, I want to thank Randall Germain, Phil Cerny, Kees van der Pijl, Lucia Quaglia, Greig Charnock, Dimitris Papadimitriou, Nicola Phillips and two anonymous reviewers for their comments and criticisms of earlier work that prompted crucial reflection. A big thank you also goes to Ben Rosamond for his advice on the completed manuscript and – especially – to Len Seabrooke for his support through the final stages. I would also like to thank the ESRC for their PhD (PTA–030–2003–01389) and postdoctoral funding (PTA–026–27–1784), which enabled the original research. Of course, I take full responsibility for the end product.

Finally, I would like to thank the group of people who help to keep me grounded. First, I need to thank my parents for their hard work and sacrifice in providing financial and emotional support through (what I affectionately call) the 'education decades'. I really could not have asked for a more loving and devoted family. Secondly, my wife Raquel has been more than a friend and partner. She is my soulmate. Her *joie de vivre* keeps me (almost) sane and reminds me that most of what is good about life has little to do with academia. Similarly – and in an age where faith is scarce and yet (in my opinion) ever more necessary – I want to thank God (Acts 17: 16–31) for undeserved opportunities time and again. What follows is dedicated to this final group in particular.

Abbreviations

AFEI   Association Française des Entreprises d'Investissements
BBA   British Bankers Association
BdB   Bundesverband deutscher Banken
BCBS   Basel Committee on Banking Supervision
BVI   Bundesverband Investment und Asset Management
BVR   Bundesverband der Deutschen Volksbanken und Raiffeisenbanken
CB   Commission Bancaire
CEPII   Centre d'Etudes Prospectives et d'Informations Internationales
CESifo   Centre for Economic Studies & Information und Forschung
CESR   Committee of European Securities Regulators
CRD   Capital Requirements Directive
EFN   European Forecasting Network
FBF   French Banking Federation
FSA   Financial Services Authority
HVB   Hypo Vereinung Bank
IFD   Initiativ Finanzstandort Deutschland
LIBA   London Investment Banking Association
MiFID   Markets in Financial Instruments Directive
NIESR   National Institute for Economic and Social Research
RBS   Royal Bank of Scotland
UBS   Union Bank of Switzerland
ZKA   Zentraler Kredit Ausschuss

Part I

EU financial market integration

1 Globalization and financial market integration

Faced by failure of credit, they have proposed only the lending of more money. Stripped of the lure of profit by which to induce our people to follow their false leadership, they have resorted to exhortations, pleading tearfully for restored confidence. They only know the rules of a generation of self-seekers.

(Franklin Roosevelt, 4 March 1933)

Introduction

The 2007–09 financial crisis has once again put finance back on the agenda. This book examines financial systems and – albeit indirectly – argues that the crisis is the logical outcome of neoliberal capitalism. The main objective of this study then is to demystify the process (or processes) of neoliberalization. More concretely it focuses on the European case study where historically averse European member states have nonetheless engaged in (variegated) processes of neoliberalization, producing convergent divergence. Finally, it focuses still more closely on EU financial market integration in the post–2000 era. This unique period has witnessed a new degree of impetus in neoliberal reform, with over forty directives aimed at integrating financial markets ratified in just a few years. With hindsight, this enthusiasm is worth questioning.

Opinion is divided, however, over the costs and benefits of neoliberalism. Western policymakers alongside mainstream economists now typically argue for labour market flexibility, the reduction of cross-border trade barriers, and more efficient capital allocation. They reason that such structural reforms produce trickle-down effects on a global scale. On the other hand, some suggest that whilst the millionaires' yachts cope well with this 'rising tide', those in rubber dinghies or – worse – deflated rubber armbands, are slowly drowning.

Despite global institutions' protestations, neoliberalism systematically fuels rising inequalities and is predicated on a credit-financed mode of capitalism since – at its core – it is an attempt to restore and confirm capitalist class rule (Harvey 2007: 2). It generates a huge redistribution of wealth effects upwards towards the working rich (notably in Europe and the US) – exacerbating income inequalities (Dumenil and Levy 2001; Froud *et al.* 2001; Montgomerie and Williams 2009: 101). Neoliberalism is therefore both precondition and product of the global restructuring of capitalism, itself predicated upon and fuelled by the realignment of social actors and the reconstitution of dominant worldviews. It is expressed ideologically in the assumptions of market rationality and the liberalization of entrepreneurial freedoms; it is embedded in relatively fixed multi-scalar institutional frameworks; it is shaped by and constitutive of the transnationalization of capitalism and associated transnationally oriented class agency; and it generates a series of fluid yet relatively path-dependent impulsions in the restructuring of global capitalism. It was therefore rooted in burgeoning contradictions in the capital–labour relation, yet displaced through financial expansion and shaped – and further propelled – through the agency of particular fractions of capital and state actors. As a result, neoliberalization is a *process*, rather than a *model* of capitalism.

The 2007–09 crisis

Thus, the dynamics of the 2007–09 crisis mirror this historic global trend. A series of short-, medium- and long-term contingencies generated the worst financial instability since 1929. The 'causes' were essentially Anglo-American: excessive leveraging in US sub-prime markets; burgeoning US current account deficits financed by foreign currencies; prolonged low interest rates fuelling housing bubbles and excessive consumer debt; profligate private banking practices and bonus cultures rewarding high-risk, off balance-sheet ventures; and the list continues. The 'solutions' have however, overwhelmingly centred on gargantuan bailout packages to restore liquidity and jumpstart global credit markets and industry. Already by October 2008, the collective figures for Western Europe, China and the US were estimated to be as high as $3,000bn (Financial Times 2008). In effect, more credit to finance the bad debt problem. As they say, you couldn't make this up.

Yet – and here's the real punchline – it's the taxpayer who ultimately foots the bill, through wage or welfare spending cuts and unemployment. For example, repossession cases in the UK rocketed by 70 per cent in 2008 (Guardian 2008), 3,960 people per day in the US filed for bankruptcy in February 2008 (*New York Times*, 5 March 2008), and Eurozone unemployment figures rose to 9.4 per cent in 2009 (and as high as 17.2 per cent in Latvia) (ECB 2009: S54, S74). Meanwhile financial elites like Richard Fuld, former CEO of Lehman Brothers, retained his personal remuneration of $480m acquired prior to the bank's collapse. This was also the case for Sir Fred Goodwin of the Royal Bank of Scotland and numerous other CEOs and high-flying traders. Further, parties of the Left and Right began announcing a series of pay freezes, pension cuts and labour market reforms to cut the deficit. In sum, this is typical of neoliberalism.

So this book targets neoliberalization, the apparent changing interests of EU member states, and the recent financial market integration efforts, as unique symptoms of wider global dynamics. These three issues require three theoretical premises and the book in turn makes three core claims. The theoretical premises derive from Gramscian historical materialism, in the form of capitalism's impulsions and crises; the strategic agency of capital; and Gramsci's notion of common sense. As we shall see, the Gramscian account departs from a rationalist emphasis on agents and institutions, and a constructivist emphasis on ideas in the hands of these agents. Instead, the book explains the dialectic of the impulsions–agency–common sense nexus with both its dynamisms and 'path dependencies'.

More specifically, the three core arguments of this study are that: first, neoliberalism is inherently *variegated* (that is, defined by its diversity and both cause and effect of the impulsions–agency–common sense nexus) rather than the 'neoliberal = Anglo-Saxon' binary implicit in the Varieties of Capitalism alternative (Macartney 2009a); second, the book highlights the strategic agency of *transnationally oriented fractions* of capital at the apex of the global restructuring of capitalism; and finally, it argues that the agency of both state and capital is embedded within a nascent neoliberal *common sense* as socially constructed worldviews open to political contestation. As a result the book contributes to the Gramscian counter-hegemonic project, emphasizing both the determined and contingent nature of neoliberalism whilst highlighting the unique window of opportunity provided by crises. The future of European integration is therefore not set in stone (Bieler 2002). Neoliberalism is *relatively* open-ended and change requires both class struggle and – so this book argues – a nuanced conception of the dynamics, agents and discourses of neoliberalization.

Why Europe?

Analysis of neoliberalization is therefore connected to prospects for national diversity. If neoliberalism were – 'in reality' – the only and the best alternative then such questions would be, at best unnecessary, or at worst, futile. This conclusion has however, been rejected. Thus the book problematizes the trend for previously *distinct* nationally organized models of capitalism, *averse* to neoliberal-type reform, to display certain obvious and alarming similarities. Of course, post-war capitalisms were always embedded within a world market but the post-Bretton Woods era has constituted a new epoch in global capitalism. This is manifest – *inter alia* – in discourses of competitiveness, market liberalization, institutional reconfiguration and corporate governance reforms. They reflect the fact that neoliberalization generates and is generated by both exogenous and endogenous pressures for change. Through historical materialist lenses, capitalism – in general – engenders unequal social relations related to the subordination of human existence to the search for profit, but neoliberalism raises certain historically specific concerns. For example, I am troubled by the obvious departure from more socially equitable models of capitalist development with extensive welfare provisions. Instead, neoliberal processes centred on the exponential expansion of credit – manifested in so-called 'financialization' – are establishing the Bucking Bronco capitalism evidenced in the 2007–09 crisis.[1]

At the heart of this study lies the following puzzle: why have historically averse states – albeit to varying degrees – pursued neoliberalization? The obvious institutionalist answer would tend to suggest a convergence of national preferences

(Moravscik 1998). The Varieties of Capitalism (VoC) approach has tended to problematize the convergence thesis arguing for multi-polar clustering; by implication this is not 'neoliberalization' but multiple and distinct trajectories (Hall and Soskice 2001). Constructivism – for all its merits – would tend to argue that, if there has indeed been convergence, it corresponds substantively to the framing of interests and the construction of dominant neoliberal worldviews. The book argues – through variegated neoliberalism and class analysis – that all three are simultaneously correct and incorrect. They all highlight formal elements of reform trajectories without connecting the dots. For example, put simply: rationalist–institutionalism would be right to note the appearance of converging national preferences but there is no a-priori reason that this should be of a neoliberal type; the VoC account would rightly note that this is not simply Anglo-American convergence, yet here they conflate neoliberalism with an Anglo-American model; and constructivism accurately highlights changing and socially constructed worldviews, yet without a class-based theory of capitalism there is no explanation of the underlying significance of these processes occurring on a global scale. I argue that these *formal* observations are embedded within changing structural conditions and their accompanying relations of power (Bieler and Morton 2008).

First, however, we must consider the evidence for the 'previously averse-states' claim. The study focuses primarily on the EU and, in particular, the cases of the UK, France and Germany. The EU has been a testing ground for neoliberalization and provides stark examples of wider dynamics. As a participant-observer of these trends in recent decades I find them to be of personal as well as intellectual significance. Further, in the UK, France and Germany we find the three archetypal national models – the Anglo-American, the *dirigiste* (interventionist) and the *soziale Marktwirtschaft* (social market) political economies – with increasing, startling similarities (and yet, obvious differences). Interests, institutions and policy directions obviously change. My concern is – in part – to explain the mechanisms from which this change derives.

Three historical snapshots

The three member states in question developed distinctive forms of Keynesian demand-management regimes in the post-war era. These so-called 'national models of capitalism' varied dramatically, influenced by – *inter alia* – ideologies on the role of the state; policies of comparative advantage and export special-ization; pre-war market conditions; interconnectedness with neighbouring states; and cultural predispositions (Crouch and Streeck 1997). John Zysman's seminal contribution characterized these as the *capital market-based system* (UK) allocating resources by competitively established prices; the *credit-based financial system with government administered prices* (France) facilitating and encouraging government intervention; and the *credit-based system dominated by financial institutions* (Germany) in a negotiated style of capitalism (1983: 18).

For Zysman, the differentiating feature lay in patterns of converting savings into investments and then reallocating these investments among competing users (ibid.: 55). Though outdated, this provides a stylized account of the differences between the UK, French and German 'models'. Within the capital market-based system (such as in the UK) a range of primary and secondary stock and bond markets operate as the main pools of finance. Here the state plays an arms-length role as regulator of market transactions whilst companies issue initial public offerings (IPOs) of company equity in primary markets and this equity is subsequently traded through secondary markets. Under these conditions,

> the textbook notion of financial markets is that prices are set by the efforts of lenders to get the cheapest money for their different projects. In this perfect market, savers are offered a variety of investment options tailored to meet individual preferences for the balance between risk and return.
>
> (Zysman 1983: 65)

The distinction, at least in principle, between a bank and a non-bank financial institution is therefore evident: a non-banking institution such as an investment firm 'invests money that it collects either in exchange for a service it performs or by borrowing it'; a bank however, 'takes in deposits and lends out more money than it takes in . . . creating money (in the form of credit) in the process' (ibid.: 59). In both credit-based systems (France and Germany), this distinction is significant. Where companies in the former would turn to capital markets and investment firms, the two latter models would (traditionally) depend on bank loans. These latter systems were typically tied to late and rapid growth requiring state assistance in organizing financial resource provision (Zysman 1983: 63; van der Pijl 2006).

Nonetheless, in reality, in both credit-based systems a degree of cohesion developed between finance (banks) and industry. This was largely absent in capital market-systems where the imperative for profit and the opportunity to pursue it will often prompt investors to dump poorly performing instruments. As Zysman himself noted 'the distinction between a capital market-system, with its emphasis on influence by exit and a credit-based system, with its emphasis on influence by voice, can be observed in the lending and investment policies of financial institutions' (1983: 64).

In both France and Germany then, historically and geographically specific systems developed on the back of credit financing. In France this was a 'financial network economy' (Morin 2000) built on interlocking directorships, cross-shareholdings and a strong degree of elite solidarity. The *grands écoles* trained cohorts of cadres who maintained connections as future managers of French banks and companies. Coupled with the shareholdings of a small group of investors from this same elite, these close relations between firms, boards and large shareholders provided a relatively coherent direction to French capitalism (Clift 2004: 93; Morin 2000: 38). The French model was also characterized by the extent of French state involvement or '*dirigisme*'. As explained above, this involved both the allocation of capital to an industrial core and the promotion of national (industrial) champions (Cohen 1995: 23–30).

In Germany the credit-based system had certain similarities and some obvious differences. It was characterized by universal banks in a 'social market economy' (*soziale Marktwirtschaft*). The central idea was for framework regulations and the enabling state to facilitate self-adjusting market mechanisms and a high degree of social equity (tightly clustered wage distribution, consensual decision-making and high welfare spending). As for credit provisions, a system of *hausbanken* allowed banks a large and sustained role in German industry; they were therefore financiers and decision-making board members (Reberioux 2002: 124). Again, the cohesion lent itself to longer-term priorities than are generated by immediate shareholder incentive structures.

The particularity of each model is clear. Further, obvious features of the 'Anglo-American model' repulsed its counterparts, notably: shareholder value; welfare austerity; and the adverse effects of short-termist foreign investment (Steil 1995). In particular, the emphasis on shareholder profits around which Anglo-American corporate governance revolved shaped resistance to the latter two.[2] Shareholder value therefore contends that since holders of shares 'bear the risk the company should be run in their interest', producing a market-based system of management (Reberioux 2002: 118, 113). Since this structure affected not only the internal organization of the firm, but inter-firm (including between finance and industry), state–firm, and management–labour relations they could potentially re-shape the very fabric of society (Morin 2000: 38–42; Reberioux 2002: 112–14; Schmidt 2002: 107).

The following summary is by no means comprehensive, but is certainly indicative. Suffice it to note that much has changed (see Figures 1.1, 1.2 and 1.3). Three indicators are provided: the amount of company shares owned by foreign investors (indicated by FDI inflows); size of stock market (measured in market capitalization); and government spending on welfare.

Of particular note are three trends: (i) all three countries have witnessed a substantial increase in inflows of Foreign Direct Investment (FDI); (ii) in all three countries the percentage of finance raised through capital markets has increased; and (iii) government spending on welfare (in France and Germany) appears to have levelled out from the mid 1990s. A further comment can be added: it appears that, in several respects, the UK has led the way. It has witnessed a tenfold increase in FDI, as compared to fivefold for France and a final sum almost three-and-a-half times the size of the German equivalent. Its market capitalization (as a percentage) far exceeds those of its counterparts. It has consistently spent less (as a percentage) on welfare than its counterparts. Figure 1.4 supports this conclusion, suggesting that – on three occasions (during the mid 1980s and early and mid 1990s) – the UK led the way in economic performance with its continental European counterparts subsequently mirroring this upswing. Thus, drawing together Zysman's account and the brief snapshots in these Figures, it would appear that – on certain indicators – both French and German systems bear similarities to the UK. This

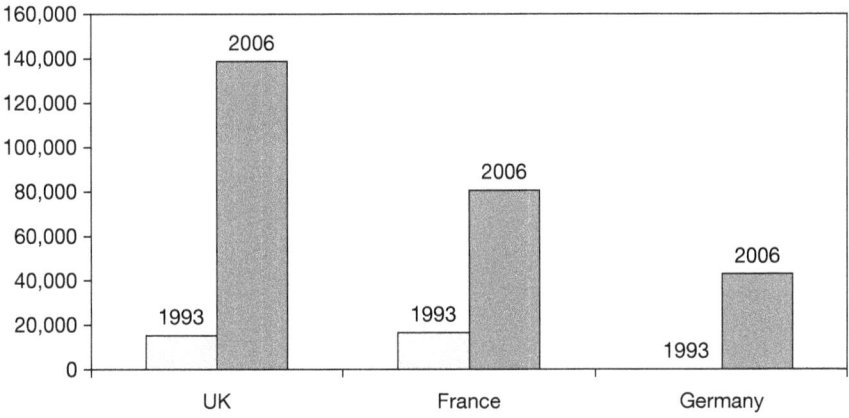

Figure 1.1 Inflows of FDI ($m).
Source: OECD.

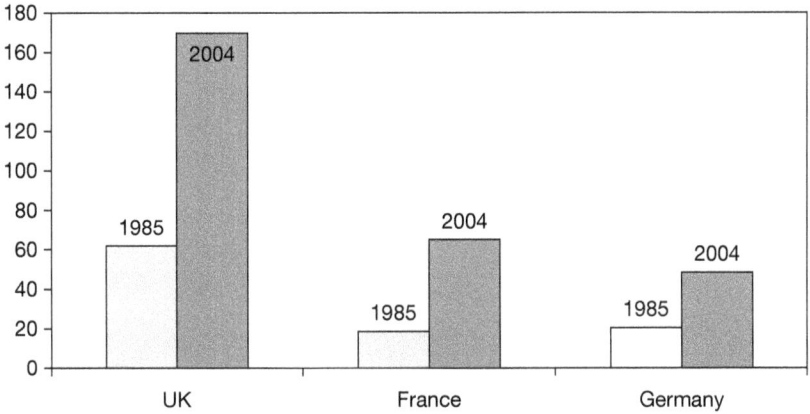

Figure 1.2 Market capitalization (% GDP).
Source: OECD.

book asks: given the historical opposition why has this occurred and, equally importantly, to what extent?

Locating finance?

This would suggest that 'finance' is at the apex of these transformations. Admittedly, the advent of the Eurozone and Economic and Monetary Union (EMU) have dramatically reshaped European capitalisms. Yet – though related to

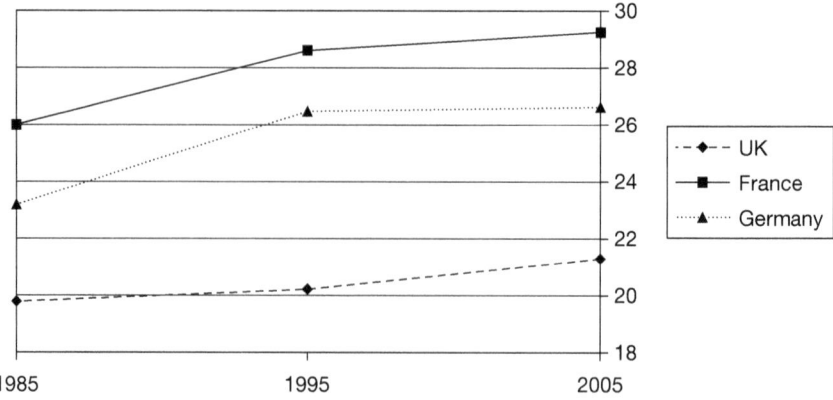

Figure 1.3 Government welfare spending (% GDP).
Source: OECD.

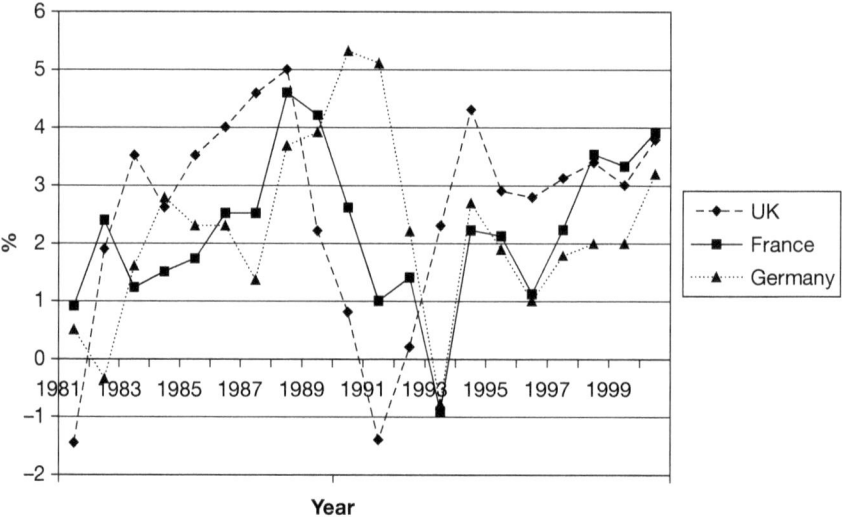

Figure 1.4 Economic performance (1981–2000).
Source: OECD.

the single market initiative – EMU is an explanation requiring a further explanation; it is a symptom of underlying processes. Nonetheless, a second factor, the integration of production processes, has also clearly reshaped national capitalisms (van Apeldoorn 2002). The crises of the late 1970s and early 1980s were manifested in global economic stagnation and an increasing awareness of the limits to the post-war Keynesian settlements. As van Apeldoorn (2002: 65) noted, European capitalisms rested on a 'class compromise' between big business and big labour which began to unravel when falling productivity came into conflict with progressively rising wage demands and increased global liquidity. Where van Apeldoorn sought to explain the renewed impetus for EU integration this study examines the shape the ensuing changes took.

EU integration is driven by capitalism's accumulation imperative: the pre-requisite for which is access to additional sources of materials, investments and labour as well as the expansion of markets. Nonetheless, since the crisis was represented in a fall in the rates of profit, the neoliberal shift which occurred – against the background of new classical, monetarist and rational expectations claims – was therefore an attempt to restore the class power of sections of the capitalist class over European working classes (Harvey 2007: 19).[3] The ensuing attempts to liberalize and integrate markets for goods, services, investment and labour predictably created both exogenous and endogenous pressures for the reform of these three models of capitalism. Yet neoliberalism pivots on a *finance-led* mode of accumulation.

Finance therefore occupies a unique position for the following reasons: the epicentres of the responses to the crises were predominantly *financial* centres with dominant financial elites; the so-called 'neoliberal shift' offset rather than resolved the crises of the 1970s through an expansion of the financial system (Macartney 2009b: 118); and the former elements – predicated on the neoliberal argument that liberalization serves 'human wellbeing' – reinvigorated a dynamic of first-mover (heartland) states and late-developer (contender) states fuelling pressures for competitive financial market reform. Chapter 2 deals with these contentions more adequately. For now I simply highlight the unique importance of finance to our study of neoliberalization.

EU financial market integration

Though EU financial market reform has been on the agenda since the 1950s there is evidence of a shift in pace and degree in the late 1990s. The difficulties encountered by the EU integration process prior to 2000 have been well documented in both academic literature and official documents;[4] here only an overview is provided. In 1988 the EU commissioned a report on the state of cross-border financial market activities which became known as the Cecchini Report. It is telling that over a decade later a second EU report highlighted largely the same set of deficiencies (Cecchini 1988: 5–13; Commission 1988: 1–4; Commission 2001: 12–15); in effect, little had changed. The second report, drafted by a self-entitled 'Committee of Wise Men', highlighted the following factors as cause for concern: the slow passage of legislation; poor implementation on the part of certain member states; significant technical or fiscal barriers left untouched by EU legislation; and impracticable compromise legislation. Together these elements severely hindered the construction of a single financial market.

Whilst significant pieces of legislation such as the Investment Services Directive (ISD) (Directive 93/22/EEC (1993)) *were* ratified during the 1990s the political impetus required to 'level the playing field' was largely lacking.[5] In a pamphlet published by the Royal Institute of International Affairs in the mid 1990s, Benn Steil (1995) noted the following shortcomings in the EU integration process. First, that 'European Community Member States continue unilaterally to implement regulations which disadvantage producers from other member states, in some cases knowingly exploiting 'escape clauses' which had been strategically inserted in European law' (Steil 1995: 2). He also claimed that integrated financial markets were impeded by member states' reluctance to *implement* legislation they had committed to (ibid.: 32) or they were simultaneously drawing up counteractive national legislation (ibid.: 31). The progress of the single financial market was being impeded by the desire to protect domestic comparative advantages. These tensions are – of course – still evident. There is, however, an increased concern for liberalization and integration – even if it means sacrificing certain domestic advantages. It is this transformation which concerns me.

Steil's claims were echoed in the work of Geoffrey Underhill (1997: 114) and Philip Brown (1997: 133) who highlighted the fears of continental European countries (including Germany and/or 'Club Med' countries) that their firms would lose out to more competitive Anglo-American rivals. Indeed a study by the Commission published shortly afterwards confirmed that, in terms of openness to capital movements, France and Germany both ranked among the five least 'open' countries; they stated that 'there remain in force in most member states a number of measures, generally of an administrative nature, designed to protect the interests of domestic markets, institutions or residents' (Commission 1997: 75). The phrasing of Steil's concluding comments is of note then. He asserted that 'the only way that multinational legislation will actually end up being liberalizing is if the member states involved see it as being in their *best interests*' (Steil 1995: 47, emphasis added). His statement suggests that during the 1990s certain member states viewed aspects of the financial integration project as contrary to these so-called 'best interests'.

By 2000 something had begun to change. Whilst this study does not aim to *explain* these changes directly it employs them as an *entry point* into the internal dynamics of neoliberal processes. The 2001 report by the Committee of Wise Men made several recommendations to overcome the legislative deficiencies of the 1990s (see above). This renewed focus on financial integration was a component of a wider agenda to remedy financial market deficiencies. The Lisbon Agenda, for example, launched at the European Council in Lisbon (March 2000) aimed at making the EU 'the most competitive and dynamic knowledge-based economy in the world, capable of sustainable economic growth with more and better jobs and greater social cohesion' (Council 2000). It was also connected to the Financial Services Action Plan (FSAP) launched in 1999, which comprised 42 original measures including over 30 directives, aimed at constructing a harmonized market in banking, insurance, investment, derivatives and commodities.[6] The FSAP was finally published on the 11 May 1999 and followed a series of Commission

Communications concerned with developing a framework for achieving the single financial market. The FSAP marks the recognition on the part of the Commission that an integrated financial market is a primary motor for European economic growth.

The FSAP targeted six areas: establishing a common legal framework; removing remaining barriers to raising capital on an EU-wide basis; moving towards a single set of financial statements for listed companies; creating a coherent legal framework for supplementary pension funds; providing the legal certainty to underpin cross-border securities dealings; and creating a secure and transparent environment for cross-border restructuring (Commission 1999). Significantly though, these developments rested upon a new degree of consensus amongst both EU institutions and EU member states on the need for hastening financial market reform (Interview Deutsche Bank). In their Final Report, the Committee of Wise Men noted that 'as a result of the consultation process, the Committee believes that there is a *strong consensus* on the need to deliver the European Commission's Financial Services Action Plan as soon as possible' (emphasis added) before adding that this was 'an almost consensual view' and that 'almost all respondents agreed' (Lamfalussy 2001: 7) to convey the degree of support for the integrated financial market. This level of agreement was reinforced by the ensuing Lamfalussy Process itself. The Process restructured the financial market legislative process, aiming to hasten the realization of the FSAP. The Committee was chaired by Alexandre Lamfalussy, the former President of the European Monetary Institute (EMI) and was tasked with assessing how best to adapt securities regulation and coordination between national regulators to ensure more effective transposition and implementation of legislation.

The Committee identified the functioning of the institutional framework as the primary shortcoming. It was too time-consuming; produced legislation which was overly complex and hence difficult to amend with changing market conditions; and was often poorly implemented and enforced (Lamfalussy 2001: 14, 18–19). In response they proposed a four-level approach[7] which was accepted by the ECOFIN Council on 22 March 2001, the European Council of Stockholm (23–24 March 2001) and the European Parliament (5 February 2002). The framework signalled a further entrenchment of rescaled governance within the EU, thereby intrinsically linked to the shifts within the member states themselves (Macartney and Moran 2008). This new process provides the basis for much of the empirical material for the ensuing chapters.

The final major puzzle for this book is thus: given that post–2000 EU financial market reform is a unique, recent example of previously averse member states pursuing neoliberalization, what can it tell us about the dynamics of neoliberalism? I argue that these lessons are significant for Gramscian counter-hegemony.

The puzzles which inform this study have now been outlined: the first is an attempt to demystify globalization and, more specifically, neoliberalization; the second takes the case of European models of capitalism and asks why previously averse states have pursued neoliberalization; the third focuses on recent EU financial market integration and asks what can be learnt from the recent change in

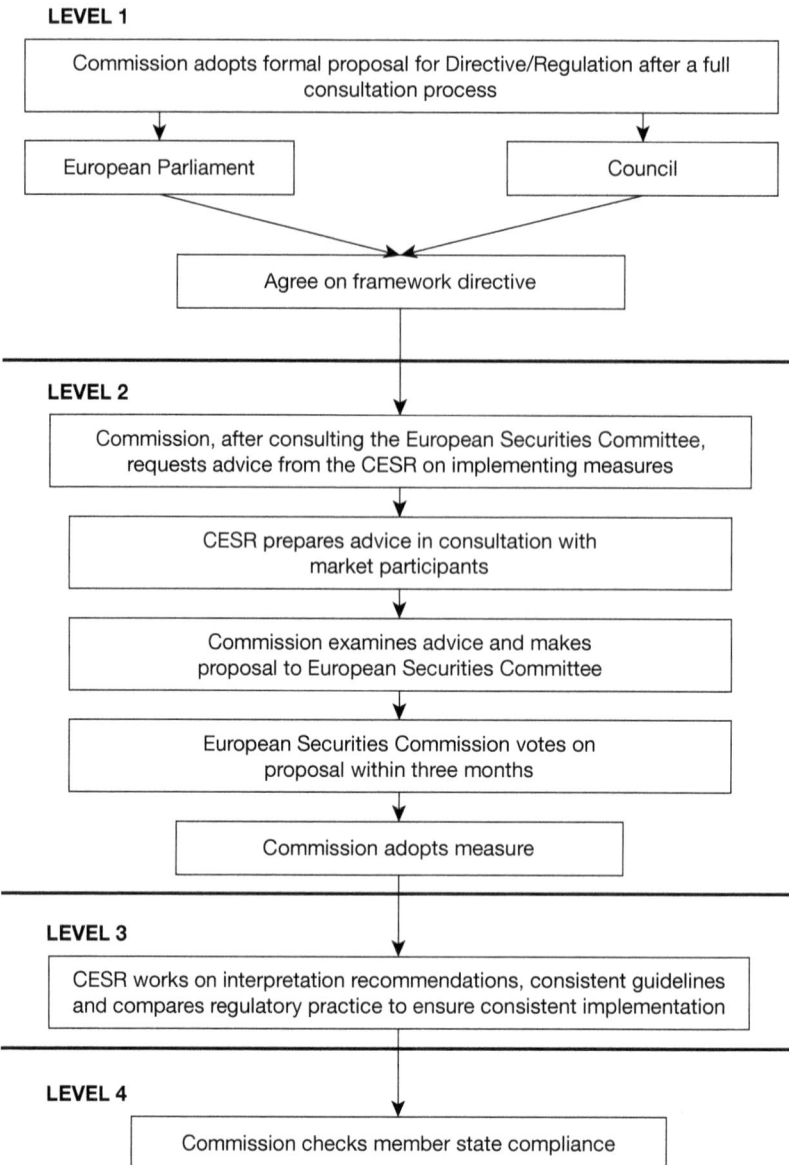

Figure 1.5 The Lamfalussy Process.

Source: Lamfalussy 2001: 6.

shift and degree of reform. The aim is to provide a nuanced account contributing to attempts to reshape the future of EU integration and globalization. Given the *timing* of the 2007–09 crisis, the rationale for a critique of neoliberalism is self-evident. Given the *importance* of crises as unique windows of opportunity, the argument of the book pre-empts future moments for class struggle.

Plan of the book

The book thus develops in stages. Chapter 2 begins by examining the questions of changing capitalisms and agency within neoliberalization. I argue that, contrary to the Varieties of Capitalism debates, neoliberalism is inherently variegated; that is, it is defined by its diversity. Not only should we expect to witness similarities (convergence) and differences (divergence) when comparing previously distinct national models but 'convergence within divergence', so to speak, is a component in the resilience of neoliberalism. Chapter 2 then highlights the following skeins within neoliberalization: I begin by exploring the expansionary and crisis-ridden tendencies under capitalism in order to situate both neoliberalization more generally and financial expansion more specifically. Then I argue that transnationally oriented fractions of capital – as particular rallying points for capital – have been strategically positioned in attempts to shape the contours of EU financial integration and, by implication, the global restructuring of capitalism. Finally, I highlight the significance of neoliberal common sense as the terrain upon which responses to repeated crises in the post–1970s era have been played out.

Chapter 3 then introduces the fractions and explains their differences. As key protagonists in EU financial market reform I argue that their interests and policy positions are fundamentally shaped by the *scale* of their operations, the *position* that they occupy within the overall circuit of capital and their relations within *socio-institutional configurations*. Chapter 4 examines the agency of these fractions in concrete terms through an analysis of financial trade associations' involvement in EU negotiations. I argue that through processes of marginalization and co-option these fractions tend to dominate the legislative processes. In particular, they construct strategic discourses – embedded within variegated neoliberal common sense – in attempts to secure political hegemony (within the power bloc at the level of the state) and societal hegemony; though interconnected the two are also relatively distinct processes. Chapter 5 outlines the contingent neoliberal consensus between the three fractions and their respective social formations (within the UK, France and Germany) which has underpinned recent EU reform.

Chapters 6 and 7 form a further part to the study, arguing that the agency of these fractions, the policies of state managers and the recent momentum in financial market integration can only be understood given the 'common sense' of neoliberalism. In Chapter 6 I focus on three national economic research centres to explore the production of ideas contributing to this common sense. In Chapter 7 I argue that the heartland (first-mover)–contender state (late developer) dynamic is reproduced within these research centres with North-American and UK academics occupying a privileged position in the dissemination of neoliberal common sense.

Finally, Chapters 8 and 9 form part of a conclusion, examining the potential lessons for resisting neoliberalization. Given the premise that neoliberalization is a project which is inherently asymmetrical vis-à-vis the lower and middle income social groups I argue that this study has several relevant implications. The most prominent of these is that accounts which emphasize the degree of unity within the agents of neoliberalization overstate the case. Here I seek to refute the notion of a transnational capitalist class – highlighting the fragility of the consensus between these transnationally oriented fractions. I conclude with a discussion of the importance of future crises as unique windows of opportunity for reshaping neoliberalization as well as considering the potential agents – including leftist academics – of reform.

2 Conceptualizing changing capitalisms and Gramscian historical materialism

This chapter examines the treatment of changing capitalisms and neoliberalization within the literature before establishing a Gramscian historical materialist apparatus. My aim is to theoretically assess the problem outlined in Chapter 1. This problem has three skeins: first, in demystifying globalization I seek to elucidate the dynamics of neoliberalization as its driving force; second, I examine these dynamics within changing European capitalisms, asking why member states previously averse to neoliberalization have nonetheless engaged in it; and third, I focus on a specific historical moment, asking how these dynamics contributed to the recent change in pace and degree of EU financial market integration.

The problem area is thus vast. I will therefore be strategically selective in my engagement. Given that our empirical focus is primarily European, here the debate on neoliberal reform has been dominated by the extensive Varieties of Capitalism literature. These accounts have provided excellent typologies of, variously, two or three models of capitalism. The debate has then tended to focus on moments of convergence and/or divergence or path dependency. I outline these theses before highlighting several lacunae: their problematic state-centrism; their binary tendencies; and their privileging form over content. I then explain what a *variegated* conception of neoliberalism adds before highlighting the important constructivist contribution to a dialectical understanding of material and ideational processes of neoliberalization. Finally, I draw on the work within historical materialism to suggest that a more nuanced conception of the impulsions under capitalism, coupled with the strategic agency of fractions of capital and Gramsci's notion of common sense contributes to our understanding of neoliberalization and the recent EU efforts.

Varieties of Capitalism (VoC)

Given the exponential increase in cross-border movements of capital, goods and services in recent years, typically entitled 'globalization', the overriding research programme of Comparative Politics/Political Economy (CPE) has focused on changes in European capitalisms (Blyth 2003: 215–25). As Chapter 1 noted, post-war nationally organized capitalisms differed in their historical trajectories.

Changing global conditions, the proliferation of public agencies and mobile private actors, and regulatory arbitrage have fuelled VoC explanations.

Chapter 1 highlighted John Zysman's (1983) seminal account of three models: the capital market-based, credit-based state-administered and credit-based universal banking systems. Though his account built upon insights by Andrew Shonfield (1965) the wealth of VoC literature has emerged since the early 1990s. In 1993 Michel Albert flagged the competing Rhineland and Anglo-American models arguing that whilst the Anglo-American model was characterized by the efficient rationale of the market economy (operating under 'neoliberal' precepts) (Albert 1993: 15), one ought not to disregard the Rhineland model which, in his reckoning, could outperform Anglo-American capitalism in both economic efficiency and social justice (ibid.: 15, 18–19). The 1997 edited volume by Colin Crouch and Wolfgang Streeck embarked on mapping moments of convergence and divergence. It questioned the implications for institutional diversity of a 'convergence' on a 'neoliberal', 'free-market' variety of capitalism (1997: i, ix).

In 2001 however, a groundbreaking contribution by Peter Hall and David Soskice established the now dominant framework for analysis of competing capitalisms and the convergence–divergence debate. Their paradigmatic account departs from previous institutional analyses and attempts to model the *strategic interactions* of economic actors, as *the* determinant factor in any political economy (Hall and Soskice 2001: 5–6). These interactions create problems of coordination for firms which are shaped by the historical–institutional parameters within their national political economy. In *liberal market economies* (LMEs) 'firms coordinate their activities primarily via hierarchies and competitive market arrangements' (ibid.: 8). Herein actors 'adjust their willingness to supply and demand goods and services . . . in response to price signals . . . [and] on the basis of marginal calculations stressed by neoclassical economics' (ibid.). In *coordinated market economies* (CMEs) however, the coordination difficulties are resolved primarily by collaborative relationships structured outside of the market. These involve relational contracting and information shared within networks rather than competitive, market-based relationships (ibid.). As such, their analysis suggests 'new formulations about the principal dimensions distinguishing one political economy from another' (Hall and Soskice 2001: 243). Though subsequently contested and reformulated, this sophisticated framework has been reproduced extensively.

I argue, however, that there are three conceptual lacunae within the VoC which impede our understanding of neoliberalization and – as a result – changes in models of capitalism: state-centrism; binary analysis; and privileging form over content.

State-centrism

In conceptualizing agency within neoliberalization the VoC offers an overtly state-centric account. Critics of state-centrism tend to highlight that, from this perspective: states act as 'containers' for societies and social processes; and political authority is territorially organized and thus circumscribed by state borders (Lacher 2003: 521). Though typically undisclosed, the VoC has certain connections with neo-realism, wherein states are clearly the most important actors (Krasner 1996: 114–15). This similarity is evidenced in the VoC definition of globalization and the a-priori analytical significance of political institutions (Bieler 2006: 25).

For example, in his study, George Menz (2005: vi) sets out to examine 'how different varieties of capitalism can, should or indeed must adapt to cope with new demands, new demographic realities, and an increasingly interlinked global economy'. Here, freer flows of investment, labour, goods and services generate pressures on institutional governance mechanisms (ibid.: 1–2). His case study of the migration of lower-waged construction workers under EU services liberalization tends to support his notion of exogenous pressures for reform. His concern then is to capture the 'national response strategies' aimed at coping with 'top-down' liberalization (ibid.: 4–6). Wolfgang Streeck and Kathleen Thelen (2005) similarly examine changes in political-economic institutions. To explain these *institutional* changes they consider: the historical setting and the type of change, be it incremental or transformative (ibid.: 2–5). Their analysis is again focused though on changes in nationally organized political economies to growing internal and external market pressures and merely charts the 'direction' of institutional reform (ibid.: 4). For Bruno Amable (2003: 1, 4) the role of institutions and the conditions for institutional change 'are at the core of the economic debate in Europe' since these institutions 'define incentives and constraints that will lead agents to invest in certain assets, acquire certain skills, cooperate or be opportunistic'. For Herbert Kitschelt *et al.* (1999: 40–41) the focus is on how national institutions mediate pressures. In all of these accounts, then, globalization is equated with cross-border movements, representing an external challenge for states and reinforcing the notion of states as societal containers through the depiction of internal and external, top-down and bottom-up incentives and pressures (Hall and Soskice 2001: 56). Further, institutions are afforded a highly problematic ontological primacy; that is, they are unquestioningly posited as a priori political forms.

The challenge is thus one of conceptualizing the (interrelationship of) spatial changes and the social content of political forms within neoliberalization. As Brenner notes and I explain later,

> The recognition that social relations are becoming increasingly interconnected on a global scale necessarily problematizes the spatial parameters of those relations, and, therefore, the geographical context in which they occur. Under these circumstances, space no longer appears as a static platform of social relations, but rather as one of their constitutive dimensions, itself historically produced, reconfigured and transformed.
>
> (Brenner 1999b: 40)

Neoliberalization, though comprising changes in state forms, is characterized by the global restructuring of capitalism. Herein the separation of state and market, political and economic is rejected, as both are simply different forms of expressing the same social relations. Here 'national states . . . are the *political* form of capitalist social relations' (Burnham 1994: 224, emphasis added), materially representing the condensation of class struggle (Poulantzas 1978: 145). This book thus adopts an entirely different starting point, focusing on the restructuring of capitalism and social relations, a component of which is the reshaping of political institutional configurations. It is therefore necessary to consider the social relations implicit within the Varieties of Capitalism (Bieler 2006: 27; Coates 2000). We shall return to this.

Binary analysis

The tendency towards a binary analysis is inscribed in the notion of two (or three) pre-defined categories of analysis – *liberal* and *coordinated* systems or *Anglo-American* (read neoliberal) and *Rhineland* or *dirigiste* models. In effect, these categories of analysis become the de facto end-states of a given continuum (Hall and Soskice 2001: 243). The pre-established conceptual categories (LME and CME) imply the existence of observable associated characteristics, acting as prerequisites for situating political economies along the VoC continuum. Categorization is then a precursor to determining the direction of change: are particular models converging (becoming increasingly similar) or diverging (remaining distinct) and, if converging, is it towards a CME or an LME variant? This tendency is presupposed in the following question: 'will institutional differences among nations of the sort we have identified remain significant or will the processes of competitive deregulation unleashed by international integration drive all economies toward a common market model?' (Hall and Soskice 2001: 55). Though sophisticated, Hall and Soskice's hypothesis is that, in contradistinction to the 'monolithic political dynamic conventionally associated with globalization . . . [they predict] one dynamic in liberal market economies and a different one in coordinated market economies' (ibid.: 57). Nonetheless, the emergence of policies or features associated with a particular model implies convergence around that model, albeit not necessarily *liberal market economy* convergence.

This criticism raises two further concerns: first, since formal analysis continues to centre on mapping convergence or divergence the social content of neoliberalism is ignored; second, the focus on tangible, material elements as both *evidence* of convergence and themselves *explanatory factors* neglects the role of ideas in neoliberalization. Before we explore the importance of ideas I will outline an alternative to the convergence–divergence account in the shape of *variegated* neoliberalism.

Variegated neoliberalism

As outlined, even nuanced readings of the VoC tend to conflate Anglo-American with neoliberal 'varieties' leading them to conclude that there are 'economic forms beyond *the neoliberal model* that can survive and prosper' (Hall and Soskice 2001: 246). By positing a neoliberal *model* – defined by its characteristics in one spatio-temporal context – they rightly note that not all political economies are 'converging' on this particular model (whatever this might mean). This book argues however, that such a monolithic, invariant conception of neoliberalism obfuscates the *processes* of neoliberalization within obviously path-dependent political economies. Further, as explored below, this mystification neglects the social content of neoliberalization as a driver of globalization.

Instead, this study argues that convergence and divergence are dialectical moments of dynamic *processes* of neoliberalization. Jamie Peck and Adam Tickell (2002: 387) argue, for example, that 'although neoliberalism privileges the unitary logic of the market while advocating supposedly universal cures and one-best-way policy strategies, it is in reality much more variegated than such self-representations suggest'. They suggest that we are witnessing *processes* of neo-liberalization rather than a neoliberal *end-state*. Neither 'monolithic in form, nor universal in effect' this is best defined as *variegated neoliberalism* (ibid.: 387, 384). By implication the similarities and differences within neoliberalization pose meaningful questions about the process itself without being conceived in isolation as the convergence–divergence debate suggests. Rejecting the Anglo-American/neoliberal *model*, neoliberalization concerns the process (or processes) of liberalizing and integrating markets, with the simultaneous construction of institutions and infrastructures apposite to functioning markets. In short, Anglo-American capitalism is thus one such institutional manifestation.

Chapters 5 and 6 discuss how the neoliberal 'new' remains infused with sediments of the 'old' creating *convergent divergence* on multiple overlapping and competing scales. Coexisting with crystallizations of former modes – of capitalism and common sense – neoliberalism nonetheless emerges as the dominant imperative. For example, neoliberalization manifests itself in the progressive breakdown of former consensuses and alliances. Put simply, neoliberalization is therefore played out differently on each national scale yet embedded within local, regional and global neoliberal impulses and tendencies. As we shall see, neoliberalism is therefore historically specific in the mode of capitalism and impulsions it engenders; its significance lies in the reconfiguration of social relations around a restoration of class power and finance-led accumulation. Moreover, this process is underpinned by the 'common sense' that freer markets are the most effective means of social provision (Harvey 2007: 2, see also Gamble 2001: 127–34).

Admittedly, *variegated* neoliberalism risks an obvious over-expansion, 'classifying otherwise different cases as neoliberal when, in fact, the differences *outweigh* meaningful commonalities' (Castree 2005: 542–43). By suggesting that spatio-temporal differences of *degree* characterize neoliberalism we risk overlooking differences of *kind*. In essence we risk suggesting that *everything* is neoliberal and that neoliberalism is *everywhere*, at which point we fail to say anything meaningful about neoliberalism. Nonetheless, as an alternative to the binary VoC account the concept is valuable; it highlights the diversity of neoliberalism as both a characteristic of (and defining element in) the reconfiguration of social relations within a global reconstitution of capitalism. Further, I argue that 'to stress the distinctiveness of the variations is to ignore the underlying theme' (Clarke 1988: 5), whilst noting the underlying theme contributes towards a counter-hegemonic agenda. In elucidating the social content of neoliberalization then – a prerogative of this study – these insights provide a *relatively* fixed analytical tool.

Form over content

The above has therefore stressed our concern with content over form. Elsewhere the distinction between analysis of the form of integration and its social content has been characterized as follows:

> For the study of EU integration, *form* and *content* are to a significant extent intertwined. Defining content as social purpose, or the *socio-economic* content of the internationalisation or supranationalisation of political authority, and form as the institutional shape this process takes.
>
> (van Apeldoorn 2002: 12)

I would only add that whilst the above might be misread as differentiating between *form-al* arrangements of institutions and their *social rationale*, historical materialism also relates to the disclosed and *undisclosed*, transcending multiple levels of abstraction. Thus, seemingly diverse, contradictory or isolated phenomena are bound together within a relatively holistic account of change. Here, theory is crucial as it provides a dialectical vantage point through which we simultaneously internalize and engage with the world around us, whilst shaping and reshaping this same totality in a process at once dynamic and path-dependent. In the writings of historical materialism and Antonio Gramsci we discover a complex yet avowedly normative apparatus through which we perceive and demystify the reified, in the aim of elucidating the struggles of the dispossessed (Morton 2007). In essence, these concerns are beyond the remit of the VoC accounts.

In his writings however, Karl Marx emphasized the naturalizing effects of an analysis of form over (undisclosed) social content, particularly in the work of so-called 'Classical Political Economy' (see for example, Marx 1990 [1867]: 762–870).[1] He argued that by focusing on fetishized *forms* Political Economy tended to miss the social relations embodied within them (Marx 1990 [1867]: 720–24). On his reading, value adopts various forms during its accumulation and circulation, yet abstracting these forms from their position under capitalism obfuscates the nature of capital as a social relation. In his words, 'the bourgeois [political] economist, whose limited mentality is unable to separate the form of appearance from the thing which appears within that form', in effect, acts as an 'ideological representative' of the capitalist class (Marx 1990 [1867]: 714, 718). Though terse, the implication is that the type of reductionism implicit in 'soft-positivist' analyses (see below) and conceptual categorization (as in the VoC) not only mystifies the social content of neoliberalization but naturalizes moments in the accumulation of capital; moments which intrinsically subjugate labour to the concentration of capitals' command (Marx 1990 [1867]: 776). This study is therefore part of a wider project of examining class struggles, hegemonic class fractions and neoliberal reform within the European political economy, contributing to counter-hegemonic analytical endeavour (Bieler 2000, 2006; Bruff 2008; Overbeek *et al.* 2007; Shields 2011; van Apeldoorn 2002; van der Pijl 2006; Worth 2008).

Soft-positivism

The origins and implications of the analysis of form (implicit within the VoC) benefit from a brief explanation of soft-positivism. With its origins in the twentieth-century physics of Einstein, late-nineteenth and early-twentieth-century formal logic, the empiricism of Hume and Mach and Kant's 'critical' philosophy, positivism in the twentieth century took its lead from the logical positivists in the 1920s and the 1950s (Hausman 1992: 283). The 'received view' of positivism in the social sciences is summarized in the following four tenets: (i) a belief in the unity of science, taken to mean that similar methods can be employed in both natural and social sciences; (ii) a distinction between facts and values where facts are essentially theory-neutral, meaning that objective knowledge of the world is possible (at least in principle); (iii) a belief in regularities in the social world as in the natural world, leading to the usage of deductive-nomological and inductive-statistical methods as forms of covering law explanation; (iv) and – given (i) to (iii) – a belief that empirical validation is the hallmark of 'real' enquiry (Smith 1996: 16). Soft-positivism is thus a loose adherence to these tenets – most especially (ii) and (iv). In the VoC it tends to inform analysis of material causal explanations, whereas the realm of ideas and underlying social content is unquantifiable and therefore taboo.

Visible, tangible and quantifiable phenomena hence become the focus of analytical endeavour (Hay 2002: 195). For the VoC, the strategic behaviour of institutions and/or firms is therefore ascribed explanatory value, whilst the emergence of features associated with a particular 'model' suggest convergence. Thus they 'prefer to study things that they can see, measure and count', whereas 'ideas seem to be the opposite – vague, amorphous and constantly evolving' (Berman 1998: 16, cited in Hay 2002: 197). Establishing causal relations between specific ideas and specific social developments is inherently problematic. Nonetheless, neoliberalization has been accompanied by a proliferation of so-called 'neoliberal ideas', manifested in economic theories of integration, discourses of competitiveness, efficient market hypotheses and the associated rise in economic research centres. Conceptualizing their significance is thus – I argue – important to an understanding of neoliberalization.

Constructivism on the role of ideas

Constructivism has made significant contributions in this respect. Though heterodox, a common theme has emerged – arguing that social reality (identities, activities, behaviour) which is often reified as relatively immutable, is in fact contingent and therefore open to change (Wendt 1992: 400–07; Hay 2002: 202). Ideas thus possess causal qualities, so to speak, in 'shaping the social, political and economic contexts we inhabit', rather than the rationalist assumption of ideas as tools of interests (Hay and Marsh 2000: 8). In addition however, more 'materialist' varieties of constructivism have emphasized that certain (material) contexts circumscribe and delimit the impact of ideas just as ideas mediate and condition their material context (ibid.: 9; see also Seabrooke 2007: 372; Sharman 2006). This dialectical approach to the material and ideational effectively expands the scope of analysis for processes driving neoliberalization.

As it relates to our problem area, constructivism offers the useful insight that actors respond to ideas and stimuli regardless of whether these stimuli are 'real' or simply 'perceived'. Unlike the assumptions of some 'soft-positivist' theories, actors do not possess objective, 'perfect' information concerning their social context but depend upon ideas as forms of knowledge. In effect, since agents interpret and internalize external stimuli based on pre-established understandings and experiences the separation between 'essence' and 'perception' is indistinguishable. Ideas are therefore both 'real' and have 'real effects' (Hay 2002: 213). Further, this account opens a political space for the contestation of particular meaning systems.

Specifically, on the turn to neoliberalization, constructivists have highlighted the significance of structures of legitimation in sustaining embedded liberalism following the fall of Bretton Woods (Ruggie 1982) and the construction of crisis narratives aimed to promote Thatcherite political projects temporally offsetting and exacerbating the 'crisis' itself (Hay 2001). Here, it is not only the underlying 'material' shifts – in power structures or the forces of production – which shape and re-shape history but alterations in epistemic conditions consisting of political doctrines and metaphysical assumptions (Ruggie 1982: 281–83; Bieler and Morton 2008: 107). Thus, as Colin Hay (2002: 201) notes, constructivism emphasizes the determinism of both material and ideational factors in shaping outcomes.

Significantly though, attempts to de-reify the purportedly immutable and avoid over-determinism render constructivism ultimately indeterminate (Teschke 2003: 27–32; Bieler and Morton 2008: 107). As a result it is unclear *why* certain narratives and certain actors succeed where others fail (Bieler and Morton 2008: 107–09; Morton 2006: 48). This is further reinforced by an 'always and already' separate and combined conception of the material and ideational (Bieler and Morton 2008: 109). For example, Mark Blyth (2001: 4) has highlighted that ideas can be powerful ideological weapons for (public or private) agents challenging existing institutional arrangements. He notes however, that crises (exogenous shocks) provide fertile ground for these changes (2007). He defines crises (and wars) as 'events which agents intersubjectively interpret as necessitating change'

(Blyth *et al.* 2007: 748). Thus, there are certain material events (here, crises) which agents do not simply respond to in predictable ways because their perceptions, understandings and responses are based on intersubjective meaning systems. Agents can both interpret and construct popular understandings of these crises in a variety of ways. Therefore '*even* exogenous shocks have to interpreted' (ibid.: 748, 749, emphasis added), yet this can only ever be the case if we accept the (false) separation of material and ideational.

A similar criticism can be levelled at Colin Hay, despite his insightful analysis of the initial phase of neoliberalization. Hay agrees that neoliberalization was precipitated by burgeoning contradictions within the Keynesian mode. Nonetheless, he also notes that neither the form of the crisis nor the responses can be derived from a 'static analysis of [these] contradictions' (2001: 204). Instead, state managers and elites typically narrated the crisis – albeit across different spatio-temporal contexts – so as to capture both widely held experiences and perceptions (ibid.: 204–09; see also Blyth 2002). Yet in so doing he opts to focus on the discursive institutional responses, neglecting the dialectical unity of material and ideational elements (so to speak). Italian Marxist Antonio Gramsci held a similar view, yet he also noted that whilst

> It may be ruled out that immediate economic crises *of themselves* produce fundamental historical events; they . . . create a terrain more favourable to the dissemination of certain modes of thought, and certain ways of posing and resolving questions involving the entire subsequent development of national life.
>
> (Gramsci 1971: 184)

In other words, crises delimit and shape the outcome. Yet, simultaneously, crises are also *products* of particular historical modes of thought and ways of organizing national development (ibid.: 177, 181, 304). Thus, a sophisticated analysis of EU integration requires a dialectical understanding of how certain ideas contribute to both the onset of and responses to crises, whilst locating agency within these nascent conditions which (re)shape their interests/ideas, themselves shaping crisis and response. Here economism – though not determinism – is rejected (Bieler and Morton 2006: 23–24). In light of this approach, I argue that the character of neoliberalization can be discerned within the crisis of Keynesianism – not simply derived from the contradictions however, but from the strategic agency of particular social forces under the conditions of an emergent neoliberal common sense. Importantly however, certain historically specific features (such as geographic location) of the crisis provided the preconditions for the latter.

Gramscian historical materialism

The following outlines a Gramscian historical materialist apparatus for our study of the contemporary period.[2] Here I focus specifically on these developments within the EU. I highlight three skeins: the historical impulses under capitalism;

fractions of capital; and common sense. I argue that through this nuanced dialectical conception an account can be established which incorporates the material and ideational, so to speak – and questions of structure and agency. Below, the first stage outlines the basis for understanding the crisis in production in the 1970s and the nature of the system – predicated on financial expansion – which emerged. The second stage lays the basis for understanding the agency at the core of the post–1970s system, leading into our later examination of this agency in recent EU financial integration. The third stage explores the 'neoliberal' common sense which emerged through the post-war period, was central to the restructuring of the 1970s, and which has been progressively naturalized thereafter. The account thus transcends multiple levels of abstraction, moving repeatedly from abstract to concrete and back again, in order to demonstrate the internal relationship of the impulsions–agency–common sense nexus. I introduce the three in relative independence only for analytic purposes.

Accumulation and crises

We have already noted then that neoliberalism emerged through crises. As Marx (1990 [1867]: 227–32, 797; 1991 [1894]: 317–75) noted, crises are both the inevitable (and necessary) product of the burgeoning contradictions inherent to capitalism and, simultaneously, moments for restructuring it. Debate has raged concerning crisis-causation (see Clarke 1993: 9–63). Given our historical focus on the post–1970s era the following reading will suffice. In contradistinction to his contemporary Political Economists, Marx rejected the natural tendency towards equilibrium in supply and demand (Harvey 1982: 75). Instead the purpose of production is the appropriation of surplus value and the accumulation of capital rather than consumption (Marx 1990 [1867]: 742). Hence capital has no regard for the 'limits' of the market which are only another 'unfortunate barrier that the capitalist has to overcome' (Clarke 2001: 75–76).[3] The imperative to accumulate however, gives rise to overproduction as markets become satiated. Thus the tendency towards overproduction is inscribed in the conditions of generalized competition under capitalism.

Crises of accumulation thus emerge, in this instance, as the circuit of capital is interrupted through breakdown between producer and consumer (Marx 1990 [1867]: 711). Already the 'social' implications of crises are apparent as the 'value of a certain portion of the capital in circulation [is destroyed] so as to equilibrate the total circulating capital with the potential capacity to produce and realize surplus value under capitalist relations of production' (Harvey 2006 [1982]: 202). This involves the reduction of social capital through wage cuts and unemployment as workers bear the brunt of this 'devaluation' (ibid.: 430). To argue therefore that crises are necessary and inherent features of capitalism is already to juxtapose the interests of capitalist and wage-labourer.

More specifically, neoliberalism requires that we theorize finance. Credit and financial systems (functionally integrated through securitization) are intrinsic to capitalism, sustaining accumulation in the temporal periods between production and consumption of commodities (Harvey 2006 [1982]: 286). The gamble implied therein requires the appropriation of additional surplus value through the expansive exploitation of labour power (Holloway 1996: 17). In the instance of a failure to secure an effective exploitation of labour a further expansion of credit is required if production is to continue. Crucially though, this credit-sustained illusion of restored accumulation is stillborn; 'the ratio of debt to surplus value will continue to increase, undermining profitability and future accumulation of capital, and so creating bad debt and financial crisis' (Bonefeld 1996: 40); and this is the time bomb at the heart of neoliberalism. Thus crises in production can be displaced into financial crises (Harvey 2006 [1982]: 236–50). These crises would tend to be manifested in expanding financial systems – concealing yet exacerbating the crises themselves.

Neoliberalization: offsetting the Keynesian crisis

In the post-war era a Keynesian settlement between capital and labour emerged across Western Europe. However, by the 1960s it was apparent that the keys to the successes of the Keynesian mode were rapidly becoming its primary limitations. Relatively immobile investments and labour created 'Chinese walls', hampering the process of accumulation. Organized labour, in the form of an extensive system of trade unions – most especially in the UK – fuelled rising wage demands which, in the face of falling profits created unsustainable conditions for capital. As Marx (1990 [1867]: 771) predicted, wage increases are sustainable only until they conflict with the pace of accumulation. The crisis of the Keynesian mode was thus manifested in rising unemployment and inflation as capital sought to restore profitability (Harvey 2007: 13–14).

The neoliberal shift therefore comprised two components: one is the recognizable 'liberalization' of former restraints under the Keynesian mode; the other is the switch to an expansion of the financial system. The former explains the opening of markets, the movement of labour, goods and investments under globalization. The latter however, serves to explain the shape that neoliberalization has taken; it is thus hugely significant to this book. To understand this shift, questions of space and timing matter. Rising oil prices produced a glut of petrodollars flooding global markets. Already apparent, limits to the Keynesian mode thus rose to fever pitch.[4] Despite the increasing mechanization of production, profits continued to fall (Holloway 1996: 22). These conditions were experienced particularly acutely in the UK where inflation surged to 26 per cent in 1975 and unemployment figures passed the one million mark. This created an epicentre, both historically and spatially. The 'Big Bang' metaphor is fittingly ironic then, given the global transformations which rippled from this epicentre.

During the 1970s therefore the neoliberal shift took hold. In the UK in 1979 a Conservative government under Margaret Thatcher began the destruction of Keynesian institutions, attacking the unions, lowering direct and indirect wages, and reducing social expenditure (Bonefeld 1996: 36). Here the emphasis of state policy changed as full employment was dropped in favour of price stability

(Clarke 1988: 5). The emphasis was now on the role of money and – in contrast to Keynesian full employment growth guarantees – market freedom and a so-called 'natural rate' of unemployment (Bonefeld 1996: 36). Following a 'coup' by investment bankers in New York seeking to attract these petrodollars to the US, the UK underwent a similar period of securities market liberalization (Harvey 2007: 45); we will return to this shortly. Already home to the Eurodollar markets and large niche areas of banking since the early 1970s the Goodison-Parkinson agreement of 1983 prompted the reform of competitive practices on the London Stock Exchange (Moran 1991: 68–71). The 'informal and consensual regulatory style' which was progressively developing made London highly attractive to both investor and procurer of capital alike (ibid.: 85).

There were however, important systemic and spatial repercussions to this process which began in the financial markets of New York and London. In brief, the 1970s reforms reinvigorated dynamics of inter-state competition with an extensive history. These dynamics are at the heart of neoliberalization. Further, the 1970s reforms established a 'zombified' system of accumulation.[5] In effect, without resolving the fundamental contradictions in the production capitalism of the post-war period, the restructuring of the 1970s established – as we shall see below – a type of 'monetary' or financial accumulation which merely displaced rather than resolved the former crises (Macartney 2009b; Bonefeld 1996: 50).

In addressing these concerns we focus primarily though on two elements. These provide the theoretical apparatus for our ensuing analysis. To understand the location of the initial reforms and the nature of the neoliberal shift we will consider (i) the agency of fractions of capital, and (ii) neoliberal common sense.

Fractions of capital

The above suggests that crises form 'turning points', 'breaks in the path of development' and 'ruptures in a pattern of movement' (Holloway 1992: 146). Put differently, crises of accumulation pre-empt the passage from one regime of accumulation[6] to another. This process is neither entirely determined nor entirely contingent (Gramsci 1971: 184). As Bieler notes, 'the end of one accumulation regime does not imply that there is only one alternative . . . which will take its place . . . On the contrary there are always various possible courses of action in times of structural change' (2000: 16).

To understand this non-economistic transition, then, the question of agency must be addressed. Here the move between levels of abstraction becomes significant (van der Pijl 1998: 49–50). Nonetheless, to posit the emergence of 'key' actors – embodied in specific forms such as fractions or capitals – risks overlooking their internal relationship to the movement of value and thus reinforce a fetishized analysis of their form (on this, see Bieler and Morton 2001b: 6). I argue that the most significant error here is thus the overestimation of contingency within agential struggles. In effect, as Bonefeld (2006: 179) argues, this implies that 'social forces struggle over the spoils of the system and they do that by trying to exploit opportunity structures, and by doing so, they shape and determine state purpose'. Instead, I argue – in this and ensuing chapters – that through examining the internal, dialectical unity of capitalisms' impulsions, moments of agency and the production of common sense, both over-contingency and over-determinism are avoided.[7] This builds on the 'systematic attempt[s] to develop an understanding of the relationship between the substance of hegemonic ideas and underlying dynamics of capital accumulation' (Overbeek 2000: 174). What emerges is an empirically supported account of how capital seeks to capture and shape,

> that which is falling and hold on to that which, under its own steam, is moving their way. It may then seem as if they had originated the process of social change, while actually they were merely beneficiaries, and may be even perverting the trend to make it serve their own aims.
>
> (Polanyi 1957: 28, cited in van der Pijl 1998: 62)

To explain this we begin with fractions of capital.

In Capital volume 2 (1978 [1885]: 109–79), Marx 'considers the different functional forms capital assumes in the circuits composing the overall reproductive circuit of capital: commodity capital, money capital and productive capital' (van der Pijl 1984: 3). Though all forms are linked within an overall circuit of capital, only productive capital is engaged in the expropriation of surplus value through the labour process. This differentiation signifies various functions or moments within the overall circuit. The formula for the circuit of money capital is M-C . . . P . . . C'-M' where the dots indicate that the circulation process is interrupted and C' and M' denote an increase in C and M as the result of surplus value (Marx 1978 [1885]: 109). In contrast however, the circuit of productive capital has the general formula P . . . C'-M'-C . . . P. The entire circulation therefore presents itself in the opposite form from that which it possessed in the circuit of money capital; now the circuit reads C-M-C (ibid.). In turn, the general formula for the circuit of commodity capital is C'-M'-C . . . P . . . C' (ibid.: 167).

Albeit in abstraction, two related points can be discerned: one concerns the formation of interests; the other concerns the overall circuit. The Gramscian claim that interests and identity are shaped through position (that is, function) within production and circulation derives from this analysis (Bieler and Morton 2001b: 17). Crudely, the money capitalist begins with an investment and looks to the return of a greater investment (Marx 1978 [1885]: 140–41); the productive capitalist begins with the 'real factors of the labour process' through which his profit is accrued (ibid.: 156) and the commodity capitalist begins with the commodity (such as coal or machinery, for example) and looks to a greater resulting amount of his commodity as a result of his respective 'circuit' (ibid.: 167). Nonetheless, though relatively distinct these interests and identities are integrated as a result of their engagement in the same overall circuit of capital (ibid.: 145–50). The result is not only interconnection but a degree of (dialectical) interdependence.

The implication for our earlier discussion of financial expansion becomes clearer: the creation of surplus value, and hence capital itself, is predicated on the exploitation of labour-power in production. Thus, even under 'normal' capitalist conditions

> profits made in the financial sector of the economy are nothing but a redistribution of the surplus product created in the productive sector ... [since] capital is a social relation. This implies that capital in the money form must be exchanged against labour to be capital at all.
>
> (Overbeek 1980: 101)

Not only does this explain the problematic expansion of finance in the absence of a corresponding expansion of the forces of production, but reveals an organic connection (a dialectical interdependence) between all fractions within the overall circuit. We return to this in our discussion of the domestic–national embeddedness of transnationally oriented capital.

More concretely, this fractionation of capital acquires a political significance. In its attempts to achieve the annihilation of space through time (Marx 1973 [1857]: 539) capital requires relatively fixed regulatory and institutional infrastructures (Harvey 1985: 145). According to Lefebvre (1978) the territorial fixity of state institutions fulfils this function. Thus the ultimate goal of class struggle is political and, further, the fractionation of capital implies yet another axis upon which intra-capital struggles rage. Marx acknowledged this tendency within inter-capitalist relations, as being defined by a so-called 'coercive law of competition'. Capitalists tend to perpetually wrestle to reduce necessary labour time, procure cheaper raw materials, create and secure alternative markets and investment, and so on, precisely because of generalized capitalist conditions (1990 [1867]: 340–416). As Marx has it, 'accumulation therefore presents itself as ... the repulsion of many individual capitals one from another' (1990 [1867]: 776).

The contradiction implied therein however, is that since the 'ultimate stakes of class struggle are political, related to the contest for power in the state' (van der Pijl 1998: 50) capital 'is continuously engaged in building coalitions transcending the particularity of "special interests" ' (ibid.). Thus, Hickel writes that 'the actual relevance of the fractioning of the bourgeoisie resides in the continuous attempt (which itself is the result of competition) of the individual capitalist to make their specific interests appear as the general interest at the level of the state' (1975: 15; van der Pijl 1998: 50). The state is therefore the material condensation of class struggle and the factor of cohesion in a social formation (Poulantzas 1973: 24–25; 1978: 145). The 'black box' state of the VoC instead embodies a series of complex and contradictory social relations and a particular social function in legitimizing and sustaining capitalism. Chapter 4 explains this conception of the state in greater detail.

Hence, in order to encapsulate both the abstract and the concrete, fractions are conceived as rallying points around which a variety of social forces coalesce. As van der Pijl notes, 'fractions' are 'the form in which capital as a collective social force made up of competitive units seeks to achieve a degree of collectivity to be able to act as a class agency' (2004: 183). These fractions construct *hegemonic projects* (to transcend their particularistic interests) which, on the one hand promote a concrete programme of objectives that explicitly or implicitly advance their long-term interests (Jessop 1997: 61–62) whilst, on the other hand, attempting to attain societal consent through relating this project to the nascent common sense (Bruff 2008: 48). Hegemony at the level of the state, is established when a leading fraction forms the necessary alliances and secures the consent or reluctant acquiescence of other fractions – and potentially working classes – within the *power bloc* (Poulantzas 1973: 237; Gramsci 1971: 182). As we shall see, then, the agency of these fractions is interwoven with both the impulsions of capitalism (see above) and the production of common sense (see below).

Finally, the transnational is therefore neither a level superimposed upon the national, commensurate with the international or supranational, nor merely the coagulation of national economies. Instead it is both scalar and relational (see Chapter 3): capitalism's expansionary tendencies drive the incessant destruction yet relative fixity of rescaled and reconstituted social relations. These create dense and multi-layered socio-institutional configurations, embedded within nested hierarchies. Thus – for our class analysis – relations and struggles within this space, embedded within competing and contradictory, yet relatively fixed institutional frameworks, become fundamental. In short, the *transnational orientation* of the fractions captures: the scale of their operations; their function (within the overall circuit of capital); and their underlying socio-institutional configurations to simultaneously make them *transnational* and *nationally embedded* social forces (see Chapters 3 and 8).

Fractions within neoliberalization

The earlier section highlighted the burgeoning contradictions in the Keynesian mode and the initial neoliberal shift. I argue that fractions of capital were central to this early period of neoliberalization and increasingly so in recent decades. As precondition, mediator and outcome of the global reconstitution of capitalism, this is of course understandable. To explain, I outline their position within the epicentre of neoliberal reform. The socio-institutional makeup of the UK model pre-dated the Thatcherite 'neoliberal' reforms by several centuries. It was characterized historically by a self-regulating market and social relations subject to the rule of law; here the state played a facilitating role underpinning market freedoms (Overbeek 2004: 126). This state–society complex was, from its conception in the seventeenth century, bound up in early periods of capitalist expansion through colonization, rapidly emerging as a hegemonic core of the developing state-system (Marx 1990 [1867]: 928–30; Overbeek 2004: 126–28). This Lockean *heartland* did not establish an autonomous market (Polanyi 2001 [1944]: 44, 71, 145) but instead provided the precursor to the modern liberal tradition of empowered market actors (van der Pijl 1998: 66–68; see also 2006: 13).

The liberal internationalism of the British state both facilitated and was supported by an Atlantic circuit of money capital in the late nineteenth and early twentieth centuries (van der Pijl 1984: i).[8] Whilst linking New York and London as the worlds dominant financial centres this 'Atlantic' fraction was also afforded considerable influence vis-à-vis the British state, reinforcing the hegemony of an economic liberal ideology (Overbeek 1990; Hall 1988: 58–60, 249; van Apeldoorn 2002: 73). Though interrupted and partially disorganized under the embedded liberal post-war architecture as nationally oriented production fractions became more prominent, Keynesian demand management, involving the expansion of the public sector and welfare provisions, was less stable in Britain than across much of continental Europe (van Apeldoorn 2002; Overbeek 1990: 136). As might be expected then, the inspiration for reforms emerged from a consortium of Anglo-American institutional investors in the City and political elites within the Bank of England, the regulatory agency (the Securities and Investment Board) and the government itself (Moran 1991: 57–63). Over almost fifteen years this consortium pushed for the removal of capital controls and restrictions on price competition (ibid.: 56), the use of state power to crush monopolistic cartels of institutional investors (ibid.: 2), and the construction of a light-touch statutory regulatory framework (ibid.: 72). Both the immediate and the historical structure of capitalism precipitated the success of this moment of agency – as did contested ideological elements (see below). The position of the City as a global financial centre thus re-emerged as the British state restored its latent liberal international traditions in a bid to compete with the recently (re-)liberalized New York markets.

In its early stages then, neoliberalization emerged as the corollary of the contradictions of the Keynesian mode, the conjuncture of circulating petrodollars and the agency of institutional investors. We will in turn consider why the project of these fractions was accepted and, more significantly for our ensuing empirical examination, the spatio-temporal dynamics which neoliberalization engendered. Importantly, though, we should note that this wasn't simply a victory of 'finance' capital but a shift establishing a system wherein (i) the distinction between production and finance capitals was progressively blurred – with production companies increasingly raising profits through financial activities – and (ii) profits became steadily detached from the messy business of surplus value extraction. As Clarke notes,

> The very distinction between financial and industrial capital is becoming increasingly anachronistic as accumulation on a world scale is dominated by multinational corporations, which take the form of financial holding companies, closely integrated with multinational banks and financial institutions, which move their capital freely between countries, between branches of production, and between productive and financial investments.
>
> (Clarke 1988: 7)

Further, the practice of paying CEOs in stock options has also tended to mean that stock value rather than the production of surplus value has become the 'guiding light' of economic activity (Harvey 2007: 32). Moreover, as Clarke (1988: 59) later points out, this financial system meant capitalists were able to secure profits – as distinct from surplus value – from financial activities: hence, 'with the development of the banking and financial system money appeared to lose the encumbrances of its attachment to the real world of commodities'. Our definition of fractions as rallying points therefore encapsulates the relative differences between coalitions of capitals whilst avoiding overstating the internal divisions.

Nonetheless, to understand how neoliberalization spread, its spatio-temporal dynamics are significant. Van der Pijl argued that state–society complexes seeking to avoid peripherilization, can be characterized as Hobbesian *contender states* (1998: 78–97). Here, political elites and dominant class fractions were typically fused and any attempts to 'successfully negotiate the modernization pressures emanating . . . from the English-speaking heartland' tended to rely on greater state involvement (van der Pijl 2006: 14; Overbeek 2000: 175). Whereas the heartland is, from its inception, transnationally integrated, contender states struggle to demarcate territories and employ forms of centralized administration which both foster a country's creative capacities and, in the long run, hinder its transnational competition (van der Pijl 1998: 79). This had two relevant repercussions in both France (the Hobbesian prototype) and Germany (which merges Hobbesian and Lockean traits); one was that the post-war Keynesian configurations were markedly different from those in Britain; and the other related feature was that these capital–labour compromises and state forms endured longer than in Britain (van Apeldoorn 2002: 73–74; Schmidt 1996; Deeg 1999).

Nonetheless, as this book argues, neoliberalization engendered a new era of capitalist development specifically configured around financial market reform. As a result, both *dirigiste* and *soziale Marktwirtshcaft* models have dramatically changed.

The French experience

Given that we have discussed the Atlantic epicentre above, I focus here on the French and German cases. Since the early 1970s the so-called 'golden years' of French economic development have given way to a crisis of the *dirigiste* model. The transnationalization of Gallic capital was both a response to and component of the global crises of the 1970s; the increasing transnational orientation of certain fractions was an attempt to compete with other emergent transnationally oriented fractions (van Apeldoorn 2002: 77). Hence, as van Apeldoorn highlighted, the result was renewed impetus for EU integration during the 1980s (ibid.). The form of responses initiated by the Atlantic heartland however, in the 'neoliberal' shift and the restoration of circulating finance capital, had significant repercussions for both French and, albeit to a lesser extent, German models. Where the Atlantic decisions were reactions to immediate recession concerns fuelled by crises within the realm of production, financial market expansion created both incentives and pressures for similar reforms elsewhere; the contender states found themselves faced with peripherilization once again. Domestic financial market reforms, the rise in equity financing and the further congealing of a transnationally oriented Gallic fraction were constituents of the French response. Further, the rescaling of EU governance under the Single European Act and the Maastricht Treaty contributed to the entrepreneurial role of EU institutions in promoting financial integration. As unemployment figures rose to around 12 per cent in the mid 1990s, the French state struggled to restructure production through increased wage moderation, reduced social contributions for unskilled workers and the development of more flexible employment contracts in the mid to late 1990s (OECD 2000: 2). These efforts were mirrored in the state-led processes of financial liberalization through public receipts of privatizations and limits on foreign investments (Schmidt 1996: 189). Gallic capital and state managers alike resisted the implications of an Anglo-American finance-led accumulation regime (Duménil and Lévy 2001: 580).

Nonetheless, both finance and production capitals perceived opportunities for profit-making through capital market reform: between 1985 and 1990 average share prices quadrupled, a result which seemed to support this perception. Simultaneously financial transactions were rapidly becoming more profitable as commission structures were established (Cerny 1989: 174–75, 181). On the other hand, foreign investment and overseas markets further compounded the sense that these reforms were necessary and inevitable. Fuelled by the Anglo-American revolutions, innovative negotiable financial instruments became increasingly more cost-effective sources of investment just as the downward spiral of liberalization fuelled the rise in foreign-owned shareholdings; these progressively undermined the French system of *noyaux durs* (Reberioux 2002). As this book argues though, the degree of fusion within the French system has meant that neoliberalization has been fiercely contested.

The German experience

The Rhenish system of bank–industry relations produced a 'negotiated style' of capitalism (Zysman 1983: 18). Unsurprisingly, the insider-dominated corporate governance structure, rigid labour markets and escalating welfare costs again fuelled a series of unsustainable tensions in the capital–labour compromise (Deeg 2005: 332). Underdeveloped capital markets, coupled with the diminishing costs of equity financing outside of Germany, made both the reform of domestic financial systems and the increased transnationalization of Rhenish capital a pressing priority (Lütz 1998). Throughout the late 1980s and early 1990s German firms began to look for acquisitions, joint ventures, and investments abroad. Again, this transnationalization of Rhenish capital highlighted that domestic 'class compromises or social partnerships [tend to] crumble when one actor has widespread global connections and extensive holdings outside of the domestic economy' (Hodges and Woolcock 1993: 338). The revival of the City of London as an international financial centre prompted Deutsche Bank, the leading German private bank, to relocate its international banking operations to London in 1985. Further, the nascent prominence of the Paris Bourse and the Paris financial futures market (MATIF) as a competitor of the London LIFFE provided the necessary added incentives for the establishment of the centralized Frankfurt exchange (Moran 1994: 174). Thus capital market liberalization and re-regulatory efforts in first-mover states like the UK fuelled a process of 'regulatory arbitrage' (Cerny 1994: 334) as capital sought out the most profitable conditions. In effect the heartland–contender state dynamic was reinvigorated.

The account thus far runs two risks. On the one hand, to argue that neoliberalization is simply the expression of properties inscribed within capital and, more specifically, the obvious or logical attempt to displace crises of Keynesianism is to ascribe to an economic determinism rejected above.[9] On the other hand, to privilege the agency of fractions of capital – and state managers – in directing neoliberalization without explaining the historical impulsions of the 1970s is to emphasize a political pluralism or, more accurately, an overemphasis on contingency. Similarly, this latter account implies both an obvious appeal of the fractions' hegemonic projects – to both state managers and wider social groups – which is not unproblematic. It ascribes both an undue coherence to our fractions and, simultaneously, a formidable ability to articulate their demands. For this reason I turn to Gramsci's notion of common sense.

Common sense

The starting point for this analysis is Gramsci's assertion that all men (*sic*, as hereafter) are philosophers (1971: 9). This is because, each individual holds an, albeit unarticulated and arbitrary, collection of thoughts about the social world which form their own version of common sense. In so doing he (man) participates in a particular conception of the world and contributes towards *either* sustaining *or* modifying it (Gramsci 1971: 9). This socially constructed conception of common sense equates to a process of socialization whereby meanings and self-understandings are diffused through societal diasporas. As Gramsci notes, for example,

> In reality, each generation educates the succeeding one . . . [because] from when children begin to 'see and touch' . . . they accumulate sensations and images which increase and gain in complexity as language is acquired. On analysis, 'spontaneity' becomes more and more problematical.
>
> (Gramsci 1995: 140)

To the extent that these individual common senses reach beyond the purely subjective and become intersubjective understandings, does common sense become universalized. Hence common sense is simultaneously embodied in 'persistent *collective* patterns of human activity and thought' (cf. Cox 1996: 514, cited in Bruff 2008: 9). The result is that the material and ideological realms are inextricably and dialectically interwoven; ideas therefore 'organize human masses, and create the terrain upon which men move, acquire consciousness of their position, struggle, etc.' (Gramsci 1971: 377; see also ibid.: 404).

Changes in common sense therefore involve struggles between sediments of remaining or pre-existing ideas; as Gramsci (1971: 181) notes, it is 'in this phase in which previously germinated ideologies . . . come into confrontation and conflict, until only one of them tends to prevail . . . to propagate itself throughout society'. Specifically, building upon Marx's (1990 [1867]: 507, 535, 569) notion of 'ideological representatives' of capital, Gramsci argued that every social group produces, organically, intellectuals tasked with unifying and promoting the interests of the group. The success of one particular common sense then depends on

> bringing about not only a unison of economic and political aims, but also intellectual and moral unity, posing all the questions around which the struggle rages, not on a corporate but a 'universal' plane and thus creating the hegemony of a fundamental social group over a series of subordinate groups.
> (Gramsci 1971: 5)

Hence, a fraction's hegemony at the level of the state remains interconnected with, yet *relatively* distinct from, societal hegemony.

In the reconfiguration and restoration of class power – central to our problem area – these intellectuals fulfil a particular social function. They are engaged actively in everyday life as agents within economic, political, social and cultural fields as constructor, organizer and 'permanent persuader' in forming or contesting hegemony (ibid.: 9–10; Morton 2007: 91–92; 2003). As such, he/she fulfils a 'directive' function (Gramsci 1971: 10): '[organic] intellectuals [therefore] have the function of organizing the social hegemony of a group and that group's domination of the state' (Gramsci 1996: 200); thus, intellectuals 'need to organize and develop the conceptions of the world present in their social group into a more coherent and collective ideology' (Bruff 2008: 55). Though journalists, lay leaders, publishing houses and writers also fulfil this function (see, for example, Morton 2003) those individuals and collectives most integrated within state apparatuses tend to articulate more lucid worldviews precisely because of their specialization in the 'elaboration of ideas' and the pragmatic demands of the policy-making process (Gramsci 1971: 334).

At times of crisis, when alternative strategies are considered, these nascent common senses are particularly prominent. Not only does the crisis likely constitute the tipping point between one hegemonic common sense and another, but fractions seek to embed their own pragmatic/corporate interests within the nascent (that is, emerging hegemonic) common sense. These *hegemonic projects* thus seek to transcend purely corporate interests promoting – at once – a concrete programme of economic reform embedded within implicit causal assumptions and worldviews (common sense), universalizing their appeal (Gramsci 1971: 181). Yet this is not to subscribe to a political pluralism or a historical idealism since the social content of the state and the underlying dynamics of these struggles are anchored in transformations in society (Poulantzas 1973: 44). Where pluralism emphasizes contingent agency and idealism ideas and discourses, here both agency and projects are framed by and mutually constitutive of capitalisms' underlying impulsions.

As a result, particular historical epochs, embedded in extant material social conditions and common senses, produce crystallizations represented – *inter alia* –

in particular institutions, infrastructures and legal systems (see Poulantzas 1978: 58). This is because '"no social practice or set of relations floats free of the determinate effects of the concrete relations in which they are located" (Hall 1996: 45) *and* the ideologies that "are embedded in collective and communal modes of living" (Simon 1991: 59)' (both cited in Bruff 2008: 52). Consequently, impulsions (see above) are the crystallizations of material condensations of historical modes of capitalism, collective agency and class struggle, and hegemonic common senses. Though not solely *material* phenomena – as if the material were entirely separate from the ideational – they present themselves with a material force and – precisely because of their formal crystallizations – are relatively path-dependent. Therefore whilst the imperative to produce is materially determined, the imperative to accumulate surplus value is historically specific to capitalism, and the idiosyncrasies of a particular mode of capitalism (such as neoliberalism) thus require the concrete abstractions of common sense and agency (as noted above). A form of 'economic' determinism implicitly assumes the false separation of ideas from material forms. On closer examination, common senses and class struggles are condensed and crystallized in these particular – historically and geographically specific – forms, with their own ensuing impulsions. As a result, societal development is both open-ended and path-dependent since socio-institutional formations, spatial fixes – as accumulation-facilitating configurations – and common sense, are both *relatively* transitory and yet *relatively* intransient.

This has two relevant implications: first, whether manifested in common senses, hegemonic projects or changing accumulation regimes they inherently and necessarily display both old and new so that *convergent divergence* is the norm (see Chapter 5). Moreover, second, this explains Gramsci's earlier comment that crises – though not *determining* outcomes – create conditions apposite to the acceptance of certain ideas and actors. In essence, certain historical and spatial preconditions are inscribed within the unfolding of crises which – in turn – shape future trajectories. This becomes apparent through our empirical analysis.

Neoliberal common sense

Whilst the production of neoliberal common sense pre-dated the Keynesian crisis it is, 'not something rigid and stationary, but is in continuous transformation, becoming enriched with scientific ideas and with philosophical opinions which have entered into common circulation' (Gramsci 1985: 421). Thus, as our notion of variegated neoliberalism suggests, neoliberal common sense displays this same path dependency and dynamism (Bruff 2008: 50). In its early stages this common sense was nonetheless a component of the crisis itself, shaping both perceptions and responses of social agents as the institutional approximations of Keynesian common sense ran aground.

Economic research centres fulfilled a specific social function then as collections of 'organic intellectuals' and as 'the institutional frameworks within and through which different class fractions (or components) of capital and labour attempt to establish their particular interests and ideas as the generally accepted, or "common sense", view' (Bieler 2000: 13). These are 'expert groups', 'who are far from autonomous, (inasmuch as such a thing exists) . . . [and] are often directly linked to concrete (transnationally oriented) social forces' (van Apeldoorn and Horn 2007: 82). In the post-war period disparate and contradictory economic ideas emerged, which would later coalesce to become neoliberal common sense.

Chapters 6 and 7 explore the research centres and the economic ideas in greater depth, suffice it to highlight here the historical importance of neoliberal common sense. In the post-war era competing research programmes on monetarism, new classical economics and rational-expectations models developed. Economists like Friedrich von Hayek, Milton Friedman, and those within the Mont Pelerin Society (founded by Hayek) argued – *inter alia* – against the expansion of government, strong trade unions, business monopoly and the threat of inflation. These theories shared an emphasis on avoiding political interference in markets, resting on the fundamental assumption of market rationality (Best 2005: 89). They argued that 'active public economic policy is either redundant or, more likely, perverse' (ibid.: 92). As full employment guarantees appeared to increasingly conflict with both inflationary pressures (a generalized concern) and profit rates (a particularistic concern of capital), the idea of a so-called 'natural rate' of unemployment had an obvious attraction. Similarly the monetarist emphasis on price stability at a time of severe currency fluctuations resonated with experiences and provided both a framework of understanding and a proposed solution to the difficulties. In effect, the crisis of the 1970s was part of a struggle for the hegemony of neoliberal common sense. Thus, the fragility of the UK Keynesian architecture (see above) was partially attributable to the historic sediments of liberal common sense in addition to the ensuing impulsions of financial expansion and elite agency.

The stagnation of the UK model, the continuing role of the City as a financial centre, and the prominence of anti-Keynesian think tanks such as the Institute of Economic Affairs and, later, the Centre for Policy Studies, contributed to the shape of the response to the crisis (Harvey 2007: 56–57). Nascent neoliberal ideas provided an ostensibly 'logical' alternative to Keynesianism, constructing a relatively simple discourse highlighting rigidities as causes of UK stagflation (van Apeldoorn 2002: 68). The push for labour market flexibility, welfare austerity and the change of governmental priorities from demand management to creating attractive conditions for mobile business (Cerny 2000) therefore began – in the European context – in earnest in the UK. Whilst the adoption of 'neoliberal' policies and the early forms of neoliberal common sense preceded the right-wing government of 1979 (Hay 2001: 209) it was the Conservative government who set about creating a relative surplus of labour by breaking trade union power (in the early 1980s) and restoring class power through the financial services revolution (in the mid to late 1980s). It is understandable then that these ideas have an obvious appeal to *transnationally oriented* capital – emphasizing both the freedom of circulation and the expansion of finance (Overbeek and van der Pijl 1993) – with fractions of capital seizing upon elements of neoliberal common sense to push for capital market liberalization and reform of the City's regulatory institutions. Capital's understanding both of its immediate conditions and opportunity structures was therefore shaped by this emerging common sense, giving neoliberalism a historically specific character as a particular epoch within capitalism.

Contender-state crises in the 1990s

The above has laid the theoretical basis for our analysis of transnationally oriented fractions (Chapters 3, 4, 5 and 8) and common sense (Chapters 6 and 7). Finally though, we should highlight the historical conditions which preceded the recent spate of EU financial market reform. As noted in Chapter 1, the arrival of the Lamfalussy Process, the Financial Services Action Plan and the Lisbon Agenda were contingent upon the wider integration project and the immediate concerns of Economic and Monetary Union. Nonetheless, as components of neoliberalization they were driven by the restructuring of global and European capitalism, prompted by: crises within the member states, the (re-)emergence of transnationally oriented fractions and the development of neoliberal common sense. As Figure 2.1 shows, where unemployment for the UK had consistently fallen throughout the period, figures within both France and Germany (compounded by reunification) remained high throughout the 1990s and early 2000s. This would suggest a prolonged crisis of these two models.

In sum, two tentative conclusions are therefore proposed: one is simply that crises will play a significant role in our ensuing analysis; the other is that we should expect to see ongoing differences – or path dependencies – within the three models. Figures 1.1, 1.2, 1.3 and 2.1 therefore reflect this convergent divergence tension: Figures 1.1, 1.2 and 1.3 displayed the increased prominence of finance and the levelling out of welfare spending characteristic of *neoliberalization*;

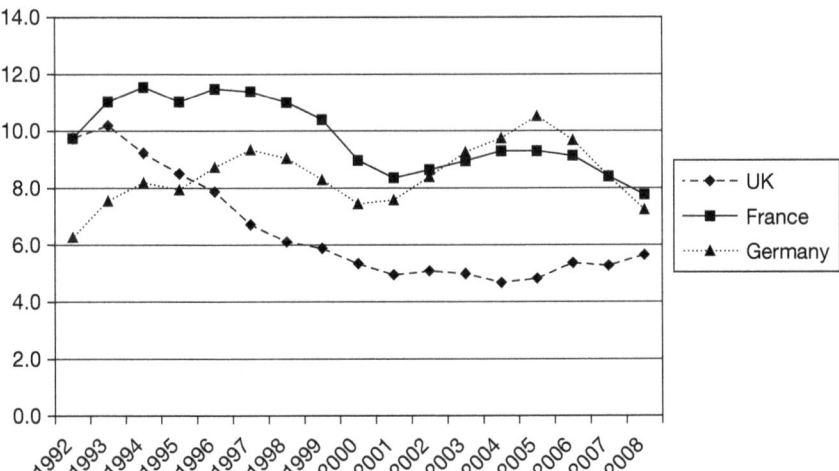

Figure 2.1 Harmonized unemployment rates (%).

Figure 2.1 reflects the ongoing structural differences characteristic of *variegation*. These two skeins provide the skeleton for the ensuing analysis.

Summary and social function

This chapter has emphasized the global restructuring of capitalism in response to the crisis of the Keynesian mode. Keynesianism had effectively contained the contradictions of the capital–labour relation until – by virtue of the rigidities and barriers to flows of labour and investment, and the maintenance of full-employment guarantees which had earlier fuelled Keynesian successes – it approached its limits. The increasing perception, fuelled by an immanent critique from new classical and monetarist economics, that stagnation could be relieved through liberalization and changing state priorities proved crucial. It framed the debates on both causes and solutions to the crises of the 1960s and 1970s, much as Keynesian common sense had shaped post-war reconstruction. The epicentre of both crises and responses was thus the City of London and New York – as an Atlantic heartland. The choice of location and shape which neoliberalization adopted was therefore partially driven by the expansion of the financial system – displacing crises through renewed profit-making and financial provision to industry – and partially, by the historical significance of London and New York as centres of 'finance' fractions. Thus, whilst EU integration has provided new investment opportunities, a reserve army of labour and new markets, it has also exported a finance-led mode of accumulation. Appearances of restored profitability therefore mask the underlying contradictions of financial expansion. Moreover, the perception that financial profits can be attained without the messy business of surplus value extraction continues to undermine capitalism's attachment to the real economy (Clarke 1988: 7); as 2007–09 revealed, this is the sugar-coated poison pill of neoliberalism.

What follows is a study of the three fractions – at the apex of neoliberalization – within the UK, France and Germany and the (re)production of neoliberal common sense in these three member states. In relation to one big question behind this analysis, I argue that these dynamics underscore the variegated nature of neoliberalism. Thus we witness convergence within divergence: neoliberal capitalist restructuring and the reconfiguration of social forces; similar trajectories and yet, reinforced national–domestic features of competing capitalisms.

This argument in turn informs the social function of the book. Having outlined the tendency for neoliberalism to place more susceptible segments of society (working classes/wage labourers) at risk – in contradistinction to the conventional 'rising tide' argument – I draw on the Gramscian notion of counter-hegemonic resistance (Gramsci 1971: 229–30; Bieler 2006). In essence, 'Gramsci called for organic intellectuals to infuse common sense with a philosophy of praxis that encourages subaltern groups' critical understanding of their subordination in society' (Mittelman and Chin 2005: 19). Here Gramsci's notion of deconstructing rather than reifying dominant worldviews is crucial. By highlighting – at once – capital's impulsions and the socially constructed character of neoliberal common sense (and discourses) I aim to provide a nuanced, accurate account of the contingencies of neoliberalism; demystifying elements which are often over-determined. I focus in particular on the concept of a transnational capitalist class often assumed to be driving neoliberalization (Robinson and Harris 2000; Sklair 2001). Here, I aim to highlight the contingency of their transnational unity, contributing to understandings of moments for political organization in rejecting or reshaping neoliberalization (Drainville 1994: 111). Further, in the concluding chapter I argue that crises provide unique windows of opportunity for the contestation of future capitalisms. This of course raises questions of 'critical' theory and leftist academics which must also be addressed.

Part II
Fractions of capital

3   Transnationally oriented fractions of capital

In this chapter we change gears, focusing in on the particularities of neo-liberalization. Here the main protagonists of EU financial market integration, transnationally oriented fractions of capital, will be introduced. I will begin by outlining their membership and organization within financial trade associations. Through a brief analysis of their accumulation strategies (developed further in later chapters) the basis is laid for understanding the 'material' factors *shaping* their interests. This term captures – for analytic purposes – the scale of their operations, their function in the overall circuit of capital, and the underlying socio-institutional configurations.

This in turn is significant in understanding the relative cohesion within the fractions, between what are essentially kindred strangers (Vogel 1996);[1] capitalists divided by the nature of competition in the world market yet engaged in coalition building – to secure institutional support and apposite political conditions – around relatively similar concerns. Significantly, through focusing on the fractions the other factors outlined in preceding chapters (impulsions and common sense) are apparent in the political agency of these key protagonists. This avoids either the economic determinism or liberal pluralism of those emphasizing *either* impulsions *or* agents in demystifying neoliberalization.

The chapter therefore begins exploring the utility of a Gramscian historical materialist account, with its nuanced dialectical approach to structure and agent, material and ideational. It argues that within these processes of neoliberalization, transnationally oriented fractions have been both integral to and, further, best positioned to capitalize on, these wider dynamics. The overall process of neo-liberalization was rooted in burgeoning contradictions in the capital–labour relation, yet was displaced through prolonged financial expansion and shaped – and further propelled – through our fractions.

The chapter begins by further exploring the concept of fractions of capital and their political agency. It then introduces financial trade associations as the institutional approximations of these fractions in the context of EU financial market integration. The membership of these fractions is examined, supporting the argument that these associations embody transnationally oriented social forces. Chapter 4 reinforces this analysis by showing how these fractions employ processes which neutralize and marginalize contending voices. Such arguments are echoed within the Public Policy literature on lobbying and interest groups. These accounts however, fail to embed these conclusions within a theory of agency within capitalism's wider impulsions and common sense production, thereby ignoring the crucial social content question.

Transnationally oriented fractions

As Chapter 2 discussed, neoliberalization has involved – as both condition and outcome – the transnationalization of capitalism. The transnational is a term often invoked yet poorly defined. As Overbeek (2003: 4) notes 'some use it as synonymous with "international", others with "supranational", and others again see it as coterminous with "global" '. In this book I use the term transnational to denote a relation produced through the simultaneously expansionary and nationally embedded character of capitalism. Capitalism's spatial contradiction is that whilst it operates under the impulsion to eliminate all geographical barriers (Marx 1973 [1857]: 539) it necessarily requires provisionally stabilized institutions and infrastructures (Harvey 1985: 128–63). Thus a relentless process of creative destruction takes place; creating, dismantling and recreating relatively fixed and immobile 'spatial fixes'. In transcending national borders and crossing typical analytical divisions of subnational, national and international the transnational therefore captures this *scalar* and *relational* set of processes within capitalism.

As political geographers have noted, a scalar conception of capitalism avoids the dualisms of a 'levels of analysis' approach; capitalism operates across multiple overlapping and intertwined scales within a series of nested hierarchies (Swyngedouw 2004). Similarly, space itself is neither a social construction – a concept, for example – nor merely a platform for social relations, but is one of their 'constitutive dimensions, itself historically produced, reconfigured and transformed' (Brenner 1999b: 40). The production and reproduction of social and political space is presupposition, medium and outcome of capitalism (ibid.: 43). Of particular note are the relations embedded within these processes. I focus primarily on this element.

Transnationalization therefore concerns the reorganization of capitalism. Avoiding the state-centrism of VoC accounts we also avoid the misrecognition of a so-called 'erosion' or 'retreat' of the state. The state remains an essential site for social, political and economic relations whilst recognizing the re-scaling of territoriality and governance on sub- and supra-national scales. Similarly, the relations upon which capitalist accumulation depend become reconfigured rather than abandoned. Despite the transnationalization of capitalism – experienced most emphatically in particular circuits of capital and by particular fractions – capital remains embedded in territorial institutional ensembles such as state regulatory institutions and technological infrastructures, as well as in social configurations such as class alliances and localized labour markets (Harvey 1985: 146–57; Brenner 1998: 463–64).

In understanding the interests of our three fractions then, these factors obtain a political and ideological relevance. Already the notion of a disembedded 'transnational capitalist class' (Robinson and Harris 2000) appears suspect; we will return to this in Chapter 8. For now I focus on the differential scales and functions of the three fractions, providing a basis for subsequent examination of their hegemonic projects. I argue that the three fractions examined – those emerging from the UK, France and Germany – are *transnationally oriented* fractions: integrated within transnational circuits yet nationally embedded. The fractions share certain similar interests (see Chapter 5) *connected to* though not *determined by* their scale, function and socio-institutional configurations. Nonetheless, they remain distinctive – as we shall see.

Fractions in trade associations

Taking fractions as our point of engagement with the empirical analysis of neoliberalization – and EU financial market integration post–2000 as a punctuated evolutionary moment – financial trade associations form our entry point. Historically, these associations have organized diverse financial interests as a precursor for engagement in political negotiations (Coleman and Perl 1999; Josselin 1996). As the diagram of the Lamfalussy Process (Figure 1.5) suggested, the incorporation of association and member firm responses in EU and national consultation processes has been on the rise.

Our conceptualization of fractional rallying points suggests that social forces with similar interests will tend to coalesce around nodal points, aiming to transcend special interests with the goal of securing political support. Financial trade associations are one such social formation, driven by the coalescence of interests and the structure of national and EU level policymaking (Josselin 1996). Here coordinated responses to proposed legislation are sought from the industry itself. The multiplicity of competing and often contradictory interests within these associations can only be understood historically through empirical engagement. This is the task of Chapters 3, 4 and 5. The core argument of Chapters 3 and 4 is twofold: these fractions have sought institutional representation, *inter alia*, through these trade associations; and this process has involved the neutralization and marginalization of dissenting and competing social forces.[2]

I begin with the trade associations and their membership. To emphasize the domestic–national differences between these transnationally oriented fractions, the labels *Atlantic, Gallic* and *Rhenish* will be applied to the UK, French and German fractions respectively. In the City of London the two most prominent trade associations in EU financial market integration have been the British Bankers Association (BBA) and the London Investment Banking Association (LIBA), as institutional approximations of an Atlantic fraction. In Germany, the private banking sector, which arguably contains the most transnationally oriented members, is represented by the Bundesverband deutscher Banken (BdB). In addition, I will argue that a Rhenish fraction has also established the Initiativ Finanzstandort Deutschland (IFD) as an action group for the private banking sector in cooperation with more internationally focused state agencies (the Federal Ministry of Finance and the Bundesbank).[3] In France, the two most prominent trade associations have been the French Banking Federation (FBF) and the Association Française des Entreprises d'Investissements (AFEI). Whilst the AFEI changed its name to the Association Française des Marchés Financiers (AMAFI) in June 2008 the empirical analysis focuses on the period prior to this change, so I retain the former acronym AFEI. These have functioned as institutional approximations of a Gallic fraction.

The Atlantic fraction is a product of the Atlantic circuit of money capital outlined previously. The historical linkages with London and New York as financial centres and the integration in transnational-*global* circuits make them prone to more overtly economic liberal policies (van der Pijl 1984: 10; Overbeek and van der Pijl 1993: 15; see also Polanyi 2001 [1944]: 141). Their membership includes banks and investment firms such as Citigroup, Morgan Stanley, Merrill Lynch, JPMorgan Chase, Credit Suisse and Royal Bank of Scotland (RBS).

The Rhenish fraction is again a product of the insider-dominated corporate governance structures historically linking German finance and industry, as well as the transnationalization of German (particularly finance) capital in the second half of the twentieth century. Though several operate globally the majority of members have a European focus; moreover, they have been particularly active in expanding investment operations in Central and Eastern Europe since the fall of Communism. The Rhenish fraction is thus characterized as a transnational-*European* fraction, with members such as the Deutsche Bank, Allianz Group, Dresdner Bank, Commerzbank and the HypoVereinsbank.

Finally, the Gallic fraction is also a product of the historical Gallic fusion of finance and production capitals. As with the Rhenish fraction, though certain members operate globally the uniquely nationally embedded socio-institutional configurations underpinning their accumulation strategies make them a transnational-*national* fraction. Their membership includes institutions such as BNP Paribas, Crédit Mutuel, Crédit Agricole, Société Générale and Dexia.

Scale, function and socio-institutional configurations as shaping factors

To substantiate the claim that the three fractions are transnationally oriented and yet predominantly global, European and national respectively, a brief analysis of their scale is offered. This is not intended to be conclusive, though it suggests a certain distinction between the three which will be expanded in later chapters. As Chapter 2 also discussed, the distinctions between the various circuits of capital is highly problematic and more so in the post–1970s period. Nonetheless, the following also uses the type and proportion of their business operations as a proxy for their function and socio-institutional configurations. Here I again outline both the relative commonalities *within* each fraction and the distinctions *between* the three. In essence, the Atlantic fraction tends to focus on finance-led strategies – manifested in an emphasis on securities-related activities and investment banking; the Gallic fraction rests, primarily, on sustained quasi-'fused' linkages between circuits of finance and production capital – manifested, *inter alia*, in retail banking

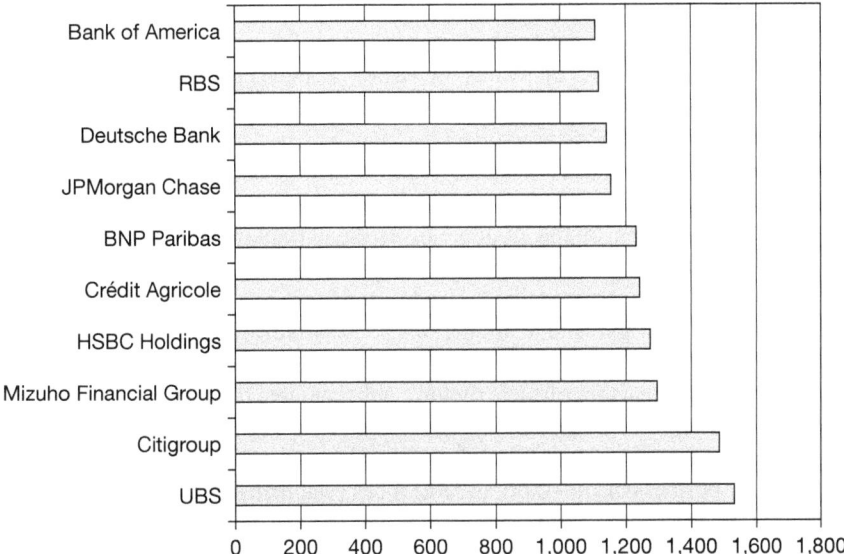

Figure 3.1 World's top ten banks by assets ($bn).
Source: The Banker 2005.

and agriculture; and the Rhenish fraction shares similarities with *both* Gallic and Atlantic strategies. The socio-institutional configurations begin to become apparent here and are discussed in later chapters.

We begin with Figure 3.1 which outlines the diverse national–domestic origins of the world's leading financial service providers (FSPs). Measured by assets the top ten banking conglomerates include the Royal Bank of Scotland, JPMorgan Chase and Citigroup from an Atlantic fraction; Deutsche Bank from a Rhenish fraction; and BNP Paribas from a Gallic fraction. As will be later argued, these 'multinational' actors have been caricatured as a Champions League of FSPs (Mügge 2008) or members of a transnational capitalist class (Sklair 2001). Instead our immediate concern is to (begin to) differentiate between these member firms as constituents of transnationally oriented *fractions*. The distinction will prove significant.

The Atlantic (transnational-global) fraction

The accumulation strategies of the Atlantic fraction have historically been underpinned by their integration in circuits of circulating money capital. With the expansion of financial systems and the further transnationalization of finance capital – and the relatively weak integration of Atlantic with production fractions – their position as a *globally* operating fraction has been further entrenched. Unsurprisingly then, an alternative measure of the world's largest banks suggests both their global prominence and their reliance on finance-led accumulation. Here, Figure 3.2 is compiled of the world's largest banks measured by market capitalization; that is, in terms of the current market value of the bank itself (current share price times by number of shares in issue), a measure which suggests the importance of equity-based financing for these FSPs. From this graph, seven of the top ten FSPs (including investment banking and asset-management operations) in the world originate in or are joint ventures incorporating North-American or British conglomerates. Since all seven are represented within either the British Bankers Association or the London Investment Banking Association a brief analysis of their rhetoric reveals the transnational-global scale of their operations. Moreover, their attachment to both London and New York as financial centres is as apparent as their global operations; so a conceptualization of Atlantic interests and identity must be related to the regulatory climate of these two locations.

A qualitative analysis of their rhetoric substantiates the transnational-global claim. Citigroup for example highlight that their central institution, Citibank, is 'a global bank but [which] operate[s] at a local level' (Citibank 2007). Since it opened for business in New York in 1812 it has established operations in over one hundred other countries and has been located in the City of London for over a hundred years (ibid.).

JPMorgan Chase shows similar traits. Whilst its corporate headquarters are in New York it is a 'leading global financial services firm' with operations in more than fifty countries (JPMorgan Chase 2007). Again however, the connection with the City of London is also apparent: Cazenove (a 'British' firm) and Chase joined

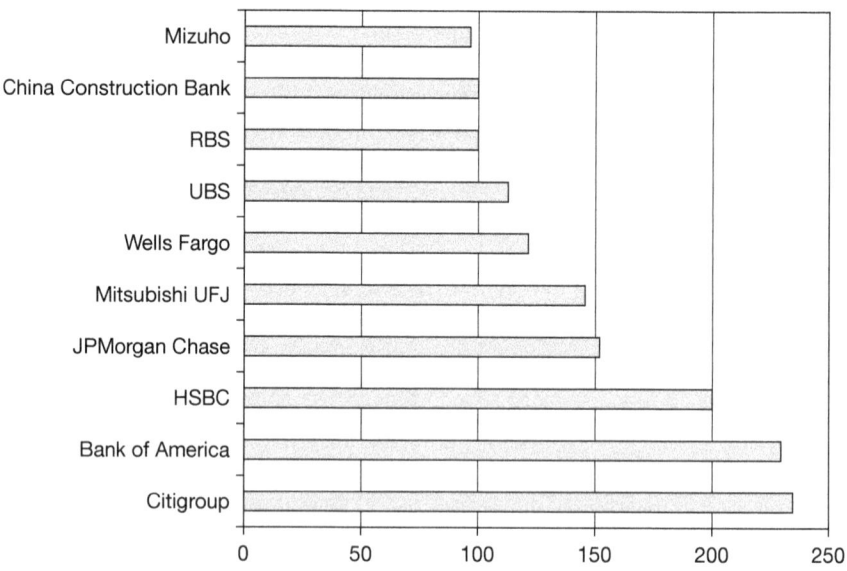

Figure 3.2 World's largest banks by market capitalization ($bn).

Source: Economist 2006.

on 28 February 2005 to provide investment banking for the UK (ibid.) and – even prior to this – Chase held significant operations in the City.

Further evidence from UBS and Credit Suisse highlights both their global operations in over fifty countries (UBS 2005) and the objective of the Credit Suisse Group 'to become the world's premier bank, renowned for its expertise in investment banking, private banking and asset management and most valued for its advice, innovation and execution'; both have headquarters in the City (Credit Suisse 2005). Finally, and of equal import, is the leading corporate bank in the UK, the Royal Bank of Scotland, which opened its first branch in the City in 1900 and currently has over 20 million customers worldwide (RBS 2004). The global operations of the Atlantic fraction are undeniable, as is their strong presence in the City of London.

Atlantic finance-led

The second step then, is to offer a brief summary of their business lines. The Atlantic fraction relies on finance-led accumulation: in short, profits through financial services. Of course, this is at the core of the neoliberal mode of accumulation. Nonetheless, accumulation strategies of Gallic and Rhenish fractions remain embedded within national–domestic configurations, giving them a qualitative and quantitative difference. We shall return to this. Suffice it to note that the finance-led strategies are evident in the Atlantic fraction's dependence on revenue through securities and investment banking. Figures 3.3 and 3.4 reveal the incomes derived from the various business lines of the aforementioned investment banks and firms.

For Citigroup the diversity of their operations is apparent, although the primacy of capital markets and banking is clear, amounting to almost $5.5 billion in annual

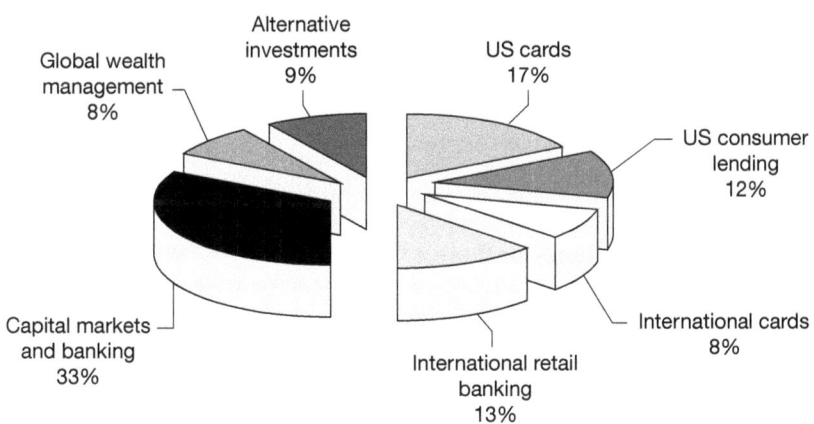

Figure 3.3 Citigroup (2004).

Source: Citigroup 2005.

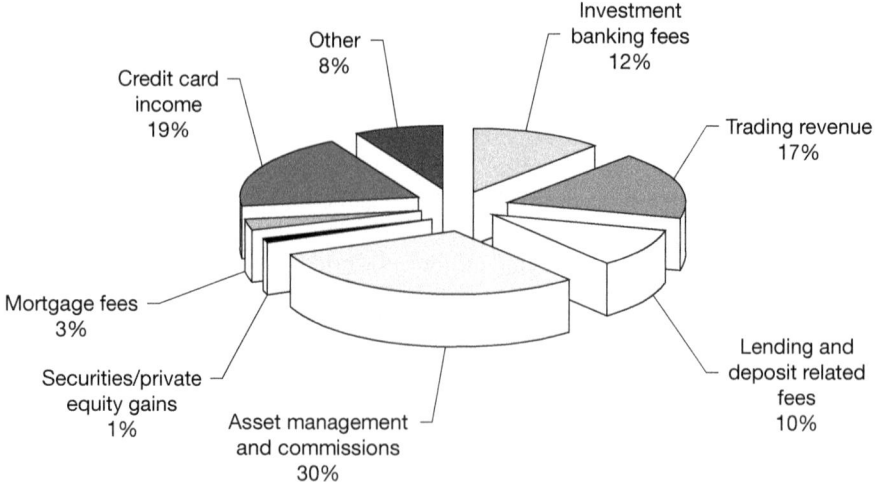

Figure 3.4 JPMorgan Chase (2004).

Source: JPMorgan Chase 2005.

revenue for the year 2004. For JPMorgan Chase a similar, yet even starker, conclusion can be drawn. For the purposes of our analysis only mortgage fees, lending and deposit-related fees, and credit card income are not, strictly speaking, directly dependent on capital markets. The result is that almost $20.8 billion of their annual revenue was derived from trading-related operations.

Again the diversity of Credit Suisse operations belies the importance of trading-related activities and hence Figure 3.5 has been simplified in order to convey the proportion of revenue accrued from trading revenues, commissions, fees and securities. Slightly ahead of the total net premiums received from insurance operations ($20.9 billion) Credit Suisse made over $23.6 billion from trading-related activities in 2004. Finally the figures for the Royal Bank of Scotland (Figure 3.6) reveal a similar picture; the single most important portion of revenue originates in financial market operations. For the RBS this amounts to approximately $4.3 billion in 2005.

The Gallic (transnational-national) fraction

As Figure 3.1 highlighted, Gallic members such as BNP Paribas and Crédit Agricole are amongst the world's leading financial service providers. Simultaneously, the fused linkages of production and finance capitals have shaped Gallic accumulation strategies along transnational-national lines (Overbeek 2004).

An examination of the French financial system suggests precisely this. Recall that the French financial system is largely dominated by credit institutions with a dominant core of five Gallic (transnationally oriented) banks (Commission

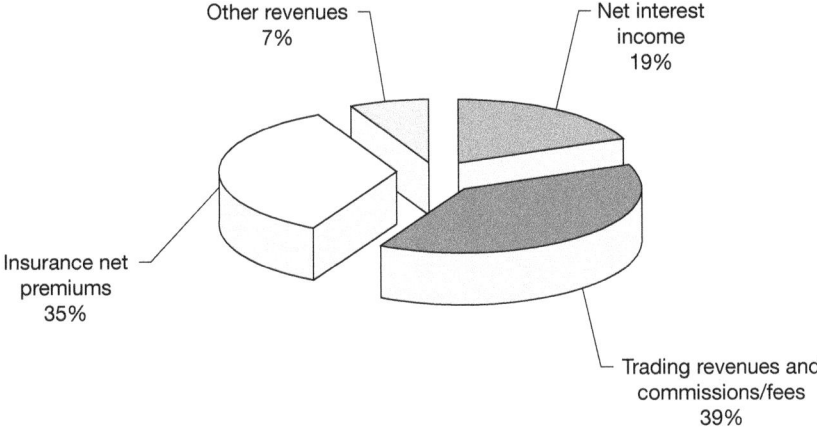

Figure 3.5 Crédit Suisse (2004).
Source: Crédit Suisse Group 2004.

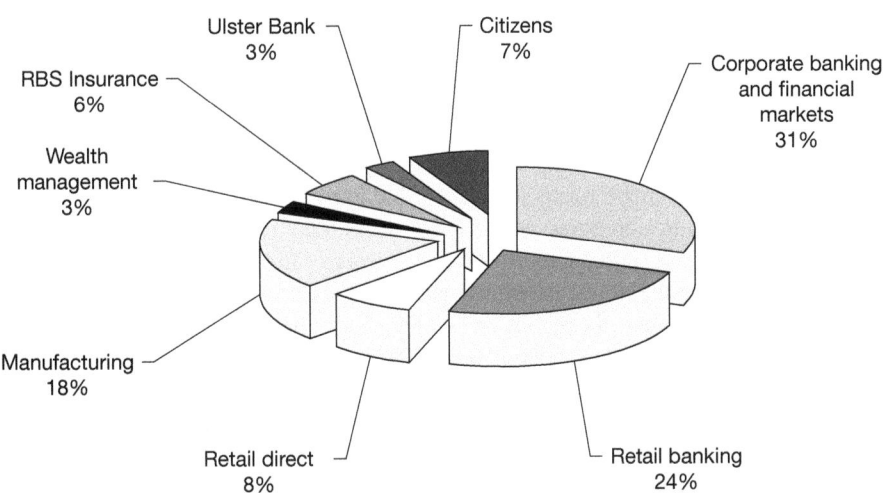

Figure 3.6 RBS (2005).
Source: RBS 2005.

Bancaire 2004). Figure 3.7 shows this data. In both housing/mortgage markets and finance provided to industry, the leading five Gallic players account for approximately 60 per cent of the total investment. Expanding the scope to include the next five largest institutions only adds an additional 20 per cent to the picture.[4]

Predictably then, the Gallic fraction comprises nationally and transnationally oriented operations. A brief examination of the aforementioned five leading banks

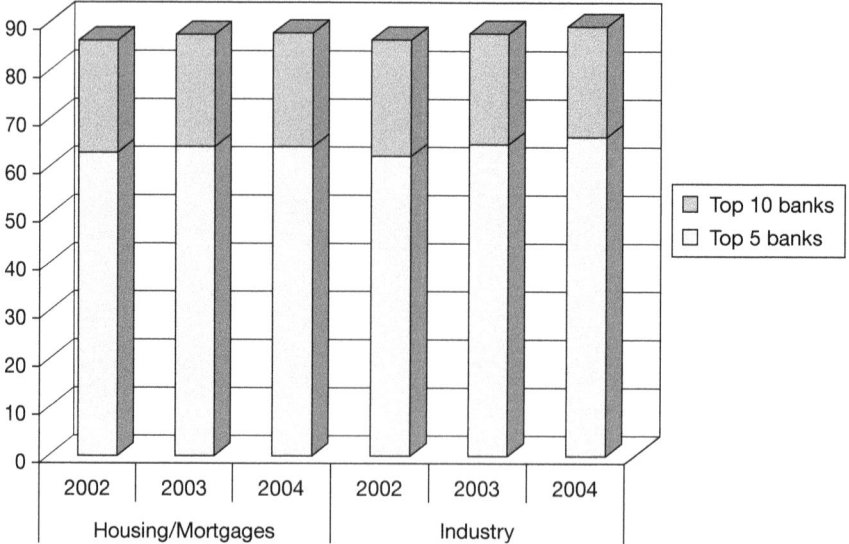

Figure 3.7 Concentration of French banking system, according to types of operations*.
Source: Commission Bancaire 2004.
Note: *These business lines are selected to provide a wide overview of banking operations.

demonstrates this. According to its own rhetoric, BNP Paribas is 'an international group . . . operating on five continents' (BNP Paribas 2005). On the other hand its primary focus is European, with 81,000 of its total 110,000 employees within European markets (ibid.). Crédit Agricole reveals a similar tendency: in its rhetoric it claims to be the 'largest banking organization in France with a presence across the entire spectrum of banking and finance activities' (Crédit Agricole 2005), describing its activities as those of 'sustainable, profitable growth through a unified approach between the regional banks and the Group's specialist business line subsidiaries' (ibid.). Whilst on the one hand they have operations in 66 different countries, of their 62,000 employees some 42,000 are located within France itself. The Gallic fraction are a transnational-national coalition.

The remaining prominent Gallic actors merely reinforce these claims. Though ranked outside the world's top ten in 2005 the Société Générale is undeniably a key transnational-*national* actor: it holds first position in the non-mutual retail banking groups in France; it is the third largest corporate and investment bank in the Eurozone and the largest bank-owned asset manager in the Eurozone (Société Générale 2005). With a majority of branches within the domestic market and almost half the number outside of France the importance of domestic sources of revenue are evident (ibid.). The final banking group of note is Dexia. Again its maxim of 'no achievement without lasting commitment' echoes the importance on social clauses emphasized in the Gallic fraction's rhetoric (Dexia 2005; see

Chapter 8). Established from an alliance of the Crédit local de France and the Crédit Communal de Belgique, Dexia ranks among the fifteen largest financial institutions in the Eurozone (ibid.). Its primary market, however, remains that of local public finance.

Gallic fusion

The Gallic strategies tend to rely therefore on the historically fused linkages between circuits of production and finance capitals, with a heavily nationally embedded content. In comparison, the lesser significance of corporate and investment banking contrasts sharply with the strategies of the Atlantic fraction. For example, Figure 3.8 reveals that one of the two leading Gallic players relies on retail banking as its primary revenue source. Of the 53 per cent of its operations composed of retail banking, services within the French market account for 25 per cent of this figure (BNP Paribas 2005). This includes 5.85 million individual and private banking clients, 500,000 entrepreneurs and 20,000 corporate and institutional clients within French borders, with approximately 31,000 of its 80,000 European employees in this division spread across a network of 200 Retail Banking Centres within France (ibid.). In comparison, the international retail banking operations only account for 42,600 employees spread across 55 territories. Again the *national* focus is interwoven with its business lines.

Similarly, with Crédit Agricole over 40 per cent of their employees are engaged in retail banking activities compared with only 11 per cent in asset-management services (Crédit Agricole 2005). Figure 3.9 supports this conclusion: whilst their operations are divided between French and international markets the dominance of retail banking in revenue terms is clear. In their capacity as France's leading retail bank they state the following:

> [we] undertook an in-depth review of the traditional mutualist values of respect and consideration and came up with a new modern-day variant: 'a lasting relationship'. Crédit Agricole is therefore positioning itself as the bank that supports its customers through good times and bad.
>
> (Crédit Agricole 2005)

The importance of so-called 'longer-term' relationships to the Gallic fraction is underpinned by their connections with other nationally oriented circuits and social forces.

Concerning these domestic social configurations, the Crédit Agricole, as its name suggests, has significant linkages with the French farming community wherein almost 90 per cent of French farmers employ its banking services (ibid.). Subsumed within this figure were approximately $6.85 billion worth of investment loans in 2005 and approximately 50,000 farms insured with Crédit Agricole's non-life insurance business Pacifica (ibid.). In turn the bank is keen to promote its position as the 'preferred partner to local authorities' providing 'nearly all budget financing for the regions, departments and communities . . . and for a large number

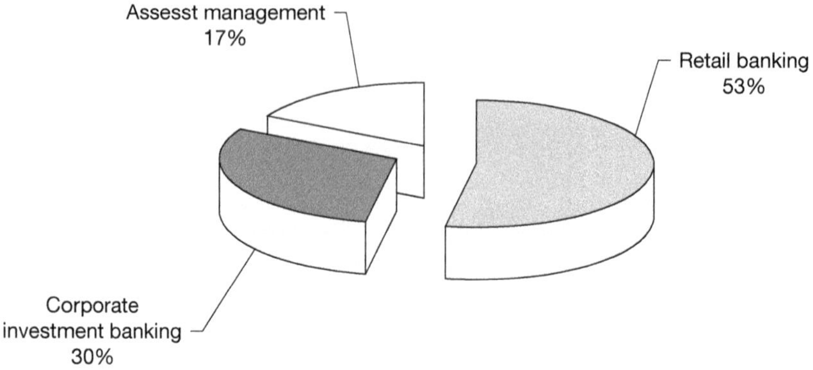

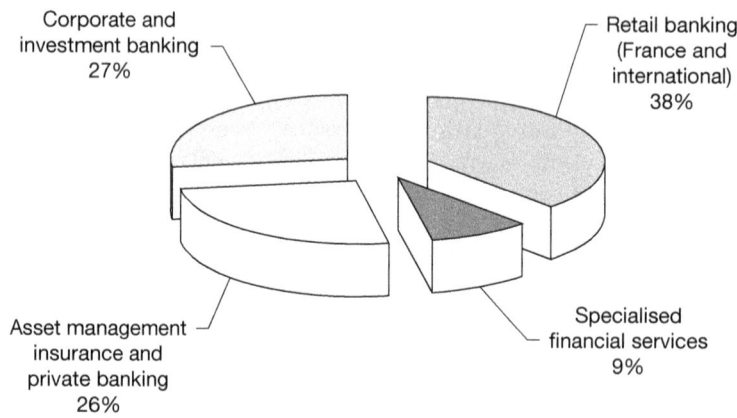

Figure 3.8 BNP Paribas (2005).

Source: BNP Paribas 2005.

Figure 3.9 Crédit Agricole (2005).

Source: Crédit Agricole 2005.

of other public-sector organizations' amounting to approximately $28 billion worth of customer assets. In brief, coupled with the ongoing acquisition of 25 per cent stakes in French companies (EDF, GDF and Sanef) in 2005 the importance of sustaining the linkages with localized circuits and forces is evident.

An analysis of several other Gallic members simply confirms this trend. The Société Générale again relies predominantly upon retail banking services, both domestic and international, with over 75 per cent of the revenue being produced from French networks. Figure 3.10 characterizes this. Again, whilst clear divisions between banking and investment operations are unsustainable, the importance of the domestic market to a leading Gallic player is clearly visible, as is the importance of retail banking.

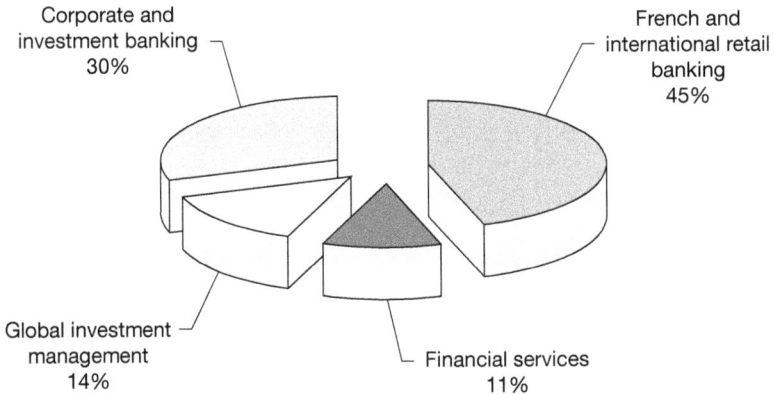

Figure 3.10 Société Générale (2005).
Source: Société Générale 2005.

As we noted, Dexia's primary market is local public finance. Therefore, though Dexia has an 'intensive presence in the capital markets' (Dexia 2005) this is substantively different from the transnational-global, finance-led strategies of the Atlantic fraction; instead Dexia employs the capital market for 'the funding and management of the Group's balance sheet, or for the engineering of sophisticated products and solutions delivered to clients of the various business lines' (ibid.); in other words to finance a predominantly nationally oriented customer base.

As Figure 3.11 reveals, over 50 per cent of their revenue is the product of public and private project financing with approximately half of that figure accruing from operations within France and Belgium. Again, whilst Dexia is clearly transnationally oriented in scale it retains a strong emphasis on French markets and localized circuits for profit.

The Rhenish (transnational-European) fraction

Returning to Figure 3.1, the Deutsche Bank appears amongst the world's leading FSPs as a global actor. Nonetheless, the historical predominance of Atlantic capital in global markets and the Rhenish transnationalization in Continental and Central and Eastern Europe make them substantially a transnational-European fraction. For example, in Deutsche Bank's rhetoric it describes itself as 'a global bank with strong roots in its German home market' (Deutsche Bank 2004). They explain their position to be that of a 'leader in Germany and Europe' whilst still 'powerful and growing in North America, Asia and key emerging markets' (ibid.). These statements are supported by the figures: in terms of staff, Deutsche employs 63,000 of whom 42 per cent are located in Germany, another 29 per cent in the rest of Europe, 18 per cent in the Americas and 11 per cent in the Asia-Pacific region (ibid.). In spite of its global operations Deutsche remains fundamentally a transnational-*European* player.

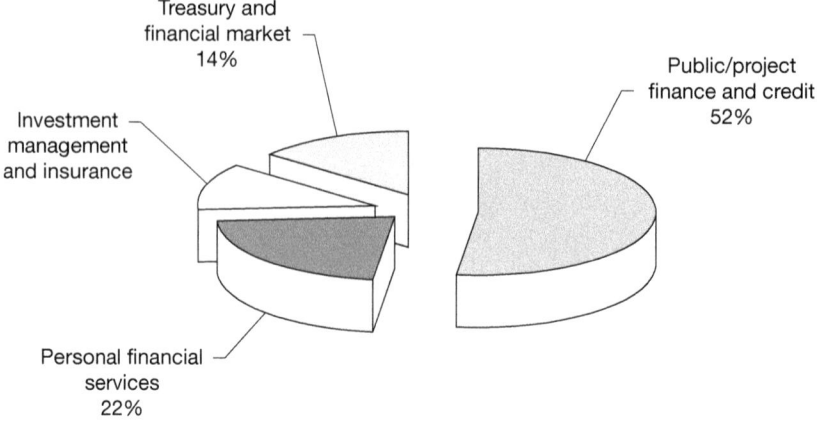

Figure 3.11 Dexia (2005).
Source: Dexia 2005.

The figures for its shareholder base support the claim that it tends to operate on a European scale with an emphasis on German markets. Figure 3.12 outlines this conclusion. Of Deutsche's 412,000 shareholders in 2005, some 52 per cent are based in Germany, with a further 30 per cent in the remainder of the European Union. The remaining 18 per cent are divided primarily between the US and Switzerland (Deutsche Bank 2005). Taken together, Deutsche is somewhat unique within the Rhenish fraction with both global operations and yet still a heavily European emphasis (Interview Deutsche Bank); fractions are, of course, fluid rallying points.

The second prominent Rhenish member is the Allianz Group. The Group is indisputably transnationally oriented with over 175,000 employees working in more than 70 countries, describing themselves as a 'leading global financial services provider' (Allianz Group 2005). Simultaneously, the Group's literature also refers to the 'home market of Europe' and 'Germany, Italy and France' as the 'most important markets' (ibid.). Founded in 1890, the Group claims to be the largest German financial institution by market capitalization and ranked number one in German property-casualty and life-insurance markets (ibid.). In their banking operations the following statement (ibid.) outlines the Group's position:

> While Dresdner Bank (Allianz Group's banking arm) focuses on selected regions worldwide, Germany is its primary market, which contains 66.1% of its loan portfolio . . . Dresdner Bank operates and distributes its products primarily through 959 branch offices, of which 927 are located in Germany and 32 outside of Germany.

> (Allianz Group 2005)

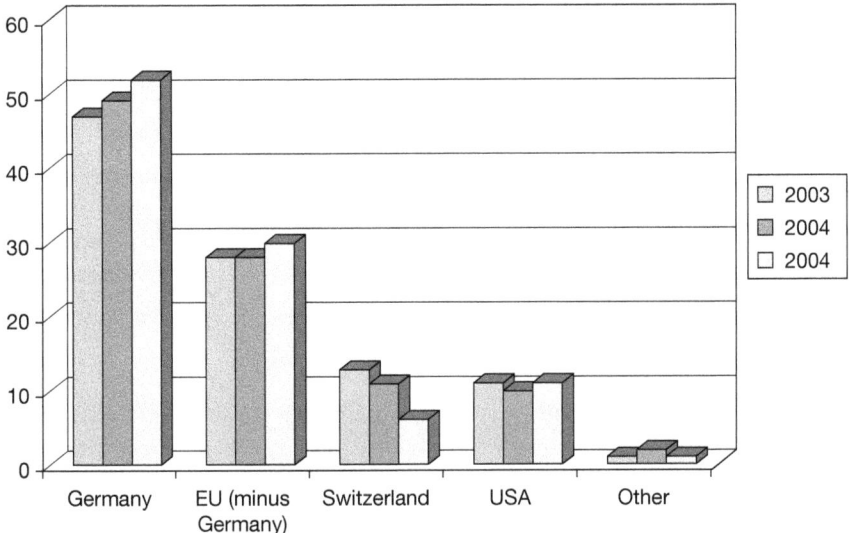

Figure 3.12 Deutsche Bank.
Source: Deutsche Bank 2005.

The third area of their operations is that of asset management, wherein they describe themselves as a 'global provider of institutional and retail asset management products and services' (ibid.).

Figure 3.13 suggests that in almost all sectors of the Group's business operations the German and European markets are consistently the largest revenue sources, aside from their asset-management operations in the Americas. Though the Allianz Group operates globally it is foremost a *European* actor with a particular dependence on the German market within its accumulation strategies.

A third Rhenish member is the Commerzbank. Founded in 1870 by a group of merchants, merchant bankers and private bankers, the Commerzbank had branches in London, Paris, Madrid, Barcelona, Brussels and New York by the early 1980s (Commerzbank 2007). It currently has over 70 bases worldwide and holdings in more than 40 countries (ibid.). The bank describes itself as 'one of Germany's leading banks and . . . among the world's fifty largest banks' (ibid.); its credentials as a member of the transnationally oriented fraction are evident.

Again, though, the prominence of its German 'origins' or 'roots' are also clear; the bank 'views itself as a reliable provider of financial services to retail customers in Germany, and as a creative relationship bank for the flourishing German SME sector' (ibid.); the fact that of its 33,000 staff more than 25,000 of them are located within Germany supports this assertion (Commerzbank 2005). As with Allianz, the Commerzbank has a European focus.

Finally, the HypoVereinsbank (HVB) claims to be one of the 'leading financial institutions in Germany', with core competencies including retail and corporate

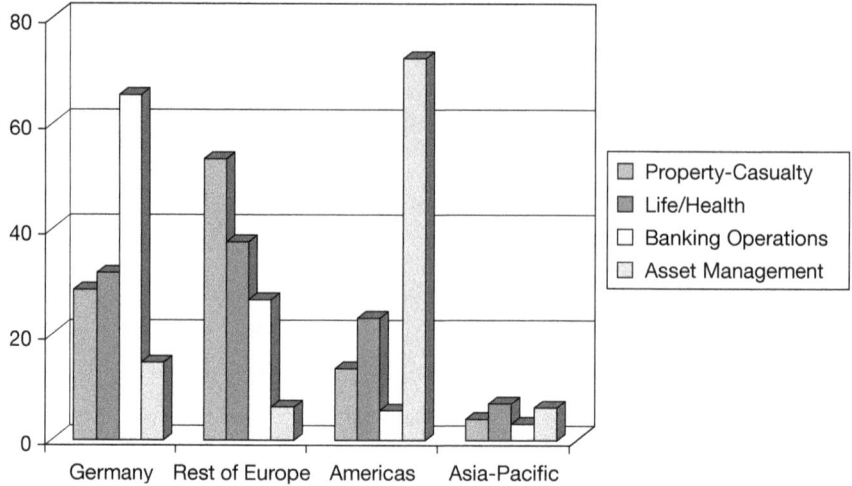

Figure 3.13 Allianz Group.
Source: Allianz Group 2005.

banking, real estate finance, capital markets and asset management (HVB 2005). It describes its position as 'undisputed number one' in the emerging economies of Central and Eastern Europe (CEE) whilst emphasizing the 'important role' played by Germany in its ambitions (ibid.). This role in the CEE countries emerged and became further entrenched following the post-Communist eastern expansion of circuits of capital (see Shields 2006). Further, in 2005 the HVB underwent consolidation with Italy's Unicredit to form the new Unicredit Group which has a total of 28 million customers in 19 countries and over 140,000 employees (ibid.); its credentials as a transnational-European actor are irrefutable.

Rhenish amalgam

As noted, the transnationalization of German ('finance') capital, visibly manifested, *inter alia*, in the rise of the private banking community, the restructuring of capital markets and the progressive demise of house-bank relationships, has meant that in scalar and functional terms Rhenish strategies share certain similarities with those of Atlantic *and* Gallic fractions. For example, in terms of the business operations which underpin Deutsche's accumulation strategies, Figure 3.14 reveals the striking prominence of corporate and investment banking operations as the primary source of revenue. This section of Deutsche's operations covers Corporate Banking and Securities which comprises all 'sales, trading and research in equity, debt and . . . bonds, commodities' both on and off exchange, as well as covering Corporate Finance and Global Transaction Banking; for our purposes the distinctions between these operations are less important than their similarities.

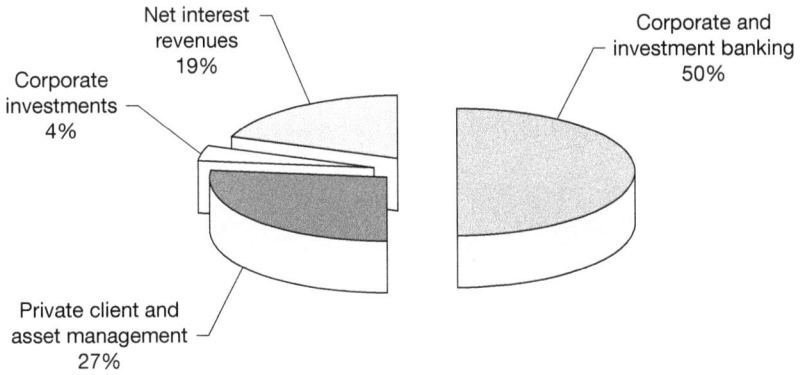

Net interest revenues 19%

Corporate investments 4%

Corporate and investment banking 50%

Private client and asset management 27%

Figure 3.14 Deutsche Bank (2005).
Source: Deutsche Bank 2005.

As Figure 3.14 portrays, over three-quarters of Deutsche's revenue for 2005 was the product of operations either directly or indirectly connected to capital market activities. As with the two other fractions, exact figures indicating how revenue was produced, that is, in which funds or securities, linked to which companies and in which particular markets, are not publicly available. Instead, Figure 3.14 provides an *indication* of the importance of Deutsche's corporate and investment banking operations.

In terms of the Allianz Group's revenue for 2005, Figure 3.15 conveys the facts outlined previously: 73 per cent of their total operations are focused on insurance markets. This merely supports the notion that the Rhenish fraction is largely composed of banks combining *significant* activities in a number of different areas; this is typical of their universal banking heritage (Lütz 2000). Again, though, it reinforces the specificity and uniqueness of each of the fractions in ways which reflect their historical origins in our three respective markets. Here we begin to perceive the significance of scale, function *and* socio-institutional configurations as shaping factors within the fractions' accumulation strategies. Allianz represents a transnational-European member clearly embedded within particularly German socio-institutional configurations and localized circuits.

Again, in similar fashion to the Allianz Group, the Commerzbank comprises a wide variety of activities under one umbrella organization; in Commerz's case this is both retail banking and asset management with corporate and investment banking. As Figure 3.16 portrays the Commerzbank derives a substantial portion of its revenue from its corporate and investment banking operations whilst still retaining significant activities in its two other fields. In relation to our argument however, Figure 3.16 is better understood with the modifications set out in Figure 3.17.

Employing the data provided by the Annual Report (2005) it becomes clear that, of the profits derived from corporate and investment banking over 50 per cent of

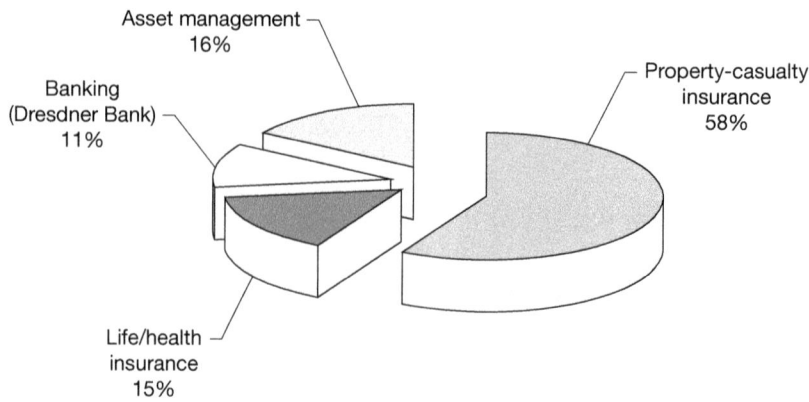

Figure 3.15 Allianz Group (2005).
Source: Allianz Group 2005.

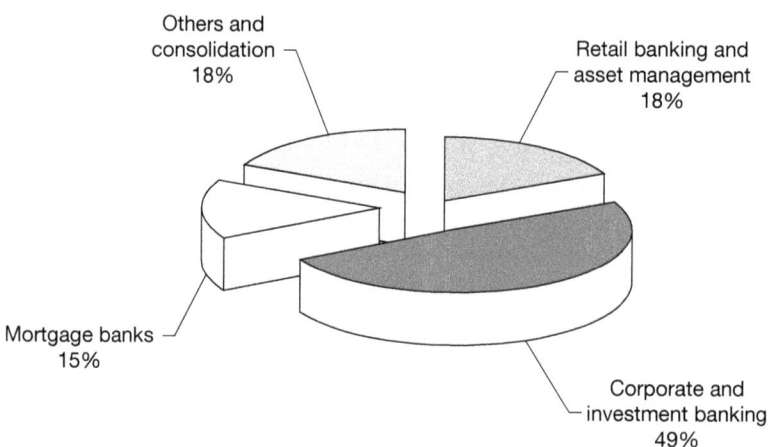

Figure 3.16 Commerzbank (2005).
Source: Commerzbank 2005.

the revenue is the product of activities involving *mittelstand* or medium-sized companies located within Germany. A further 25 per cent of the corporate and
investment banking revenue derives from *international* corporate banking. The
transnational-European status of the Rhenish fraction is increasingly apparent; they
are an amalgam of significant transnationally oriented operations and strong
linkages with 'German' social forces and their circuits, meaning that their
accumulation strategies are firmly rooted in the German market.

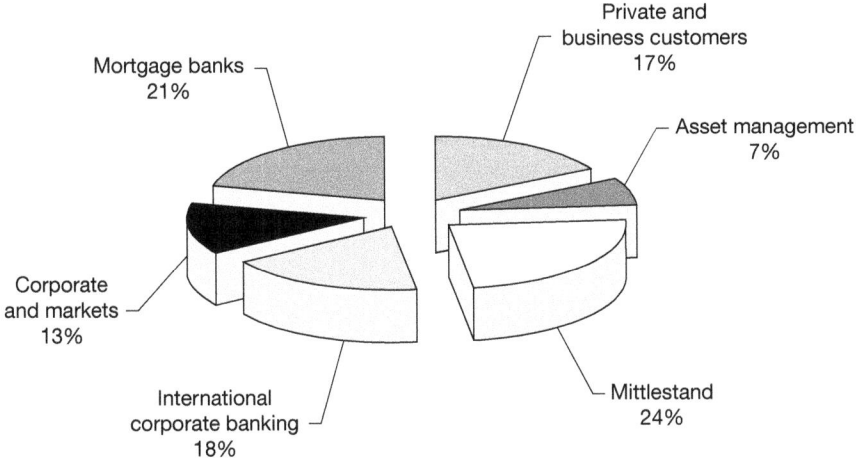

Figure 3.17 Commerzbank (2005).
Source: Commerzbank 2005.

Summary: Shaping factors

The preceding sections have introduced the three transnationally oriented fractions. The argument of the book is that they are key protagonists within processes of neoliberalization. In one respect they simply capitalize on a series of wider dynamics within which they themselves are both engendered and constituents. In another, they struggle to shape these wider processes to their advantage (van der Pijl 1998: 62). Crucially, the overall trajectory of neoliberal reform is therefore not simply the product of *their* agency, but the result of the impulsions–agency–common sense dialectic. Nonetheless, in our search to demystify neoliberalization we identify transnationally oriented fractions as arguably its core beneficiaries; the main focus then is on identifying the processes, expressed materially and ideologically, which underpin their social agency.

With interests and identity shaped through position within production and circulation the above introduction has identified significant commonalities: namely, their transnational orientation. It has also highlighted significant differences: their global, national, and European scales respectively; and their differential circuits and socio-institutional configurations. Of course the tacit distinction between scale, circuit and configuration is only of limited didactic value. These similarities and differences, however – encapsulated within variegated neoliberalism – form the basis for much of this study. Fractions embody attempts by individual capitals to build tacit coalitions in order to secure political hegemony. These coalitions have tended to achieve these goals at the national level through the construction of relatively cohesive hegemonic projects and underpinned by a nascent neoliberal common sense (Chapters 4, 5 and 6).

These positions have, in turn, been represented by national governments in intergovernmental negotiations at the EU level, though this remains beyond the remit of this study. This contingent neoliberal consensus amongst state and fractions of capital has thus provided the basis for renewed neoliberal restructuring and rescaling (see Chapter 5). Having outlined the consensus then, Chapters 8 and 9 focus primarily on the differences or so-called 'divergences' within this consensus, emphasizing the disunity of the incorrectly labelled 'transnational capitalist class'.

4 Political agency of transnationally oriented fractions

The previous chapter introduced the membership of the three fractions. This chapter now reinforces the claim that these fractions are represented institutionally within their respective trade associations and similar lobbying bodies. The first aim of this chapter is to disclose the internal dynamics of these bodies, revealing the tendency to neutralize or marginalize competing social forces. The second aim is to briefly consider the struggles of these fractions at the national level and at the EU level. It does not chart the passage of neoliberal policy from the fractions to the state since neither is the state the *instrument* of the ruling class, nor does this fit with the impulsions–agency–common sense nexus. Yet transnationally oriented fractions utilize regulatory processes, embedded within dynamic yet unequal social formations at national and EU levels, in attempts to shape regulatory politics. Neoliberalization is driven by the above nexus, yet the key protagonists – and, by implication, the dispossessed – are here made apparent.

Social function of trade associations

This section discloses the dynamics of coalition building represented by the trade associations and similar bodies. Individual idiosyncrasies apply, yet similar processes of neutralization and marginalization are evident. I focus primarily on the *internal structure* of these bodies. Having outlined their membership I now explain how the fractions are represented institutionally; the social content of these institutions is therefore anchored in societal developments. Here the consensus-view of trade associations serves hegemonic struggles, receiving additional political 'weight'. Diverse, competing interests tend to be excluded or neutralized, so the *function* of the association (as a representative body) and its *social function* (as an instrument of fractional hegemonic struggles) are at odds.

Thus, the functional organization of fractions of capital around financial trade associations is both an (abstract) attempt to secure the hegemony of a relatively common set of interests[1] and (more concretely) a technical feature of the structure of EU and national legislative mechanisms which necessitate coordinated responses to consultation papers. For example, according to the associations, their function is to 'share ideas' and enable their respective banking and investment industries to 'speak with a unified voice' (Interview AFEI). Similarly, the Bundesverband deutscher Banken states 'it is very helpful to have a *common view* because then you can say, this is the common voice of the banking industry in Germany' (Interview BdB, emphasis added). Significantly, the argument that large private financial interests dominate regulatory politics is longstanding within Public Policy accounts (see, for example, Coen 1997; Quaglia 2008). Further, these accounts also highlight that interest groups seek to present their particularistic interests as representing a wider membership of the industry (Bouwen 2002). Nonetheless, their conclusion that EU interest politics is simply an *elite pluralist* environment (Coen 1998, 2007) is misleading. The assumption is that this is a necessary and inherent component of majoritarian democracy. Instead, the capitalist state – though comprising genuine labour interests and concessions – is constantly asymmetrical. The state is thereby anchored in unequal (capitalist) social relations, whether manifest in the capitalist mode of production (more generally) or neoliberal finance-led accumulation (more specifically).

Public Policy accounts tend to fall within a rationalist (and soft-positivist) conception of ideas and, subject to the critique of *form-al* analysis (Chapter 2), these accounts simply reify the norm. Beginning with the observation that the 2007–09 crisis appears to disclose fundamental inequalities under capitalism, our Gramscian analysis proposes a demystifying, normative engagement with these same processes. Though – at this early stage – the argument bears similarities to the Public Policy account, here the agency of capital ('interest groups') is embedded within wider 'structural' dynamics. This more nuanced, critical account is crucial to the counter-hegemonic arguments made in the conclusion. Suffice it to note that the representation of the particular as the universal masks the class struggles through which transnationally oriented fractions emerge as dominant voices. These chapters therefore address political agency.

Fractions, hegemonic projects and the state

Simply, demystifying neoliberalization requires a more pronounced understanding of state–capital–labour relations. Unfortunately, the state has aroused disparate accounts and the purported 'retreat' of the state is itself an ideological component of neoliberal hegemony. In contrast, historical materialism has, alongside other accounts, tended to emphasize both the ongoing relevance and the transformation of the state (on historical materialist accounts, see Burnham 1994; on other accounts, see Cerny 2000). In effect, these accounts tend to argue that the state both drives and responds to capitalist restructuring on sub- and supra-national scales (Shields 2008: 447).

More specifically for our European-focused account of neoliberalization, we are concerned with: *how* and *why* fractions pursue class struggles at the level of the state and at the EU level; how neoliberal hegemonic projects (Chapters 5 and 8) translate into neoliberal policy; the relationship between the state and working classes; and how this affects our case studies.

A linear, causal account is rejected, yet four salient points emerge in descending order of abstraction. First, the capitalist state is a *precondition* of capitalist accumulation. Capitalism comprises competing capitals; however, despite this rivalry they rely on generic conditions, such as general infrastructure, the maintenance of property rights and frameworks of regulation, and the ability to 'legally' enforce discipline on those groups who do not 'consent' either actively or passively. Thus a *relatively* autonomous power is required (Gramsci 1971: 12; Engels 1978 [1884]; Poulantzas 1978). This is not to replicate the infamous state–market dichotomy of IPE. Instead the state is imbibed within and *internally* related to capitalist social relations (Burnham 1995: 136; Bieler and Morton 2003: 470–71). As Poulantzas notes, 'as is the case with every power mechanism [read institution], the state is the material condensation of a *relationship*' (1978: 145). The contours of struggles *within* capital and *between* capital and labour are therefore inscribed within the state apparatus, so the social content of the state is thus anchored in societal developments (Poulantzas 1973: 44; see also Gramsci 1971: 52). As a result, transformations within the impulsions–agency–common sense nexus engender both emergent hegemonic class fractions and reconfigurations of and within the state.[2]

Second, therefore, the state is the *factor of cohesion*, maintaining 'the unity and cohesion of a social formation by concentrating and sanctioning class domination' whilst being irreducible solely to the economic interests of the ruling class (Poulantzas 1973: 24–25, 44). The result is that 'political power is founded on an unstable equilibrium of compromise' (ibid.: 192). Thus a 'continuous process of formation and superseding of unstable equilibria' (Gramsci 1971: 182) ensues where the 'line of political demarcation between domination and subordination cannot be marked out from the viewpoint of a "dualist" struggle between dominant and dominated classes' (Poulantzas 1973: 229). The state is no instrument of the ruling class.

Instead, a *power bloc* emerges, comprising both dominant and dominated classes, yet: within which particular fractions constantly struggle for their project to become and/or remain hegemonic; the hegemonic fraction secures the consent or reluctant acquiescence of others to an economic and political agenda in line with this fraction's interests; and finally, which is nonetheless constantly asymmetrical vis-à-vis labour. This is because 'the dominated classes exist in the state not by means of apparatuses concentrating a power of their own, but essentially in the form of centres of opposition to the power of the dominant classes' (Poulantzas 1978: 142).

Thus, hegemony at the state level is not the exclusive dominance of one fraction but the 'hegemonic class or fraction is in fact the dominant element of the contradictory unity of politically "dominant" classes or fractions, forming part of the power bloc' (ibid.: 237). In contrast to a pluralist-inspired account, though the state presents itself as a neutral instance expressing the general will of the people, it is a site of class conflict and the 'suppression, deceleration and deflection' of subordinate groups (Gallas 2009: 2; Poulantzas 1978: 156). This means that whilst the state is *relatively autonomous* vis-à-vis the various fractions of the ruling class the hegemonic fraction assumes a leadership role within the power bloc. The leading fraction secures hegemony at the level of the state through a hegemonic project (Chapter 2) constructing alliances, granting concessions and appealing to perceived interests of competing forces. Already it is clearer *how* and *why* the class project of neoliberalization emerges through the state.

As a result, however, the contradiction-laden character of policymaking is reflected in state policy. Similarly, a linear analysis tracing particular interests to particular policies is problematic – given the relative autonomy of the state and the multiple social forces within the power bloc. Instead, this book focuses, on the one hand, on policy positions and hegemonic projects, whilst on the other, outlining the overall trajectory of (variegated neoliberal) policy emerging from state and EU institutions.

Third, political hegemony at the level of the state, and societal hegemony are therefore interconnected yet relatively distinct processes. Hegemony at the level of the state is a necessary but insufficient precondition for societal hegemony (Gramsci 1971: 235, 365; Bieler and Morton 2003: 483). Put differently, since the state constitutes the unique factor of cohesion between the various levels, securing 'sufficient power in the state to organize a central project' is vital (Hall 1991: 124). A fraction's hegemonic project thus seeks to build alliances with other fractions and working classes, securing – at best – their endorsement, or – at worst – their reluctant acquiescence (Bruff 2008: 60; Poulantzas 1978: 144). The dominant hegemonic project therefore also captures both domestic and international interests, proposing concrete strategies of corporate appeal on a 'universal plane' (Gramsci 1971: 181). As Chapters 6 and 7 explain then, organic intellectuals function as intermediaries between political and *societal* hegemony through the production of a common sense which engages not just political agents, but also civil society.

Finally, the EU – as another institutional ensemble – is also a material condensation of class struggle and social processes. Thus hegemonic projects, alliances and rival power blocs emerge, shaped by and reshaping the global reconstitution of both capitalism and dominant common senses. Thus, in the following sections we witness transnationally oriented fractions exploiting trade associations, embedded in constantly evolving struggles at the national and EU levels, yet seeking political support for their respective projects. In this way our fractions are at the apex of the neoliberal political project.

More concretely, within the UK power bloc, the Atlantic (predominantly finance) fraction has occupied a relatively unique hegemonic position. With the demise of British industry, production capital adopted a secondary role such that the institutions of the UK state gradually crystallized around the Atlantic fraction and a *liberal* neoliberal project (van der Pijl 1984, 1998: 106–16).[3] In France, the power bloc has historically incorporated both nationally and transnationally oriented production and finance (so to speak) fractions, relatively fused with the strong state (Overbeek 2004: 126). Fractures within the power bloc have been limited, with the Gallic fraction focused primarily on promoting a so-called *social* neoliberal project at the EU level. In Germany, the power bloc has traditionally incorporated a greater degree of labour representation typical of the consensual model. Thus, transnationally and nationally oriented, production and finance, capital and labour social forces had a strong presence within the state (van Apeldoorn 2002: 74–75). Unsurprisingly, this has contributed to both the inertia of structural reforms (Dyson 2008) and the growing alliances between transnationally oriented fractions and internationally minded state agencies, around what can be termed a *socio-liberal* neoliberal project.

Policymaking: a historical perspective

Beginning with the UK, though, where capitalism has long incorporated transnationally oriented (finance) capital within its liberal internationalist state, this agenda-setting capacity therefore extends beyond the associations. In the City of London for example, so-called *haute finance* capitalists became institutionalized in a meso-corporatist, 'inner circle' of internationally minded public institutions (Useem 1984). The demise of production within the British Isles and the Thatcherite breaking of labour during the 1980s reopened the door to the Atlantic fraction as a dominant force in UK policymaking.

One result has been the implementation of strategies by the regulator, the Financial Services Authority (FSA), which overtly privilege transnationally oriented capital. For example, during consultation periods concerning the Capital Requirements Directive all firms were given opportunity to respond although the FSA 'actively sought' responses from 'key' (read transnationally oriented) institutional investors (FSA June 2000); the FSA claimed that this was due to a lack of time and resources. Notably however, the Atlantic fraction were institutionalized in a series of standing groups endowed with policy formulating capabilities. The following statement is taken from one such standing group where certain UK firms

> complained that the authorities were not getting industry-wide views, but had focussed on certain institutions that were already willing to implement the proposals. They suggested that the wrong data might emerge, as a result of studying larger banks. The authorities would need to talk to *smaller firms* not just the *larger institutions*.
>
> (FSA June 2000, emphasis added)

In response the FSA 'agreed that a small number of institutions had [indeed] been driving this debate' (FSA January 2001).

A brief look at the membership of the CRD standing group supports this claim. Of the thirty-one members, nineteen represented either transnationally oriented investment banks or trade associations and the remainder were Treasury or FSA officials. Members of the Atlantic fraction included Rothschilds, Barclays, Merrill Lynch, Salomon Smith Barney, Goldman Sachs and Citibank (FSA December 2004). The claim is obvious: the privileged position of the Atlantic fraction within UK policymaking agencies simply reinforces Atlantic hegemony in the UK power bloc.

In Germany, the institutional arrangements within which state–finance and capital–labour relations were traditionally negotiated were described as

Rahmenbedingung, literally, 'framework conditions' or framework regulations. This typically provided a relatively secure context which allowed 'actors to expend their resources on bargaining for advantage within the system rather than trying to destroy other actors or to bypass the system altogether' (Wever and Allen 1993: 184; Offe 1985). Further, the coordinating and policy-shaping roles of peak (trade) associations have a considerable history, as bodies like the *Bundesvereinigung der Deutschen Arbeitgeberverbaende* (Confederation of German Employer Associations), the *Bundesverband der Deutschen Industrie* (Federation of German Industries) and the *Deutscher Industrie- und Handelskammertag* (the Federation of German Chambers of Industry and Commerce) were effectively incorporated into the formulation and even implementation of public policy initiatives (Streeck 1983: 265); that is, effectively fulfilling a public policy function (Wever and Allen 1993: 184; Shonfield 1965).

Crises of accumulation and a nascent neoliberal common sense have had two prominent effects on this consensual model: the first has been the breakdown of previous accords both within capital and between capital and labour; the result has been both increased attempts by transnationally oriented fractions to neutralize, co-opt in or marginalize more nationally oriented fractions, as well as attempts to secure consensual rule through the production of neoliberal common sense. The second feature has been the rise of new bodies, such as the *Initiativ Finanzstandort Deutschland* (IFD), which overtly construct policy proposals outside of traditional coordinated pathways and avoid the complexities of trade association negotiations. New social formations – embedded in, yet distinct from, former ones – are emerging.

In France, the myth of a strong, centralized bureaucracy dominating policymaking and fiercely resisting particularistic interest group pressures was short-lived (Dunn and Perl 1994: 312). Instead, it is clear that the French system of *grands projets* and national champions was founded on the basis of integral coordination mechanisms between large enterprises, whether publicly or privately owned (Parker 1999: 65). In line with a neo-corporatist tradition France therefore relied less on lobbying by business than it did on the presence of institutionalized access to the decision-making process (Wilson 1983: 896). Even so, the degree of state activity across the network economy, both as coordinator and financier, gave it a degree of autonomy and authority unlike either the German or British state (ibid.: 900).

This underwent transformation, though, as crises began to take effect during the 1980s Socialist era, bringing both an increasing emphasis on small and medium-sized enterprises (SMEs) and an erosion of state involvement in industrial development (Cohen 1995). As we shall see, however, the centralization of the Gallic system, the relatively enduring alliance of production and finance fractions, as well as the transnational-national character of the Gallic fraction including strong linkages with more nationally oriented fractions, have contributed to the following contradiction: the inertia of historic accumulation regimes, yet an overt (and almost visceral) resistance to more liberal degrees of neoliberalization.

The neoliberal elements, so to speak, of the Gallic hegemonic project have therefore been balanced with, or arguably countered by, elements of social protection.

The Gallic fraction

Having contextualized the different historical arrangements for state–capital negotiations we return to the French and German material to examine the dynamics of exclusion, neutralization or co-option employed by these two fractions. As contender states they display most evidence of struggle to avoid peripheralization and thus form our analytical focus. Much like the Atlantic fraction then, the Gallic fraction remains firmly embedded within the French network economy and the (still relatively) interventionist state. Though the trade associations again display an institutional bias towards the Gallic fraction there is less evidence of dramatic change in recent times. Thus the fusion and centralization of the Gallic system as well as the transnational-national character of the Gallic fraction are reflected in the French associations. The internal structure of these organizations again enables a single dominant voice to speak for the French investment industry (FBF 2002a). The French Banking Federation described this process as, 'clarify[ing] the thoughts of the Paris financial centre' with regards to financial market integration (FBF 2002b).

Composed of over 500 banks and financial institutions, the FBF is represented through twenty-one regional committees and eighty-eight local committees (FBF 2004). This has a dual effect: it means that the cumulative voice of the French banking industry is represented in different regional and local institutions such as the Chamber of Industry and Commerce (ibid.). Of greater concern for our analysis is the tension between, on the one hand, the centralization of French banking views on integration – with the obvious ability to marginalize contending social forces – and, on the other hand, the resistance to extensive neoliberal reform exacerbated by this closely integrated network of diverse fractions and interests. The contradiction suggests that – through transnationalization – the perspective of the Gallic fraction 'will tend to move away from social protection and towards that of economic liberalism' (van Apeldoorn 2002: 29), thereby conflicting with more protectionist interests embodied in the associations; yet simultaneously, the Gallic fraction – fused as it is with domestic production forces – continues to rely fundamentally upon these circuits and actors.

This is where the internal structure of the associations matters most. At the head of these localized committees sits a joint committee of senior bank executives. These emanate from transnationally oriented actors such as BNP Paribas, Crédit Mutuel, Crédit Agricole and Société Générale and form a committee where, of the sixteen members, only one place is given to the representatives of foreign or smaller sized credit institutions (FBF 2002a). So we find the Gallic fraction (i) with increasingly neoliberal interests yet (ii) with accumulation strategies firmly embedded within national–domestic forces whilst (iii) being institutionally represented at the head of the trade associations and thus able to push forward *neoliberal* elements of their project. In every way they are at the apex of these underlying social processes.

The structure of the *Association Française des Entreprises d'Investissements* (AFEI) produces a similar trend, over-representing the interests of the Gallic fraction. The AFEI implicitly emphasizes this tendency by responses of the following sort:

> Is it imaginable that CESR could give the *same weight* to all the responses to its consultations, without considering how representative the correspondent might or might not be? Obviously, we object strenuously to such a possibility. First, because it would deny the *special role* of representative professional organisations, which, when they provide comments to CESR, present a position that expresses the *consensus view* of their members.
>
> (AFEI February 2004, emphasis added)

By implication, the consensus view achieved over-represents the Gallic fraction whilst as a 'representative organization' this cumulative response view holds greater 'weight'. As noted, however, both the structure of the association and the underlying social configurations shape policy positions. Yet the AFEI themselves note that,

> There are . . . 'big players' . . . driving all the changes in the financial marketplace. At the same time the process of producing regulations that are increasingly international . . . are developed for the . . . [transnationally oriented] financial players . . . because they do more business across borders.
>
> (Interview AFEI)

In so doing we present a more nuanced picture of the contradictions and struggles within the associations, surpassing the Public Policy account of strategic micro-interactions influencing policy positions; here we embed key agents within social structures. Yet, this view also explains how transnationally oriented fractions are positioned at the apex and thereby key protagonists of neoliberal reform.

The Rhenish fraction

In Germany there have been overt struggles, greater crises, and greater social breakdown, and though the transnationally oriented fraction is institutionally represented by the associations the struggles have 'broken out' into new and alternative forums. At both political and societal levels the hegemony of the Rhenish fraction is highly contested, as schisms within the German power bloc deepen. Again, this merely exacerbates the contradiction between transnationally oriented yet national–domestically embedded modes of accumulation. We begin though with the associational structures. Here the marginalization of subaltern groups has been increasingly conducted through the private banking association (the *Bundesverband deutscher Banken*), the umbrella association, the

(*Zentraler Kredit Ausschuss*), and by the *Initiativ Finanzstandort Deutschland*. We focus initially on the BdB and the ZKA. The result has been – for example – that positional papers tend to display a bias towards the Rhenish fraction.

Whilst, in principle, the *Zentraler Kredit Ausschuss* operates as the central 'representative' body, in practice this function has been progressively challenged. It has no staff or offices of its own; instead, supervision and support duties are passed among members on a yearly basis (Interview Deutsche Bank). In fact though, whilst the ZKA represents five associations the coordinating role only passes between the three largest associations: the *Bundesverband der Deutschen Volksbanken und Raiffeisenbanken*, the *Bundesverband deutscher Banken* and the *Deutscher Sparkassen- und Giroverband*, already limiting the potential for contending 'voices' to be heard (ibid.). In effect the politics of achieving a common voice within the individual associations are therefore writ large through the ZKA.

This becomes significant when responding to EU consultations since, in these negotiations, the Rhenish fraction have been able to respond individually through individual firms' responses, collectively through the BdB *and* collectively through the ZKA; this amounts to three avenues for expressing its interests. The following statement is typical of a BdB response to the CESR:

> The Association of German Banks is a member of the *Zentraler Kredit Ausschuss* (ZKA), the joint committee of the central associations of the German banking industry. We fully support the Joint Comments of the ZKA which you will find enclosed.
>
> (BdB January 2004)

In effect, the interests of the Rhenish fraction are both over-represented in policymaking processes and, again, presented as the 'common position' of a wider variety of social forces, thereby achieving a greater weight.

One such example can be seen in the BdB responses during EU consultation processes. A cursory examination of the Deutsche Bank response to an EU report entitled 'Which supervisory tools for the EU securities markets?' reveals precisely the same responses as were offered by the BdB in their 2004 Banking Survey and various responses to CESR consultations. Deutsche stated that the following elements ought to be included in the nascent EU framework: pan-European efficiency as the goal of European financial market integration; international competitiveness as a benchmark for regulation; increased usage of self-regulation; the promotion of competition; and competitive neutrality on the part of political authorities (Deutsche Bank 2005). In brief, the rhetoric emerging from the German trade association tends to represent the project of the Rhenish fraction as a common position.

This should not be overemphasized, however. Once again, the social configurations of German capitalism continue to shape the interests of the Rhenish fraction – themselves firmly embedded with national–domestic strategies. Yet – as Chapter 5 explains – whilst German corporatism initially proved quite resilient (van Apeldoorn 2002: 71) the gravity of crises, the transnationalization of Rhenish capital, and neoliberal common sense, have led to attempts to circumvent the institutionalized struggles within associations and shape regulatory politics independently. The Rhenish fraction have thus assisted in constructing alternative institutions on the back of a nascent social formation; the IFD is perhaps the most formidable example. Founded in 2003 the *Initiativ Finanzstandort Deutschland* created a coalition of Rhenish members alongside internationally minded state institutions. Of its eighteen members the following are included: Rhenish members like Deutsche Bank, Commerzbank, DZ Bank, Munich Re, Allianz-Dresdner Bank, HVB; the private banking association (BdB); and several (Atlantic) associate members in the form of Morgan Stanley, Citigroup, Merrill Lynch, Goldman Sachs and JP Morgan. These are then joined by the Deutsche Bundesbank and the Federal Ministry of Finance.

Its primary aim has been to 'develop numerous projects and measures' to provide a 'stimulus for growth' (IFD 2008); the spectre of the ailing post-war model lingers. Elsewhere it notes the need to 'transcend . . . all partisan interests . . . [and] formulate its common interests and assert them externally' (IFD 2005). Precisely in ostensibly overcoming partisan or fractional particularities does the transnationally oriented fraction obfuscate their dominance. Though all three pillars of German banking (cooperatives, private institutions and public corporations) are represented as part of this reconfigured power bloc, the agenda of the IFD is wholly neoliberal.

This is reflected in its positional papers which speak of international competitiveness as the EU's benchmark, strengthening competition and a greater reliance on self-regulation (IFD June 2004). We will return to these in greater detail in Chapters 5 and 7, suffice it to note that competitiveness discourses have often been linked to transnationally oriented capital (Overbeek and van der Pijl 1993; van Apeldoorn 2002). According to Deutsche Bank the IFD intends to 'form a common view on where we want the financial market to be' and to 'raise the importance of Germany as a financial centre in global competition' (Interview Deutsche Bank). In this sense the IFD was clearly the 'brainchild' of the transnationally oriented fraction and part of a wider attempt to extend the propagation of the Rhenish project beyond the institutional channels of the BdB and ZKA (ibid.). That said, there remain obvious traces of the embeddedness of the Rhenish project within national–domestic configurations (Chapters 5 and 8).

The first section of this chapter has therefore begun to explore the political agency of the three fractions. As rallying points for a variety of social forces these fractions attempt to transcend particularistic interests in the bid for political support. All three are incorporated within state frameworks and power blocs yet reveal the ongoing struggles with state, labour and intra-capital. In effect, we briefly examined these processes of co-option, marginalization and neutralization. This section has argued however, that in both national and EU-level (neoliberal) reform agendas – and, specifically, on financial market expansion – trade associations embody the contradiction and tension between nationally and transnationally oriented fractions, whilst still situating the three fractions at the apex of these policymaking processes; the variegation of neoliberalism is anchored in this tension. For now, our aim is to examine the agents of neoliberalization.

Struggles for political support

Struggles at the national level

Suffice it to note that, in the UK and France where (though for different reasons) less change has occurred in the underlying configurations there is also less evidence of struggle and systemic change at the level of the state. First, the Atlantic fraction remains embedded within the liberal internationalist UK state and has maintained its hegemony within the UK power bloc. Second, in Germany there is significant evidence of change in all three 'elements' of the dialectical nexus; hence we find national struggles and new institutional formations (such as the IFD). The German power bloc has shifted as the Rhenish fraction has secured a tentative hold on political hegemony whilst societal hegemony (Chapters 6 and 7) is also still highly contested. Finally, the Gallic fraction remains embedded within the interventionist French state. That said, crises (impulsions) and (neoliberal) common sense are at work in reshaping the French system (Chapters 6 and 7). Further, the transnationalization of Gallic capital has shifted the balance of power and interests within this hegemonic configuration. In a later section we examine the Gallic struggles which have been focused at the EU level, resisting the Atlantic finance-led project.

Whereas the previous section outlined the social function of the associations by focusing on their internal structure and intra-capital struggles, this section focuses on the *ideological expression* of their policy positions in their struggles with states and at the EU level. These discourses – as part of wider hegemonic projects – are neither detached from material conditions, except in a crude analytical sense, nor constructed *de novo* by the associations (van Apeldoorn 2002: 113). Instead, as ensuing chapters explain, they are adapted and re-articulated in light of the pragmatic concerns of the fractions. Thus the discourses appear as both embedded within the wider 'structural' changes under neoliberalization and, given the role of our fractions *within* the struggles over these changes, the discourses themselves have a shaping role in neoliberalization (ibid.: 158).

The second point for Gramscian counter-hegemony is apparent now. Having situated these discourses within a reading of common sense we, the observer-participant, understand the strategic threat of relocation as both *ideological* construct and *material* reality (so to speak). By implication though, we contribute to studies de-reifying the seemingly objective assessments of – *inter alia* – capital flight as a strategically constructed threat on the part of capital. Through this book, the material essence of these threats (the *actual* potential for relocation, for example) is balanced against, for example, the embeddedness of capital (that is, the *constraints* on relocation). The limits to neoliberalization as exogenous, immutable and irresistible force become apparent.

These strategic discourses have nonetheless had discernible effects. For example, in a consultation paper on capital requirements the UK Financial Services Authority (FSA) stated that 'in response to firms' concerns we have appraised our proposals . . . The proposals . . . that we have set out in the CP (190) are less prescriptive than those . . . we put forward in CP 136' (FSA 2002). The rationale for the change in policy direction lies in the rhetoric employed by the associations during previous negotiations. During consultation, the BBA and LIBA rightly noted that the FSA was 'likely to considerably exceed the international norm in the application of Pillar Two' (BBA and LIBA June 2003b). They acknowledged that in operating globally they favoured a single set of international standards; the associations' rhetoric was employed, however, to suggest that the UK becoming an 'international outlier in the manner in which it applies and interprets Pillar 2' (ibid.) might threaten the City's attractiveness amongst the international community of banks and investment firms (BBA and LIBA June 2003a). Transnationally oriented firms contended that if the FSA applied the EU rules more stringently than other member states they would come under pressure to liberalize because of the *potential* migration of capital and actors (FSA September 2000). The hegemonic project of the Atlantic fraction is reinforced by their perceived ability to relocate operations outside of the City of London; whilst the UK state largely supports the neoliberal agenda, if its policy proposals diverge dramatically from the pragmatic concerns of the Atlantic fraction these 'strategic' discourses become formidable political instruments. Here the individualistic and corporate are presented as the universal. Within the UK power bloc then, Atlantic hegemony is unceasingly renegotiated yet relatively stable.

As noted, in Germany a process of coalition building has allied 'reform-minded' elements of the German state with the Rhenish fraction as part of the nascent political/social formation (Dyson 2002). These state managers within the Federal Finance Ministry and the Bundesbank have allied with the Rhenish fraction to secure the consent of other state officials and subaltern groups. As Chapters 6 and 7 will explain, economists, functioning as organic intellectuals in German research centres and the IFD itself, are central to this process of transcending the particularistic interests of the Rhenish fraction and engaging with previously germinated common senses. In this capacity, the IFD provides a regular forum for 180 market experts and economists responsible for proposing political initiatives to counter the ailing German economy. These initiatives typically focus on increased securitization and expanded capital markets.

These proposals will be examined more fully in Chapter 5. Suffice it to note that their production is symptomatic of the social formation emerging around Rhenish hegemonic struggle. Together their reports and policy proposals contend that 'The positive effects of deeper and broader financial markets are now a *received wisdom* from empirical financial market research' (IFD 2005, emphasis added). They therefore logically suggested that, 'the key to unlocking [German] potential lies in shifting the focus more towards the capital markets' (ibid.) under the assumption that the capital market will bring better prospects for *all* portions of society. In this way, political hegemony and societal hegemony are interwoven: dominance within the power bloc focuses more on policy reforms, concessions and alliances; societal hegemony focuses more on securing the universal plane and establishing a hegemonic common sense. The state–capital–intellectual formation of Chapter 6 also therefore emerges. Further, the neoliberal agenda relates its expansive, EU-related concerns to the provision of domestic public goods: the integration of European financial markets is perceived as fundamental in the 'competition for global capital to the benefit of employment and growth' (Koch-Weser 2005).

The suggestion is that the Rhenish fraction have, under wider global restructuring, secured tacit political dominance at the national level. For example, Hans Eichel, Federal Finance Minister (and member of the IFD) noted in his speech on 'Structural Reforms for More Growth' that,

> Following sometimes difficult negotiations, we were able to make what is, overall, an important breakthrough in reaching a compromise with the opposition on these reforms . . . moreover the debate . . . has ensured that almost *all social groups* now accept the need for reforms, even though the reforms themselves may not be so popular.
>
> (Eichel 2004, emphasis added)

His comments suggest reluctant acquiescence rather than spontaneous consent (Gramsci 1971: 12). Elsewhere he stated that 'in common with many other countries [Germany] is facing two crucial challenges: demographic change and globalization. And we cannot succeed in mastering these two long-term challenges unless we achieve higher sustainable growth' (Eichel 2005). In both cases he argues that there is a generalized crisis of previous accumulation regimes; general in the sense that all social groups are affected by it.[4] He then posits the 'solution' to this crisis as increased financial market openness and competition, since 'it is clearly evident that countries with well-developed financial markets grow faster than others' (ibid.).

These discourses therefore reveal Rhenish (and state) attempts to capture so-called 'exogenous pressures' fostered by the neoliberalization of the heartland. As I argue, these 'externalities' are themselves generated both by actual tendencies of the historic-geographic epoch in capitalism as well as the socially constructed neoliberal ideas and worldviews materially represented therein. The Rhenish project thus merges 'external' elements as both *stick* (the need for reform) and *carrot* (positive growth impact) whilst transcending corporate interests through reference to all portions of society. Already, the ideological content of hegemonic struggles in the contested emergence of neoliberalization is therefore apparent. Hence, the IFD is evidence of an institution inscribed with the interests of the emergent hegemonic class fraction (Poulantzas 1973: 190). Rather than simply an amorphous black box the social relations embedded within the German state are evidenced in the IFD, as are the subjectivities and contingencies in seemingly objective policy discourses. Since the Gallic fraction have primarily focused attention at the EU level, it is to EU-level struggles that we now turn.

Struggles at the EU level

Above we noted that institutions are anchored in societal developments; the same is true of the EU. Though functioning on a *supra*-national scale, changes within the impulsion–agency–common sense nexus will be embodied in EU processes as a material condensation and factor of cohesion – albeit at a different level of social formations. Here, hegemonic fractions at the national level typically secure state support in multilateral EU negotiations. Simultaneously, the fractions struggle at the EU level (see below). The contradictions and complexity manifest at the national level – between sediments of past and emerging common senses, institutional crystallizations of former modes, and tensions attached to transnationally oriented–nationally embedded interests – are merely expanded.[5] Similar, rival, overlapping power blocs and projects emerge comprising labour and fractions of capital. Again however, this unstable equilibrium – though incessantly renegotiated – is also perpetually asymmetrical vis-à-vis labour and, moreover, institutionally biased towards better resourced and coordinated transnationally oriented business. For this reason, amidst the complexities of EU policymaking the following is noted: (i) that the EU is not simply the agent of a ruling class formation and – importantly – (ii) to argue that the trajectory of EU reform is neoliberal is not to imply that the Atlantic fraction dominates EU policymaking. Instead, EU trajectory derives from the multi-layered, multi-scalar unfolding of the impulsions–agency–common sense nexus which, more specifically, positions transnationally oriented capital at the apex of political negotiation.

Of the three, the Gallic fraction are therefore particularly instructive. A Hobbesian contender historically dependent on state-led development, the functional, institutional and sociological fusions of the French system have fuelled resistance to extensive, rapid, and economic liberal processes of neoliberalization. As a result, Gallic struggles for social protection within neoliberalization have been more focused at the EU level. Analyses of EU lobbying have noted the increased activity of those groups with most 'at stake': they argue that 'interest groups make . . . calculations concerning the allocation of lobbying resources as between possible lobbying targets – deciding which public institutions to lobby' (Coen 1997, 1998). Increasingly, groups are aware of the 'potential gains from transnational [read European level] lobbying' (Richardson 2000: 1014). Gallic accumulation strategies are most overtly dependent upon national factors (localized circuits and socio-institutional configurations) which are threatened by the dominance of cross-border capital market financing at the heart of the Atlantic project. Though increasingly neoliberal, the Gallic project has prompted efforts at the EU level for the insertion of so-called 'social clauses' (see Chapters 5 and 8). We will consider the three fractions in turn, emphasizing the uniqueness of Gallic efforts.

All three fractions, have therefore sought to gather political momentum for their particular project through traditional lobbying and consultation pathways. In the post–2000 period for example, all three sought representation from their respective national governments through the European Parliament and Council of Ministers in the formulation of Level 1 framework directives.[6] Moreover, all of the fractions have responded to the consultation processes coordinated by the Committee of European Securities Regulators (CESR) at Level 2; that is, where the crucial 'details' are fleshed out within the framework directive. Here, the fractions have responded collectively within the trade associations and individually through their member firms. Finally, all of the fractions have also sought to establish international linkages with other associations in order to achieve the perception of a truly multinational position on certain policy initiatives. These alliances are components of nascent supra-national power blocs. Against this background, Gallic efforts stand out.

In Level 2 consultations, the scale and economic liberal interests of the Atlantic fraction have underpinned strategic discourses not dissimilar to those at the national level. Hence, they have emphasized the potentially excessive costs of conflicting multi-jurisdictional requirements (BBA January 2005a). For example, in negotiations over the Markets in Financial Instruments Directive they were concerned that overly restrictive transaction pricing obligations would create dual requirements: they stated that, 'Overall, in view of the fact that a significant withdrawal of liquidity from European markets would be very damaging, our members consider that regulators/the EU should err on the side of caution in setting the parameters for the universe of shares' (BBA January 2005a). Significantly, the threat to Atlantic accumulation strategies was only an issue because of their global scale; ironically however, the strategic discourse appears to embody a 'threat' precisely *because* they are organized globally rather than solely under the auspices of the CESR within the EU.

As noted, however, the Atlantic fraction have also exploited technical features of the Lamfalussy Process. Atlantic membership for example, lends itself to representation through both UK and international trade associations; the diversity of both their financial operations and the nationalities comprised within the Atlantic fraction foster such linkages. Often then the London Investment Banking Association cooperates with other associations in formulating joint responses. For example, they have regularly joined with the International Swaps and Derivatives Association (London), the International Securities Market Association (London), the Futures and Options Association (London), the Association of Norwegian Stockbroking Companies, the Bankers and Securities Dealers Association of Iceland, the Danish Securities Dealers Association, the Finnish Association of Securities Dealers and the Swedish Securities Dealers Association in EU consultation responses (see, for example, LIBA *et al.* March 2004).

Their rationale is twofold: first, it *replicates* the phenomenon apparent at the national level in subsuming dissenting projects and social forces, and offers another avenue to press Atlantic interests. Second, it again *reinforces* the phenomenon, implying that a common voice warrants greater attention than individual national associations. These tendencies are implicit in the following response by the LIBA:

> We respond jointly in order to assist CESR by providing one document rather than eleven. For the purposes of its analysis of responses, CESR should

however count this response as coming from eleven respondents, representing a significant proportion of investment firms active in Europe's securities and derivatives markets, especially its wholesale markets, and *weight it accordingly*.

(LIBA *et al.* October 2004, emphasis added)

Further, the Atlantic fraction have also sought to promote their project through international trade associations such as the European Banking Federation (EBF) (BBA July 2004).[7]

Again, there are commonalities between the Rhenish and Atlantic fractions. As was apparent in the IFD, a tacit consensus has emerged between German capital with neoliberal concerns – in our terms the Rhenish fraction – and the Atlantic fraction. These similar interests relate to both their accumulation strategies and embedded patterns of financial market organization, as Chapters 5 and 8 explain. One such example is taken from the market participants (consultative) panel[8] of the Committee of European Securities Regulators. The following example concerns the price transparency clauses in the Markets in Financial Instruments Directive (MiFID). As was highlighted, the different perspectives on price transparency underscored the differences between (investment) banking-dominated market systems – like the UK and Germany – and stock exchange-dominated systems – like France.

In a meeting in mid 2003 Dr Rolf Breuer of Deutsche Bank argued that, since 'price formation is an ongoing process' it was impossible to determine a 'best price' for customers in a given financial investment; the draft directive had suggested however, that enhanced price transparency would enable regulators to ensure that consumers achieved *optimal prices*. He stated that the, 'proposed pre-trade transparency regime harms both investment firms offering internalization and clients seeking off-exchange execution' by virtue of the fact that over-the-counter trading[9] itself served a particular need for the customer. Further, certain investors are more concerned with rapid execution than the execution price, hence financial markets need to be organized to allow for this trade-off; this meant that internalization served a specific purpose in the financial market (CESR June 2003). This position, derived from financial markets dominated by investment/private banks, was common to both Atlantic and Rhenish fractions. Similar patterns of market organization have promoted coordinated efforts on certain policy issues. This 'contingent' consensus will be explored in the next chapter; suffice it to note that there is evidence of alliances between Atlantic and Rhenish fractions, contributing to EU financial services industry negotiations, and policy outcomes.

The Gallic fraction, as the most distinctive, have responded to the rescaling of governance in the EU by refocusing their hegemonic struggles on three fronts: first, attempting to secure the cooperation of other associations with similar interests; second, physically relocating lobbying efforts to the geographical centres of EU policymaking; and third, attempting to secure the support of political agents through direct contact.

Unsurprisingly, the Gallic fraction have also recognized that 'positions expressed via a consensus of professional organisations of different nationalities have a better chance of being heard by European authorities' (AFEI 2002) and hence have 'forged links with [their] counterparts elsewhere in Europe sharing the same concerns' (AFEI 2003). Furthermore they state that 'the success of action taken at this level *hinges* on the ability to put across a *transnational viewpoint* and, in so doing, to bring participants from different countries together behind a common idea' (AFEI 2004, emphasis added). These 'sister' associations have included the *Association Belge des Membres de la Bourse* (Belgium), *Associação Portuguesa de Sociedades Corretoras e Financeiras de Corretagem* (Portugal), *Associazione Italiana Intermediari Mobiliari* (Italy), *Bundesverband der Wertpapierfirmen an den deutschen Börsen* (Germany) and the Association of Private Client Investment Managers and Stockbrokers (AFEI March 2005). As noted, this suggests that rival yet overlapping power blocs have emerged. These linkages have developed an 'escalating importance' as the Gallic fraction have attempted to promote their interests in EU negotiations (ibid.).

In addition, the Gallic fraction have sought to establish headquarters in the centres of EU policymaking. This has meant developing an extensive presence in Brussels (FBF June 2002). They explain their rationale as follows:

> It is nevertheless Brussels that is laying the foundations of the legislative and regulatory framework for banking and financial institutions. For this reason, FBF set up a team in October 2002 in the Belgian capital in order to strengthen its presence at all levels of the European decision-making process.
>
> (FBF 2002b)

Elsewhere they also noted that,

> Opening an office in Brussels enables the Federation to follow European projects more closely from the outset, explain the reality of the banking industry to those responsible for drawing up the legislation and contribute to the creation of a European banking model.
>
> (FBF 2002b)

The growing importance of Brussels is evident as it performs several of the policy-relevant and legitimization functions commensurable with a form of state. Hence it is fundamental to regulatory processes within neoliberalization. Given the *variegation* of neoliberalism, however, the EU becomes yet more significant as it shapes pan-European accumulation through compromises secured between different fractions (and labour) with (as we are seeing) projects shaped by nationally embedded factors. Understandably, the 'higher' the tier of governance the more fragmented and contradictory the socio-political formation embodied within the institutional forms. The tensions between impulses, agents and common sense, unfolding on multiple competing and overlapping scales (locally, nationally, regionally and globally), are thus represented in the EU. Yet as Chapter 5 argues, the consensus between these rival projects and blocs provides sufficient commonality to prompt neoliberal integration in the EU.

The third element of the Gallic fraction's attempts has involved a specific focus on political agents at the EU level. Whilst these attempts were part of a generic strategy formulated in 2002 they assumed a particular importance in the formulation of the MiFID. In 2002 at their General Assembly the French Banking Federation noted the need to develop increasingly close relations with the European institutions and, specifically at that time, the European Parliament (FBF June 2002). By 2003 the 'chairmen of the eight largest French banks that make up the French Banking Federations Executive Committee' (FBF 2003) had met in Brussels with various European commissioners including Commission President Romano Prodi to present their 'guiding principles and vision for Europe' (FBF June 2003); in Gramscian terms, their hegemonic project.

With the progress of the MiFID, certain key elements of the three fractions' concepts were brought to the fore. As a result the Gallic fraction were compelled to engage even more vehemently in inter-fractional struggles. The AFEI stated that they organized 'no fewer than thirty-six meetings, with twenty-seven MEPs representing ten nationalities and seven shades of political opinion' through the course of 2002 as well as continuing their 'active efforts to raise awareness at the Council of Europe and the Commission' concerning price transparency (AFEI 2002). In addition the Chairman and the Chief Executive of the AFEI both spoke at a conference in Copenhagen attended by numerous Commission and industry representatives (ibid.). Evidently the Gallic fraction have been exceptionally active in promoting their interests and securing alliances in the EU. To the extent that their project coincides with hegemonic common sense at the European level, they have been relatively successful. By implication, though, institutions such as the European Parliament and Council comprise members of 'national' socio-political formations – the remit and parameters of the Commission for example, introduce a greater degree of 'relative autonomy' at the EU level than is present nationally. The result is more frantic struggles – on the part of different fractions and labour – and the greater risk of contradictory, self-defeating compromise legislation – on the part of EU institutions.

Summary: Political agency

This chapter has briefly outlined the struggles of the three fractions in relation to other fractions within their national–domestic contexts, at the national level, and at the EU level. Two key arguments of this study are therefore emerging. The first is that, as respondents to, mediators and agents of, wider structural changes within the global economy, these transnationally oriented fractions are key protagonists within neoliberalization. Their ability to deploy strategic discourses, rooted in common sense, and to construct alliances with other fractions and political agents, underpin their agency. All three fractions have sought to capture so-called 'exogenous' pressures and incentives. Though focusing on the fractions then, neo-liberalization is more than simply an elite-driven project; struggles to secure hegemony recognize the necessity of working-class acquiescence, secured 'ideologically' through projects and common sense, through alliances and concessions at the state level, and through 'material' forms like access to cheap credit. Finally however, the spatio-temporal specificity of neoliberalization within the EU, characterized by the heartland–contender state dynamic, elucidates features of the three fractions' struggles.

As a fraction within the heartland, ideologically represented in the emergent hegemonic neoliberal common sense, the Atlantic project has sought to capture these tendencies to both maintain and/or reinforce a more liberal skein of neoliberalization. The Rhenish fraction, in the context of a contender state in the throes of crises of accumulation and less rigid socio-institutional configurations than the French model, have sought to both respond to and reshape neoliberalization – on national and supranational scales – and their struggles for reform of the German model are traced in the contours of the IFD. The Gallic fraction, within the archetypal contender state, are an emergent transnationally oriented fraction yet deeply embedded within the French 'fused' model. Despite evidence of – albeit limited – transformation at the national level, their project and struggles have thus been characterized by attempts to secure social protection (Chapter 8) through EU institutions. The significance of the three fractions and the variegation within neoliberalization are manifest. The next chapter supports this by exploring the (contingent) consensus between them which has underpinned neoliberal policy within the EU and helps us understand the recent spate of financial market integration. The second nascent argument, though, is that significant struggles *between* the three fractions already reveal the relative 'disunity' of a purportedly *transnational capitalist class*.

5   A contingent neoliberal consensus

Having outlined the three fractions (Chapter 3) and their political agency (Chapter 4) this chapter now zooms in on the recent period of EU financial market legislation. As the introduction highlighted, post–2000 EU integration has marked a punctuated moment within neoliberalization warranting particular attention. This chapter does not primarily seek to explain the flood of EU directives. Instead I use the post–2000 period to highlight the emergence of a contingent and *variegated* neoliberal consensus among the three fractions. Here I focus on the policy positions themselves before Chapter 8 widens the lens to situate these positions within hegemonic projects. Embedded within the global reconstitution of capitalism – through changing modes of accumulation and neoliberal common sense – I argue that recent EU efforts have been underpinned by this consensus (Macartney 2009a). Here it is evidenced in the discourses of the fractions yet progressively materially condensed in social formations and institutions across the EU, the Lamfalussy process being an obvious example.

Positing a neoliberal consensus might appear tenuous, as if imposing similarities between the three fractions where none exist. Nonetheless, the emphasis remains on the *contingency* of this consensus rather than its coherence (see below). Elsewhere this consensus has been, so I argue, misconstrued as a hegemonic project in its own right, pertaining to a transnational capitalist class (van Apeldoorn 2002). For this reason this chapter examines the parallels in the three hegemonic projects whilst keeping in view the obvious dissimilarities. The remainder of the book then deals with the wider implications for our understanding of neoliberalization.

Here we focus on the policy positions of the three fractions, specifically those on the Capital Requirements Directive (CRD) and the Markets in Financial Instruments Directive (MiFID). These responses are focused at both national and EU bodies as well as drawing on resources (such as annual reports) produced by the associations and their members.

The neoliberal consensus

In order to posit a neoliberal consensus however, we must first return to the overexpansion of neoliberalism question (see Chapter 2). In essence, since our methodology for determining a neoliberal consensus necessarily employs discourses, a series of conceptual and empirical difficulties arise. Conceptually, a dialectical understanding of the material and ideational means, of course, that one can neither read the ideational from the material nor the material from the ideational. Furthermore, empirically, there is no neat historical separation between Keynesianism and neoliberalism. Let me explain.

In effect, the two difficulties (above) mean that: just because fractions speak of 'level playing fields' and competitive reform, it does not follow that they agree on what this means; further, these discourses are often employed strategically without implying an *actual* interest (intention) in undergoing competitive reform. As Crouch (2009: 388–89) notes for example, neoliberalism is not synonymous with neo-classical economics, since neoliberalism often accepts monopolies – for example – as the product of Darwinism inherent in free markets. Consequently, positing a neoliberal consensus is problematic – though neither impossible nor futile.

The following can be noted: given the emergent argument concerning the national–domestic embeddedness of our fractions, the consensus logically comprises both cross-national comparative and nationally embedded elements. Put simply, cross-national comparisons are problematic because pinning down what neoliberalism means nationally is also problematic. Yet the consensus arises from the conjuncture of these nationally embedded, albeit distinctive, projects. As a result, since the neoliberal consensus is anchored in the contradictions of the capital–labour relation outlined earlier, and offset (with the relevant spatio-temporal impulsions) through financial expansion and transnationalization, the binary between these impulsions (as primary explanation for neoliberalism) and class agency (as primary explanation) is inherently misleading. Instead, as indicated by our three-part nexus, neoliberalism is an attempt to restore and/or secure class rule by capitalizing on this global reconstitution (see Chapters 1 and 2). Material and ideational elements are inextricably interwoven in explanations of neoliberalization.

The two analytical keys to unlocking these contradictions are therefore already apparent: one is the emphasis on *fractions* at the apex of these social processes; the other is *variegated* neoliberalism. Highlighting the position of these fractions explains how, imbibed in the global restructuring of capitalism, their primary concern is to secure and consolidate class rule. Their hegemonic projects embed pragmatic concerns within common senses – epitomized in the usage of terms like 'competitiveness' and 'liberalization'. Put differently, neoliberalism – in the case of each fraction – is related to the liberalization and integration of markets and the profit-related opportunities afforded by finance-led accumulation. Yet our fractions pursue this project from an individualistic perspective; their concern is not full-blown cross-border competition but rather the liberalization of constraints imposed on their own accumulation strategies. Those fractions most transnationally integrated therefore typically display neoliberal elements to their projects whilst *liberalization* should not be read as synonymous with *free market* competition (Overbeek and van der Pijl 1993). This has meant the emergence of class projects comprised of 'oligopoly and protection for the strong and a socialization of their risks, market discipline for the weak' (Gill 1995: 405). The fractions seek liberalization and integration insofar as it aids their insatiable thirst to accumulate; yet this obviously involves *retaining* certain national–domestic arrangements, thereby simultaneously limiting liberalization.

Second, however, the neoliberal consensus is inherently contradictory and therein – within the notion of *variegated* neoliberalism – lies the key. Again, let me explain. Variegated neoliberalism is rooted in the contradiction that we witness in the transnationally oriented–nationally embedded class fractions; namely that full liberalization (so to speak) would undermine the very conditions (such as socio-institutional configurations and localized circuits – rooted in the national) which underpin their accumulation strategies in the first place. Consequently, the transnationalization of these fractions lends itself to neoliberal interests (hence the consensus) yet this consensus can only be contingent since it is comprised of distinct and competing *accumulation strategies* and *hegemonic projects*. As a result, this contradiction runs to the very heart of the 'transnational capitalist class' thesis and supports one core argument of this book.

With this in mind we return to the fractions themselves. In effect, the variegated neoliberal consensus between the three fractions reflects the struggles outlined in the previous chapter. It therefore has supra-national – that is EU-level or global – and national-level elements. Again, distinguishing between the two is only ever a poor analytical device, as our scalar conception of the transnational suggests. Yet, the differential transnational orientations and path-dependent national–domestic configurations engender the following: the Atlantic fraction, though hegemonic at the national level, display the aforementioned contradiction between liberal interests and protecting comparative advantages, evidenced at the intersection of EU-level and national-level policy; the Rhenish fraction, fiercely contesting hegemony at the national level have sought socio-liberal neoliberal reform both nationally *and* at EU level, and often as a means to break the deadlock at the national level; the Gallic fraction, embedded in more inert domestic configurations have sought social neoliberal interests primarily at the EU level, and often to retain domestic arrangements. This is the obvious contradiction outlined above; that variegated neoliberalism can appear at once both *liberal* and *protectionist*. Chapter 8 explains this in greater detail. The conjuncture of the projects however, has given rise to a neoliberal consensus underpinning European financial integration.

Variegated neoliberalism: Atlantic project

As a transnational-*global* fraction, Atlantic interests extend beyond the jurisdiction of the EU. Their engagement in circuits of finance capital, coupled with their organization on a global scale, underpins their distinctive economic liberal project (van der Pijl 1984: 7). Their concerns in EU integration have therefore focused on avoiding the excessive costs associated with the multi-jurisdictional operations of their accumulation strategy. This engenders an obvious tension between EU and global operating standards, and here their liberal interests are most apparent. I therefore focus on the intersection between these EU-level and national policies.

The tension between European and global regulation is perhaps best displayed through the requirements of capital adequacy legislation, since EU Capital Requirements Directives were precipitated and impelled by changing global requirements surrounding the Basel II Accord (2004). Basel II, entitled 'International Convergence of Capital Measurement and Capital Standards: A Revised Framework', focused on improving the risk sensitivity of capital allocation, distinguishing between different degrees of risk associated with the different market operations of a bank (see Quaglia 2007). Though non-legally binding it established a framework for global regulatory standards. For financial market governance in the Eurozone it therefore contributes to the overlap and friction between national, EU-level and global requirements (Moran 2002: 257).

This raised concerns upon implementation at the national level. Atlantic responses to consultation processes were characterized by two appeals: first, concerning capital adequacy,[1] they objected to the degree of national discretion permitted within the Basel regulatory framework on capital requirements; second they argued that whilst the Accord was intended to move towards a 'greater dependency . . . on qualitative and discretionary standards', the Financial Services Authority had implemented restrictive, inflexible rules (BBA and LIBA December 2002). Both had global and national implications.

'*Super-equivalence*'[2]

Industry responses to capital adequacy directives were therefore littered with allegations of 'super-equivalence', targeted at various aspects of the FSA's interpretation of the Basel and EU standards. Attention is drawn to one clause in particular; namely the FSA's intention of raising the capital requirement above the 4 per cent minimum established in the EU text (BBA and LIBA June 2003a). Here the tension between global (Basel II), EU (CRD) and national standards is palpable. Simply, both the EU draft directive and the Basel Committee's proposals employed a separation of different forms of liabilities and required correspondingly different ratios of capital to underpin each set of liabilities. According to the FSA consultation paper (CP 155) the regulator intended to raise the capital requirements for liabilities issued under Tier 1 significantly higher than the 4 per cent minimum required by EU legislation and excluded certain financial instruments from an issuer's calculations; the effect being that – in specific cases – issuers would be required to retain greater amounts of capital (ibid.).

The BBA and LIBA's concerns over super-equivalent standards were, however, primarily related to the dual regulatory criteria that such measures would provoke. This was reinforced when the FSA issued CP 136, laying out its proposals for Individual Capital Adequacy Standards (ICAS), designed to fit within the framework constructed by the Basel Committee for Banking Supervision. Within this framework, specifically designed to promote international convergence, the BBA and LIBA noted that the FSA was 'likely to considerably exceed the international norm in the application of Pillar 2' (BBA and LIBA June 2003a). In operating globally they favoured a single set of international standards and, as Chapter 4 noted, the associations' rhetoric was strategically employed. They suggested that the UK might become an 'international outlier in the manner in which it applies and interprets Pillar 2' which would threaten the City's attractiveness amongst the international community of banks and investment firms (ibid.); a fact which was of course analysed in Chapter 4. The possibility of any of the three regulatory authorities (FSA, EU or BCBS) implementing incommensurable requirements would compel global operators to comply with several potentially conflicting sets of criteria. This prompted the (variegated neo)liberal responses of the Atlantic fraction. One such example is Citigroup. In its response to CP 189, it stated that,

> a primary concern of Citigroup is the maintenance of a *globally* competitive playing field for its business . . . We (Citigroup) are mindful that we do not want the burden to be duplicative. This is of the utmost importance to an organization such as ours where we *operate in multiple regulatory jurisdictions* and the cost of 'dual' applications is likely to be a significant cost burden.
>
> (Citigroup 2003, emphasis added)

Similarly, the Royal Bank of Scotland (RBS) stated its case for the global convergence of capital requirements, arguing that, 'the FSA should consider how the US and UK approaches can be aligned more closely' (RBS 2003). In this case the concern for mobility is central to Atlantic accumulation and, as before, regulatory cost burdens present themselves as just another barrier to be removed (Marx 1973 [1857]: 539). The umbrella terms 'liberalization', 'level playing field' and 'integration' are therefore infused with (concrete) pragmatic concerns of a – more abstractly – neoliberal type yet (in negotiating with the British state) embedded in common sense assumptions concerning the provision of public goods. At once, their liberal interests in market integration were also fused with protecting domestic–national advantages. Here I focus only on the liberal element.

Principles-based regulation

The Atlantic fraction also called for *principles-based* as opposed to *prescriptive* legislation. Again, the distinction is significant, both for the economic liberal skein of neoliberalism it reflects as well as revealing the embeddedness of the Atlantic fraction within the UK.[3] The premise underpinning principles-based legislation/regulation, so I argue, is that it encourages a form of so called 'market-led'[4] integration. This is a distinctive feature of the liberal internationalist state form–common sense within the UK. Moreover, it most closely corresponds to the ideological preferences of finance capital as outlined earlier (van der Pijl 1984: 10).

Again, this was manifest in negotiations at the national level. In their joint response to FSA CP 136 the associations commented that, 'there is no need for the regulator to take a prescriptive view of the process a firm might adopt' in establishing its capital requirements (BBA and LIBA June 2003b). Instead they stated that, 'the industry favours a principles-based approach to the implementation of the new Accord and the Capital Adequacy Directive' (BBA and LIBA December 2003). Further, in relation to Individual Capital Standards, the Atlantic fraction argued in favour of 'firm-specific self-assessment' (ibid.). The rationale for these requests was that, according to the Atlantic fraction 'Commercial pressures and market forces achieve greater choice and flexibility of execution without a need for intrusive regulatory intervention' (BBA October 2004; see also LIBA December 2004; Barclays December 2004). These requests have a haunting resonance, given the lack of regulatory scrutiny contributing to the 2007–09 crisis.

In sum, we have already noted that any relatively abstract conception of neoliberalism is problematic when we move to a more concrete level; that is, in examining policy positions in state–capital negotiations. Here it is obvious that these interests are not simply reducible to a form of neo-classical economics but are primarily driven by the pragmatic concerns of capital: under the competitive impulsions of capitalism here we witness capital's attempts to remove any barriers, legislative or otherwise, to accumulation (Marx 1973 [1857]: 539). More specifically, the transnational-global orientation of the Atlantic fraction lends itself to *liberal* neoliberal interests. As noted, I focus primarily on establishing the neoliberal consensus.

Variegated neoliberalism: Rhenish project

As Chapter 4 also noted, similar embedded patterns of market organization fuelled certain commonalities between Atlantic and Rhenish fractions. Further, the notion of a late developer, contender state is also useful in understanding the neoliberal elements of the Rhenish project: the concerns of the Rhenish fraction are explicitly contextualized against the crises of accumulation within the German system. Finally however, the integration of production–finance, capital–labour, transnationally–nationally oriented fractions shapes the specificities of what I provocatively earlier called liberal protectionism. In short, the Rhenish neoliberal skeins are manifest in: an emphasis on self-regulation; less intervention by the state; and a principles-based, flexible approach to regulation (BdB 2004); and these again incorporate EU and national skeins.

First, however, I contextualize these interests. Recall that crises provide preconditions for class struggles over hegemony and changing accumulation regimes. It was also noted that certain spatio-temporal dynamics are inscribed within crises which tend to delimit outcomes and responses. The reports emerging from the largest German banks reveal the importance of the ailing German economy in both prompting and shaping the subsequent restructuring process.[5]

For example, in his opening statement the chairman of the Hypo Vereinung Bank stated that,

> The economy performed less dynamically than expected [in 2003–04], so that business conditions for banks remained difficult, especially in Germany, and despite lower credit risks. Lending growth for the year was well below average, demand for financial services was generally slack, and movements on the capital markets were minimal.
>
> (HVB 2004)

The report continued to spell out the ways in which HVB was restructuring to promote its 'profitability' and competitiveness in the German market.

Similar comments emerged from other transnationally oriented financial institutions. In its annual report, the DZ Bank explained how it had already undergone significant restructuring in order to lower its cost base and improve the quality of its lending portfolio (DZ Bank 2004). It also noted the steady decline of its consumer loan market because the 'cooperative financial services network did not have the requisite modern and efficient products to offer'; the response was to 'make their own offering more competitive' (ibid.). So the liberal interests of the Rhenish fraction (below) are already embedded in the transnational orientation–national rootedness dialectic, manifest here in discourses on national crises. Thus the neoliberal character of competitiveness discourses emerges in the shape of increasing financial instrumentation and capital market reform. I examine this further in the concluding section of this chapter. There has been a progressive shift then, from forms of nationally organized credit-based financing to transnationalized, capital market-dependent strategies in response to worsening economic conditions. In the words of the BdB, crises 'have led to the realization that Germany's current economic and social problems cannot be solved by a *traditional* approach' (BdB January 2004, emphasis added).

Principles-based legislation, self-regulation and state withdrawal

The Rhenish fraction's neoliberal agenda is therefore evidenced in these three elements: principles-based legislation; self-regulation; and state withdrawal. As with the Atlantic fraction, the Bundesverband deutscher Banken stated that 'information about investment firms . . . should not be too detailed', an approach which would give 'national regulators sufficient room for manoeuvre' in negotiations on the MiFID (BdB January 2004). In their 2004 Banking Survey the BdB (2004) emphasized the need for, 'a discussion about . . . a *principles-based regulatory concept* that, for example, takes more account of *European banks' competitive position* in the international arena', they also noted however, that '*intervention in the market* [should be kept] to a minimum' and that allowing 'more room for *self-regulation* could give a major, new boost to the integration of markets for financial services'. As a result, European banks' liberal interests are evident in their concern for legislative flexibility – presupposing their multi-jurisdictional operations – yet their comments on political intervention are also linked to a structural reform agenda within Germany.

So their variegated *neoliberal* skeins are anchored in the transnational-national dialectic: promoting (i) requests for non-prescriptive governance on an EU scale and (ii) attempts to avoid excessive intervention in their domestic–national market. In a positional paper to the EU, the BdB again claimed that 'state intervention in market activities should be kept to a minimum' (BdB March 2004). Likewise, in addressing structural changes to the German market, the BdB challenged state ownership of German banks as one of the primary explanatory factors stunting growth; in their words 'only the withdrawal of the state and privatization of public-sector banks will ensure the German economy is provided with financial services in an efficient and market-driven manner' (BdB 2004). So the individualistic, accumulation imperatives of the Rhenish fraction are framed in competitiveness discourses. For example, in place of state guarantees the association championed the governing mechanisms of the free-market economy (BdB 2002). State guarantees were simultaneously at the core of former German financial provision and an immediate focal point for the liberal agenda of the Rhenish fraction.

So the transnational-national dialectic, manifested in individual projects of a liberal protectionist type, have given rise to a variegated neoliberal consensus. Here the Rhenish fraction – engaged in struggles at the national level over structural reform (economic) and securing hegemony (political) have also sought a similar agenda at the EU level. Nonetheless, our goal at this stage is simple: to establish the common neoliberal interests between the three fractions.

Variegated neoliberalism: Gallic project

Expectedly, Gallic neoliberalism stands apart from the previous two projects in its emphasis on social protection. Recall though that the 'separation' of neoliberalism into three, so-called variants, is only ever an unsatisfactory analytical precursor to our later analysis of the three projects as particular moments within processes of *variegated* neoliberalization. Neither is it satisfactory to align Gallic neo-liberalism with a transnationally oriented fraction as somehow distinct from nationally oriented fractions with interests in social protection. Our conception of accumulation strategies (comprising a (shaping) matrix of scale, function and social configuration) and power blocs (comprising competing yet allied frac-tions) precludes this crude dichotomy. The fusions of the French system thus reveal themselves in the character of Gallic neoliberalism, as do the loci of class struggles. Put differently, this strand of variegated neoliberalism is less *economically* liberal and has primarily been expressed at the EU level.

Market expansion

For example, the Association Française des Enterprises d'Investissements (AFEI) stated that the Gallic fraction share 'the same interests' as other transnationally oriented fractions and have a similar concern for cross-border financial market activity in Europe (Interview AFEI). They asserted that the single financial market was proceeding as a result of the 'cross-border nature of market practices and a relatively clear consensus' concerning its benefits (FBF June 2003). Further, in their annual reports the French Banking Federation (FBF) goes as far as *insisting* that the increased competitiveness of markets for investment is fundamental to the progress of both EU and French economies and hence 'must be pursued' (FBF 2004).

The transnationally oriented operations of the Gallic fraction *clearly* promote neoliberal concerns. Like the example of Citigroup cited above, they too aim to avoid dual standards and unnecessary costs; responding to the CESR they state that 'many ISPs (investment service providers) belong to corporate groups that operate across Europe and use common reporting tools. It is therefore vital that the reporting requirements imposed by different authorities are not superimposed onto these intra-group procedures' (FBF 2003). As stated, a similar concern over the progress of the single financial market is apparent amongst all three fractions; hence the reference to a (contingent) consensus.

More significantly, there is certain evidence that cracks may be appearing in the Gallic system and of the slow erosion of protection in the Gallic system. For example, one of the key impediments to cross-border competition has historically been the 'concentration principle'. Recall that it had been a central feature of the French financial system during the development of French capital markets in the early 1990s, ensuring that the traditional credit-based (banking) system did not lose competitive advantages to foreign capital. This meant that foreign investment firms were unable to trade on their own account and instead forced to utilize a regulated market.[6] This relatively opaque 'anti-competitive' practice came under pressure early in the MiFID negotiations, and the Gallic fraction reluctantly agreed to its abolition (FBF 2003). As we noted in Chapter 1, the Gallic fraction have progressively perceived neoliberalization as being in their 'best interests' – even where certain costs are attached to the integration project.[7] This is due to both exogenous pressures – of investment opportunities abroad – and endogenously generated pressures – through the transnationalization of Gallic capital, as well as being shaped by neoliberal assumptions about economic development.

Prescriptive legislation

As noted, however, the fusion of the French system has tended to be embedded in material social practices, such as cultural and ideological differences (Bruff 2008: 53, 58). For example, within EU financial market negotiations the Gallic fraction have sought integration through *harmonization* with an emphasis on 'investor protection'. In contradistinction to integration through flexible, principles-based regulation the Gallic fraction have preferred 'harmonization' or convergence-through-prescription (AFEI June 2004). This would allow the desired liberalization and integration proposed at the EU level, whilst enabling protection at the national level. In short, this position was underpinned by pragmatic concerns associated with historical features of the French financial system. Already the distinctiveness of the three projects is emerging, yet this is a necessary evil in positing the neoliberal consensus; it is as if to say, the Gallic fraction too have neoliberal interests, though in demonstrating this it also becomes apparent how their project differs.

An example of this approach was the AFEI's response to the consolidation of transparency information in the Markets in Financial Instruments Directive, referring to increased visibility of market information on the part of market vendors. The AFEI noted the existence of two alternatives, 'achieving consolidation through CESR', or through 'leaving it to market forces', before asserting that, 'the idea of giving free rein to market forces is not necessarily the most obvious answer' (AFEI October 2004). This is starkly juxtaposed against the Atlantic position outlined above. Nonetheless, the (neoliberal) notion of prescriptive means to achieve integration was both acceptable and desirable to the Gallic fraction.

Ostensibly their concern is that unless specific measures are determined at the regional level, greater flexibility risks overriding important domestic legislative measures (FBF April 2003, October 2003). They noted, for example, that the key to 'achieving a level playing field between market participants . . . will hinge on the detailed content of the Level 3 measures drafted by CESR' (AFEI June 2004). Essentially, though expanded accumulation requires both greater cross-border access and new, rescaled regulatory infrastructure, pragmatism also requires the retention of certain features of the French system enshrined in detailed legislative measures. They note for example, that 'French banks would like orderly competition, which genuinely guarantees the protection of investors and business finance, and thus favour free competition amongst the different trading systems in place across Europe'. In effect, their concern for 'free competition' is only acceptable with necessary ('orderly') clauses designed to defend Gallic strategies (FBF 2002b). Later chapters will examine one such set of clauses, concerning investor protection, which, if absent from EU measures would disadvantage more stringently regulated financial markets (AFEI December 2004). For now, however, it is sufficient to note that – albeit distinctive – the Gallic fraction too have neoliberal interests related to the transnationalization of their strategies.

Summary: Contingent consensus

This chapter has therefore concluded the first part of the book: the three fractions were introduced in Chapter 3, wherein their similarities as transnationally oriented social forces became clear, as did their differences, stylistically characterized as global, European and national fractions. Chapter 4 examined the political agency of the three fractions, institutionally (over)represented in financial trade associations and similar bodies, at the national and EU level. This fifth chapter has argued that, despite obvious differences which will be further examined in Chapter 8, a neoliberal consensus is apparent between the three fractions. Moreover, the specificities of their accumulation strategies and the nature and loci of their class struggles can now be seen to shape this variegated neoliberal consensus. I argue that this consensus, coupled with the agency of our fractions within nascent social formations, has underpinned recent EU financial integration, thereby addressing a major *problématique* of this study.

This claim must not be misinterpreted, however: the tacit consensus is relatively unstable and contingent; *variegated neoliberalism* seeks to capture this as a concept, reflecting the transnational–national contradiction. Two key arguments of this text are therefore apparent: one is the relative fragility of this neoliberal consensus; the other is that the consensus, and by implication variegated neoliberalism itself, is nested within a more encompassing or fundamental process of common sense production.

Yet this first part of the book also sheds light on three further interconnected issues: the relation of material and ideational revealed through these hegemonic projects; the question of determinism; and counter-hegemony. On the first, we note that neoliberalism is neither solely prompted by a rational–objective assessment of external material conditions nor a carefully framed narrative employed by big business to convince state and public alike. Again, these are merely analytic attempts to discern causality through the separation of material and ideational elements; leading to the problematic separation of interests and ideas. Instead, through our dialectical approach, what becomes significant is the way social actors themselves perpetuate this same illusory separation; in effect, the way ideas frame perceptions of self-interest and the way agents employ discourses as interest-laden ideological instruments. This is because social agents themselves cannot distinguish one from the other (Hay 2002: 213).

For example, in the Rhenish case, capital here perceived damaged profit margins as a product of material factors such as inefficient products. For them this is no ideological construct but a 'hard fact' evidenced in balance-sheet losses. In turn, their responses also appear based on the 'hard facts' of domestic and international experience, where 'competitive' liberalization and particular 'efficient' products have proven track records. What is missing then is an awareness of the *internal* and *imperceptible*. For instance, they are oblivious to the ideas and worldviews which gave rise to these now defunct financial products and the 'new' ideas framing their future strategies. The point is this: the distinction between *real* interests and *ideas as instruments* of these interests is meaningless. Social actors *perceive* the world as both external and material, formulating activities and discourses about the world as such, when – despite claims to the contrary – they are continuously involved in *constructing, destroying*, and *reconstructing* material–ideological reality as simultaneously exogenous–endogenous. This leads into the determinism question.

The determinism question thus elicits two responses: first, *both* the 'tangible' effects of crises and the fractions' hegemonic projects drive neoliberalization; yet, it is the specific material condensations of past and present material–ideological conditions which fundamentally constrain and shape the contours of future potentialities. This is, as noted, partly because actors perceive the world as material and external, and partly because social reality itself reproduces and reinforces this appearance. Thus, genuinely 'material' elements (so to speak) are afforded further influence by their internalization-as-material by social actors. As Gramsci

(1971: 34–35) notes, the 'contemporary world [is] a synthesis of the past, of all generations, which projects itself into the future'.

So, for example, capital is neither able to discern – for obvious reasons – whether its falling profit margins are genuinely related to *material* factors nor does it – empowered with this knowledge – construct discourses to simply conceal this separation. For reasons largely beyond either its understanding or its concern, it is driven by the search for profit, and barriers to this end-goal are (from its perspective) simply responded to with business strategies (of which policy responses are but one) employing already tried and tested measures for restoring profitability. The internal relations of material and ideational, interests and ideas, are simply elided into one.

Second then, this again reinforces that our fractions are not puppet masters of the global restructuring of capitalism, but themselves engendered through and imbibed in processes they neither solely initiated nor necessarily understand. Finally, this of course suggests that successful counter-hegemonic efforts would require cataclysmic events to rupture these underlying processes. Capturing state agencies or focusing on restraining capitalist agency would simply be misguided in the absence of more fundamental 'ruptures in [the] pattern of movement' (Holloway 1992: 146). We return to this in the concluding chapter.

In sum, departing from the state-centrism of VoC accounts we find those capitalists – engendered through and themselves preconditions of processes of neoliberalization, embedded within alliances at the level of the state and EU, and at the apex of neoliberal reforms. Further, although European working classes are present in these alliances we better understand *how* capital seeks to shape national and EU regulatory politics asymmetrically. Here, rejection of VoC's soft-positivism helps explain both the 'power' of discourses – rooted in material social changes – and simultaneously demystifies elements of these strategic threats. Moreover, rejection of pluralism's agent-centricity embeds the agents of Part I within the global reconstitution of capitalism itself. Finally, the variegation of neoliberalism – rejecting the VoC binary – thus allows a nuanced account of the 'underlying theme' of post-Keynesian reform whilst highlighting its spatio-temporalities as inherent and necessary features. We must now examine the changes in hegemonic common sense which help explain the efficacy and content of these hegemonic projects and the attempts to consolidate class rule at the heart of neoliberalization.

Part III
Neoliberal common sense

6   Organic economists as producers of neoliberal common sense

The previous two chapters examined the three fractions and their political agency, arguing that they are key protagonists within processes of neoliberalization and yet, simultaneously conditions, mediators and outcomes: recent EU financial integration provided a case study of these dynamics. Specifically, however, I argued that the content and impact of their policy positions – within hegemonic projects – can only be understood given the production of neoliberal common sense. In effect, the fractions seek to transcend their pragmatic individualistic interests in order to secure or maintain political support. Both the immediate shift to neoliberalism in the 1970s and the hegemonic struggles of capital are therefore infused with 'ideological' struggles. This chapter begins with a further exploration of Gramsci's writings on common sense. It then introduces economic research centres as collectives of organic intellectuals producing neoliberal common sense (Macartney 2008). Finally, it examines this common sense embodied in the research findings of the three centres introduced.

Chapter 2 outlined the basis for an examination of neoliberal common-sense production through a focus on economic research centres. These centres and their research have risen to prominence in post-war decades as both cause and effect of claims of ailing accumulation regimes. Gramsci's insights have a particular relevance then in the contemporary era. In recent decades economic research has developed an unparalleled importance in plotting trajectories of growth and development. On a global scale, central banks have been granted autonomy over monetary policy; at the helm are the world's leading economists in so-called 'epistemic communities' of central bankers (Kapstein 1992). A particular 'scientized', opaque policy discourse has emerged with all the hallmarks of objective scientific analysis and deliberately reminiscent of the natural sciences (Marcussen 2008). Further, this analysis is evidence of the ongoing dominance of 'positivism' within economics (see Chapter 2; see also Fine and Milonakis 2009). Not only are economic policies now underpinned by a complex mix of neo-classical, monetarist, rational market-oriented research but this eclectic hybrid has adopted the status of the *only* sensible policy programme for contemporary capitalisms (Hay and Rosamond 2002). Significantly though, this policy pro- gramme has been connected to the rise of circulating, 'finance capital' (Overbeek and van der Pijl 1993). The parallels with Gramsci's critique of immanent, universalized worldviews as subjective and particularistic are obvious.

Organic economists

In our three country case studies we thus witness two interwoven processes at work: on the one hand, national economic research centres linked to the three transnationally oriented fractions have produced similar neoliberal claims specifically targeted at the condensations of common senses in their respective member states; again, this is an important feature of *variegated* neoliberalism. On the other hand, the international connections of these economists and a variety of disciplining techniques reveal the importance of the Atlantic heartland in the production and dissemination of neoliberal common sense.

Figure 6.1 provides a stylized account of the common structural features of the three research institutes. Each one incorporates: a scientific council or committee responsible for overseeing research findings; a board of directors comprised of either economists and/or representatives from business; various sources of funding, corporate or otherwise; a collection of economists producing the research itself; and a variety of end-users receiving the outputs of the research centre.

The National Institute of Economic and Social Research (NIESR)

By definition, 'policy research aspires to pragmatic usefulness in the sense that it should be able to provide information that (if heeded by policy makers – which is another question altogether) could contribute to the design of effective and feasible

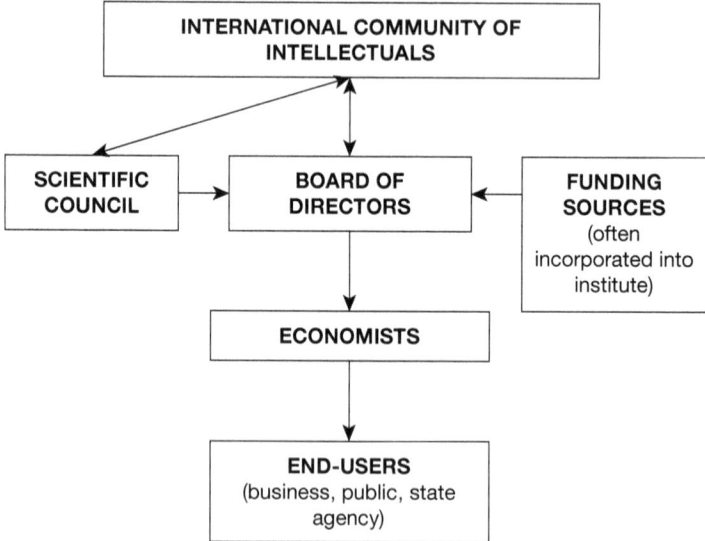

Figure 6.1 International community of intellectuals.

policy responses to given societal problems' (Scharpf 2000: 764). Within the City of London there are a number of prominent research institutes aiming to fulfil this (social) function. Significantly though, these institutes tend to fall within the US 'think tank' tradition of organizationally independent bodies (Gellner 1998: 83).

Though societies such as the Fabians predate the twentieth century, the majority of UK research centres emerged in either the inter-war or post-war years and fell within the broad 'Keynesian consensus' (Denham and Garnett 2004: 235). The primary distinction between first- and third-wave centres like the Fabians or the Institute for Economic Affairs, and second-wave centres like the NIESR, is that second-wave centres overtly aimed to be non-ideologically motivated, simply producing *empirical* research (ibid.: 243; see also Denham and Garnett 1998: 30). As we shall see, the claims to objectivity of neoliberal common sense are linked to these so-called 'scientific standards'. Significantly though, unlike German or French systems the UK was dominated by a so-called 'monopoly model' of economic research centres; that is, where only one dominant worldview tends to underpin the majority of economic research in one historical epoch (Scharpf 2000: 772). This led to a watershed in the 1970s where the dominant Keynesian paradigm was jettisoned in favour of what I characterize as a neoliberal one.

That said, the National Institute of Economic and Social Research (NIESR) is important because of its connections with the Atlantic fraction *and* research institutes in other member states. These latter connections are a feature of the diffusion of neoliberal common sense from within the heartland. Further, the NIESR claims to be 'Britain's premier *independent* economic research institute' (NIESR 2007, emphasis added) and is one of the oldest (established in 1938) and largest, with a staff of 54 (Denham and Garnett 2004: 233) suggesting its prominence above other potential case studies in the City of London. Perhaps more significantly though, it pre-dates the economic liberal or so called 'New Right' policy institutes (such as the Institute for Economic Affairs) and was typically viewed as a Keynesian stronghold (ibid.: 236). I argue that its emphasis on neoliberal ideas is therefore a symptom of the hegemony of neoliberal common sense. As will be seen, its research is targeted at both business and state elites and its empirically grounded research claims are central to the demystification of the universality and rationality of neoliberalism as a spatio-temporally contingent representation of the interests of transnationally oriented capital.

Since the claim is that Germany and France are contender states (effectively) responding to processes initiated within the Atlantic heartland this chapter focuses greater attention on these two continental European case studies; Chapter 6 then focuses on the role of the heartland itself. The Munich-based Centre for Economic Studies und dem institut für Wirtschaftsforschung (CESifo) and the Paris-based Centre d'Etudes Prospectives et d'Informations Internationales (CEPII) are significant for three reasons: first, their research is primarily focused on the international economy and its relation to the national, employing empirical or quantitative methodologies. Second, they reveal clear connections with research institutes in other member states which will prove to be a conceptually insightful feature of the contemporary economics profession, seen through historical materialist lenses. Third, they too have formidable linkages with both capital and the state in Germany and France respectively. As we noted previously, this is symptomatic of our nascent social formations.

The Centre for Economic Studies und dem institut für Wirtschaftsforschung (CESifo)

In Germany, the state was historically less extensive than its French counterpart, hence it lacked the capacity for an overarching industrial policy. As Streeck notes, 'in compensation [therefore] it offer[ed] firms and industries a wide range of general infrastructural supports, like high public spending on research and development' (1997: 38). Further, the 'organizational culture' of German capitalism had historically allowed for 'applied research conducted by research institutes'; in effect, publicly financed institutes or the so-called 'Blue-List' received equal support from federal and regional tiers of government (ibid.: 46). The result was that, throughout the 1990s for example, the German state recorded spending more on R&D in the higher education and government-related sectors as a percentage of GDP than most of the other OECD countries including the US (OECD 1997, cited in Beise and Stahl 1999: 401). Interestingly however, there has historically been significant conflict between state-funded research and the data, explanations and policy recommendations of in-house research institutes within big businesses. The often contradictory results were therefore typically 'debated in the financial press' with often inconclusive outcomes, meaning, however, that German research institutes have a clear orientation towards media outlets (Scharpf 2000: 772; Thunert 2004: 84). Thus, whilst under routine conditions research centres tend to provide research for business and political elites, 'periods of crisis provide [them] with an *entrée* because their voice and competence is required to assist agenda-setting' (Gellner 1998: 83). I shall argue that though crises provide unique moments, the production of neoliberal common sense has been an ongoing process prior to, during and following these specific historical junctures. Crises thus represent both the burgeoning contradictions of former accumulation regimes and the struggle for hegemony over competing common senses and their material social forms.

With this in mind, the CESifo Group is our focus within Germany. It consists of the Centre for Economic Studies (CES), an independent institute at the University of Munich, and the Institute for Economic Research (ifo) also situated in Munich. It brings together the theoretical work of university academics and the empirical work of a leading economic research institute (CESifo 2007). The fact that the CESifo is one of Germany's leading economic research institutes and one of the most frequently cited in the media, suggests its prominence both as state-funded institute and widely accepted disseminator of policy proposals and economic ideas (ibid.).[1]

The institute sits at the apex of relations between state, finance and production capital,[2] combining a national and international focus. The exigencies of the political process demand that the version of common sense espoused become less amorphous, unconscious and contradictory the closer to the state we look (Bruff 2008: 61–62). Thus, the positioning of a research centre contributes to its social function. As per article 91b of the German constitution the ifo is included on the 'Blue List' of publicly subsidized institutes, financed 'within the framework of research assistance' (CESifo 2007). Although there are officially eighty-three Blue List institutes, six larger bodies dominate the group; the CESifo is among these six. As a result, since 2000 it has received institutional funding as a 'research-based service institution' (ibid.) suggesting its acceptance in the field of economic research within Germany. The ifo supports this by claiming that, given the challenges of adjusting to globalization its policy advice to the public sector has 'developed into a core task' (ibid.). Again, globalization is constructed as an exogenous – and therefore irresistible – pressure, a skein picked up in the projects of the three fractions. Situating the origins of these projects is thus the concern of the next two chapters.

Also, whilst the CES is linked to the university research community it combines with the ifo on its international activities (ibid.), suggesting a dual research interest in national and international affairs. Finally it is precisely this 'blend' of traditional and contemporary research institutes which is seen to epitomize the current state of flux of the German financial market (Thunert 2004: 75). Whilst the ifo was established in 1949 by Professor Ludwig Erhard, architect of the post-war reconstruction, the CES was founded in 1991 and has connections with numerous prominent economists within the Atlantic heartland (see Chapter 7).

The Centre d'Etudes Prospectives et d'Informations Internationales (CEPII)

Again, research institutes within the French system are closer to the German type than US-style think tanks. Here the tacit distinction between intellectual and political endeavour in the US is, at best, blurred in the French case.[3] Unlike German institutes, however, French bodies are typically smaller, geographically concentrated and, paradoxically, receive less state funding yet are more closely integrated within the framework created by a strong, centralized, unitary state (Fieschi and Gaffney 2004: 109). Nonetheless, crises have contributed to the declining Bonapartiste tendencies of the French state, which previously paid less attention to research institutes, and have heralded a rise in prominence for research institutes. As Fieschi and Gaffney note, and as was the case in Germany, 'renewal is the think tank's role, crisis the event which calls it forth' (1998: 57).

Though several state-funded institutes do exist, such as the Centre National de la Recherche Scientifique (CNRS), the majority are not state-funded. In effect, the state-funded bodies are an extended part of the state apparatus (Fieschi and Gaffney 2004: 117), hence we focus our attention elsewhere. At the other extreme, as in the UK, more recent, avowedly ideological centres of the New Right (such as the Groupement de Recherche et d'Études sur la Civilisation Européene) have engaged in more overt 'cultural struggles' to displace *dirigiste* economic policy (ibid.: 119). Within this context the Centre d'Etudes Prospectives et d'Informations

Internationales (CEPII) presents itself as a prominent yet – ideologically speaking – mainstream alternative.

The CEPII also sits at an apex between public and private actors, production and finance capital relevant to the analysis. Whilst there are an increasing number of French Anglo-Saxon joint venture policy institutions apparent in Paris,[4] the CEPII represents a mainstream, historically embedded research centre. As Gramsci noted, organic intellectuals are typically woven into the very fabric of bourgeois rule, part of a nascent social formation witnessed in our analysis of state–capital–labour relations (1971: 376). Hence, the CEPII claims to be France's leading institute for research on the international economy, again suggestive of its popular acceptance. Further, it is also intimately connected with the state through the French Planning Agency, indicative of the ways in which contemporary economic policy is underpinned by so-called 'scientific' research (CEPII 2007). Further, the CEPII also has connections with research institutions in other member states, most notably the National Institute for Economic and Social Research (London).

Having introduced the three research centres we will now turn to examining their linkages to both state and transnationally oriented capital, supporting the economists as organic intellectuals claim. The chapter then concludes by exploring the neoliberal common sense produced and the dynamics therein.

Organic linkages

The NIESR

Three features have been central to the NIESR's role as a collective organic intellectual to the Atlantic fraction: the internal structure of the institute, its membership and its funding sources. The internal structure of the institute comprises two tiers. One is composed of economists engaged in econometric research and the other is made up of directors. It is the NIESR Council of Management which is of primary concern at this stage, and a historical snapshot reveals an institutionalized 'unity' of academic, capitalist, and state. For example, of the twelve Council members in 2004, there were two practising academics, Professor Charles Goodhart and Dr Sushil Wadhwani, who were also formerly members of the Bank of England Monetary Policy Committee; and another three were economists on public bodies, Professor Charles Bean, Colette Bowe and Professor Willem H. Buiter, employed by the Bank of England, the Statistics Commission and the European Bank for Reconstruction and Development respectively.

Of equal interest however, is the interconnection between (transnationally oriented) business and intellectual. Over half of the twelve members emanated from international banking and insurance: Nicholas Barber, Sir Brian Corby, Sir Peter Middleton, Sir Michael Scholar, Lord Adair Turner, and Sushil Wadhwani are or have been Chairman of Bolero International, Royal Sun Alliance and Barings Bank, Chairman of Prudential Insurance, Chairman of Barclays Bank, Chairman of Legal and General and previously Barclays, Vice President of Merrill

Lynch Europe, Chase Manhattan Bank, and finally chief economist at Goldman Sachs respectively (Who's Who 2004; NIESR 2007). In addition, one of these members, Sir Peter Middleton, was also the Chairman of the British Bankers Association. As directors they shape the direction of future NIESR research around pragmatic, policy or business-oriented agendas (NIESR 2007). As specialists in organizing and articulating particular conceptions of the world then, the NIESR is embedded within the bourgeoisie, acting as 'ideological representative' of capital (see Marx 1990 [1867]: 535–36).

Not only does capital contribute to shaping the NIESR agenda but also provides significant finances to support the NIESR research programme. There has, since its establishment in 1938, been a history of corporate funding; the Rockefeller Foundation provided the initial capital for its first research projects. More specifically, in 1946 – following negotiations with bankers and industrialists – the Institute first began to receive support from business interests. The influence this source of funding had on the nature of the work undertaken was evident from the outset; the funding was provided in order for 'research on industrial structure and productivity' to be supplied (Jones 1998: 10). This research was specifically aimed at informing the decision-making capabilities of capital.

More recently, this pattern has been on the rise. Alongside public sector support and research grants there are also a number of Corporate Members and Financial Supporters. Amongst them are a series of financial institutions, both nationally oriented and transnational-global, most notably Abbey plc, Barclays Bank, Morgan Stanley Dean Witter Europe, Nomura Research Institute, Cazenove and the Bank of England (NIESR 2004: 26). Of the £7.1 million income the Institute received between 2000 and 2004, £266,000 was the product of direct contributions by corporate supporters, equating to almost 4 per cent of annual funding, with significant additional contributions derived from NIESR workshop participants and subscribers to the various publications and resources provided by the institute (ibid.: 27).

Further, over the last four decades there has been a gradual increase in the percentage of funding acquired from private sources. Whilst in 1976 only 20 per cent emanated from the private sector, by 1986 the figure had risen to 45 per cent and by 1996 to 54 per cent. This relationship prompted the NIESR to launch a Corporate Membership scheme in 1994 to 'facilitate closer links between the institute and its major corporate supporters' (Jones 1998: 30). Hence, by 2004, the Institute noted that public research grants were insufficient to cover the costs of more detailed forecasts of the UK; 'the costs of producing [them] are underpinned by the support [we] receive from [our] Corporate Members' (NIESR 2004: 2). This was, in part, a product of the tightening constraints on state expenditure and yet, simultaneously, emphasizes the importance placed on articulating and organizing pragmatic, policy-related ideas by capital. The result is that the NIESR is positioned within the nascent state–capital–intellectual social formation, simultaneously dependent on and functionary of the others.

Finally, as disseminator of neoliberal common sense the most prominent, nationally based forum was the Westminster Economics Forum (WEF) located within the City of London, targeted at policymakers and businesses. On average around forty to fifty individuals attended each WEF lecture with more than half coming from multi-jurisdictional financial institutions (Kellawan 2006). On the issue of financial market integration, the institute explicitly undertook a European Financial Markets Research Programme to consider the 'practical effects of integration, and their implications for policy' (NIESR 2007); a programme which was supported by a 'consortium of public and private sector interests' (Arrowsmith 1998: i). It is therefore worth noting that trade association members and trans-nationally oriented financial institutions were the foremost subscribers to this NIESR programme (Grisham 2005).

This chapter is not seeking to establish causal linkages between policy research and state policy or our fractions' strategies; such a claim would merely reinforce the false separation of ideas and materiality through a quantitative analysis of ideas as independent variables. Instead, common sense is as much a part of the changing global structure of capitalism as material changes (so to speak) through regimes of accumulation. Nonetheless, the first section of this chapter situates the research institutes as organizers and articulators within and between the state, capital and labour.

The CESifo

A similar analysis of the CESifo reveals analogous traits. Again, we examine its internal structure, membership, sources of funding and methods of dissemination. Incorporated in the organizational structure is the 'Friends of the ifo Institute', otherwise known as the Society for the Promotion of Economic Research. In 2007, its sixty members were leading figures from the business world, corporations, banks, insurance companies and trade associations. Whilst its function is to offer corporate funding to CESifo projects, it simultaneously aims to ensure that the research targets practical questions being asked by market participants; hence ensuring its relevance (CESifo 2007).

The membership of this body is particularly insightful, as the Executive Board and the Board of Trustees reveals. These comprise research directors, chief economists and supervisory board members from Commerzbank, HVB bank, the German railways company, Porsche, Credit Suisse, Dresdner Bank, Swiss Re, Siemens and the Deutsche Industriebank. The institutionalized representation and funding of the transnationally oriented fraction are suggestive of their interest in CESifo research and the *social function* of the institute as 'mediator' of capital (Morton 2003: 29). Further the interconnectivity of production and finance fractions (so to speak) in the German system is reflected in the membership.

The forums, meetings and publications of the CESifo are yet more revealing. The institute holds regular, informal 'Business Club' lectures in conjunction with the University of Munich. Focused on the pragmatic implications of economic findings, the meetings are attended by approximately fifty representatives of business and banking sectors (Interview CESifo); the institute therefore plays a role in the 'everyday life' of the transnationally oriented fraction (Morton 2003: 30).

Of particular importance though is the annual Munich Economic Summit. The Summit is a joint initiative of the CESifo and the BMW Foundation Herbert Quandt and, unsurprisingly, receives significant corporate funding. Whilst the Summit is aimed at 'bringing together academic scholars and decision-makers in politics, industry and finance to discuss vital European issues' it is noteworthy that only a limited number of participants are 'invited' (CESifo 2007). According to the explanatory rhetoric of the institute this is to ensure a 'private atmosphere' (ibid.).

A representative analysis of attendees can be derived from the 2005 Summit which focused on the achievements and failures of the Lisbon Agenda.[5] Of the 149 participants, three features are especially relevant: first, they comprise members of financial and production communities as well as policymakers and media representatives; second, they are of multi-national origins; and third, the sponsors of the event are again characteristic of this private and public international diversity. Not only is the CESifo situated within a social formation comprising state–capital–intellectual but, compared with the NIESR, it displays a greater degree of engagement with parallel institutes. We will return to the social purpose of these networks shortly.

In terms of composition 17 per cent (26) of the participants were members of the transnationally oriented financial community, including banks, insurance companies and investment firms. These included representatives of the Spanish bank BBVA, the German subsidiary of ABN AMRO, Goldman Sachs, the re-insurance company Swiss Re, and several German banks including the HVB Group, Commerzbank and the Bundesbank itself. Approximately 18 per cent (27) were members of industry, a category used here in its broadest sense to cover firms as diverse as Siemens, Boeing Germany, and Deutsche Telekom. The largest proportion, 29 per cent (43), were public officials from across Europe, representing both Federal and Länder tiers of German government as well as the European Parliament, the World Bank and EU experts on the Lisbon Agenda. Others were representatives of academia and the media. In total, twenty-two different countries were represented (CESifo 2007).[6] Moreover, the attendees at the Munich Summit indicate the pervasiveness of the CESifo research on both the international and national scale. This connects to one big issue behind our study: the recent spate of EU integration. I argue that the immanence of the research (common sense) espoused by the German institute is symptomatic of the neoliberal consensus underpinning financial market integration.

The CEPII

Finally, the CEPII also displays similarities to the NIESR and the CESifo: situated within a (Gallic) state–capital–intellectual formation, and with international linkages. Again, we shall briefly examine its membership, structure and these linkages. The institute is organized into three tiers: the CEPII Council; the economists themselves; and the Scientific Committee (see Figure 6.1). Again the Council determines the research programme and, according to the Director of the CEPII, this particular governance structure (ostensibly) ensures the 'independence' of CEPII research (Fontagné 2006).

The Council is composed of twenty-one individuals, both *de jure* members and qualified experts. It is immediately evident that these individuals have undergone processes of 'Gallic' socialization. This, of course, matters to the simultaneously dynamic and path-dependent character of variegated neoliberalism. For example, six were students of the *écoles supérieures*, with four of those having attended one of the *écoles d'ingénieurs*. More significantly, two-thirds of the members graduated from the *Ecole nationale d'administration* (ENA) or the *Institut d'études politiques de Paris* (IEP) (Who's Who France 2004). These schools and training colleges have a history of conditioning French social forces (Cerny 1989).

Concerning their linkages with capital and the state, the CEPII Council comprises former delegate generals of the Gaz d'Electricité de France (GEF), Ministers of Industry, Labour Ministers, Foreign Economic Affairs Ministers, the General Inspector of Finance, the former French administrator for the International Monetary Fund, former members of the Directorial Committee of BNP Paribas, members of the French Planning Agency, Scientific Director at AXA insurance and the president of COFACE, an organization for exchanges amongst businesses (CEPII 2007).

In disseminating research, several strategies are of note. The CEPII operates a forum fittingly entitled *Le Club* (the Business Club) which convenes approximately thirty times a year as a forum where 'business leaders, economists and financial experts may discuss their experiences and analyses' (CEPII 2007). The Club brings together industry, banking and financial institutions. As above, an analysis of the Board of Directors demonstrates the ties with both capital and state actors. Comprising ten members, the Board includes the Director-General of Groupama Asset Management, the Chairman of the Rothschild International Council, the Director for Economic Studies at BNP Paribas, and directors of economic research at the Société Générale as well as other banks and insurance associations.

The Club's membership includes a similar array of finance and production interests. It has forty members, including transnationally oriented financial interests such as BNP Paribas, CM-CIC Securities, Crédit Agricole, Crédit Commercial de France, IXIS Corporate and Investment Bank, Compagnie Financière Edmonde de Rothschild and CPR Asset Management. In addition companies such as Renault SAS, Electricité de France (EDF) and Peugeot Citroen represent industry. Finally, a total of six public bodies are represented, the most significant of which are the Commissariat du Plan (the French Planning Agency), the French Agency for the International Development of Businesses and the French Agency for International Investment (CEPII 2007). In short, the CEPII is closely connected to the state and transnationally oriented capital through the provision of scenarios for future economic trends and insights into 'the workings of the international economy' which it deems '*vital to strategic planning*' (CEPII 2007, emphasis added).

This book aims to demystify the dynamics and agents of neoliberalization. More specifically it questions why, in the EU context, member states previously opposed to neoliberalism now increasingly see neoliberal reform as in their best interests.

The argument has been that crises of accumulation, the strategic agency of particular fractions of capital and changing common sense underpin these processes.

More specifically, an understanding of what social forces (political, capital, or subaltern groups) perceive as their 'best interest' is fundamentally shaped by their conception of the world. This generates a series of dialectical interdependent relations and processes between our fractions and the research centres as organic intellectuals. Thus far we have focused on the national dynamics therein. The transnationalization of capital brings with it as both agent and outcome the rise of nascent transnationally oriented fractions of capital in our three member states and organic economists institutionally represented in our research centres (Gramsci 1971: 5). On the one hand, these intellectuals and fractions possess a degree of autonomy such that overt collusion in hegemonic struggles is neither necessary nor obviously visible. On the other hand, however, these emergent social forces are mutually reinforcing: our fractions understand the historically specific constraints and incentives of accumulation under neoliberalism through inter-subjective meanings generated – most formatively – by organic intellectuals; simultaneously, the intellectual seeks to explain and resolve the apparent contradictions of the nascent epoch of capitalist development – as if objectively – yet, in reality, that which he/she analyses represents the behaviours of agents dependent upon his very outputs. To the naked eye then this dialectic appears not only as independent behaviours but as rational processes, given the seemingly objective impulsions of contemporary capitalism. The contradiction (or indeed, the irony) is therefore that, in overlooking the material–ideological dialectic materialist readings of – *inter alia* – historical materialism, further reify the object they are at pains to critique. As noted in the conclusion of Chapter 5, misrecog-nizing the material–ideological dialectic has serious implications, perpetuating the illusion and neutering resistance to neoliberalism.

This first section has examined three research institutes, situating them within social formations and beginning to outline their function as producers of neoliberal common sense. We now move to examine the common sense claims they espouse.

Neoliberal common sense

Unsurprisingly then, neoliberal common sense is predicated in the first instance on (positing) a causal link between pro-competitive reform and economic growth.[7] Here the purportedly 'scientific', empirical character of the research is funda-mental. Based on the positivist separation of subject and object the research institutes aim to analyse past economic developments in order to identify causal mechanisms. These mechanisms are then offered as policy 'prescriptions' for market actors and public authorities. Rejecting the separation of subject and object, though, positing a dialectical understanding of structure and agency, reveals how social context shapes man's self-understandings which in turn enable man to reshape his social context, thereby emphasizing the contingency of the neoliberal 'logic of no alternative' (Gramsci 1971: 346, Hay and Watson 2003).

The language of neoliberalism is therefore ideologically laden, not just 'words grammatically devoid of content', but instead reifying a 'specific conception of the world' (Gramsci 1971: 323). For Gramsci this entailed the establishment of a 'fixed or fixable yardstick ... given by the past, by a certain phase of the past or by certain measurable aspects' since 'progress [itself] is an ideology' (ibid.: 357). The 'disciplining' effect of this knowledge is then apparent, as are the internal relations of struggles both with competing ideologies and over what Gramsci called the 'universal plane'.

Crises of accumulation throughout Western Europe have fuelled attempts by capital to restore profitability, through rising unemployment, and state policies on the flexibilization of labour and the expansion of financial systems, enabling modes of accumulation through financial activities. These visible features are manifestations of attempts to restore capitalist-class power, by shifting the burdens of the crisis. Of note however, is the relative lack of organized and effective resistance – in all three of our case studies – to these obviously painful reforms. Sporadic, short-lived strikes and protests have provided little barrier to the passage of neoliberal reform. At least part of the answer lies in the fragmentation of the working class already engendered through several decades of transnationalization in production. Moreover, the expansion of credit – driving consumerism through access to cheap credit and rising housing equity – has acted as a neutralizing agent on class antagonisms (Bonefeld 1996). Nonetheless, I also argue that the production of neoliberal common sense has provided both carrot and stick for securing or sustaining forms of consensual rule. Of course, this is linked to the national struggles our fractions engage in, yet has international components (Chapter 7) transcending our particular fractions. As a result, whilst less dramatic changes are evident – for example – in the Gallic power bloc and accumulation regimes, the combination of crises and neoliberal common sense foster both exogenous and endogenous pressures for neoliberalization.

The production of neoliberal common sense therefore comprises two stages: first, the concept of 'public goods' is constructed against the background of these widely held perceptions and experiences of crises; second, the construction of economic imperatives and the logic of no alternative reinforces the 'necessity' for neoliberal reform (Hay and Watson 2003). The juxtaposition of ('good') growth-enhancing, efficient neoliberal policies against ('bad') unsustainable and inefficient former policies is typical.

Recall then that the primary impulsion under capitalism is towards the annihilation of all barriers to the accumulation and circulation of capital. New opportunities for investment, alternative sources of capital, expanded markets for commodities and the rise of the reserve pool of labour are thus central to the displacement of capitalist crises. In one respect then, the ideologically laden claim that pro-competitive (neoliberal) reform restores certain public goods by offsetting the *immediate* effects of crises is an accurate depiction. On the other hand, the new 'compromises' secured between labour and capital realized through state or state-like institutions merely subject labour to a new set of conditions apposite to their subjugation vis-à-vis capital; in our case this predominantly relates to forms of social breakdown in and through a finance-led mode of accumulation.

Competition–growth tenet

NIESR

Competitiveness thus becomes the relatively opaque benchmark against which all member states are measured. From a qualitative analysis of the NIESR research this derives from a tacit link between empirical evidence and normative assumptions. Note the following, for example:

> National markets have become more contestable, with competitive pressures encouraging product innovations and a reduction in excess capacity and operational inefficiencies. The *prospects for economic growth are also likely to have been improved*, with domestic investors now able to raise finance from a larger volume of savings using a wider variety of instruments.
>
> (Pain and van Welsum 2002: 1, emphasis added)

Evidence is presented depicting the diversification of financial instruments as promoted by and itself enhancing competition in financial markets. The terminology used to describe this process is, however, value-laden. Here the words 'improved', 'larger', 'encouraging', and 'enhancing' convey the effects of increased competition as a 'positive' phenomenon with phrases such as 'reduction in excess capacity' and 'operational inefficiencies' depicting the market environment prior to increased competition (ibid.: 2–5). In the economists' words therefore, 'the introduction of measures aimed at deeper integration of European financial services markets stems primarily from a perception that enhanced financial development will improve the prospects for future economic growth' (ibid.: 6). On the basis of a 'wide range of studies' the NIESR thereby forms an, albeit tacit, causal link between competition and growth (Barrell and Choy 2003: 3).

Developing this connection still further the institute contends that integration fosters 'efficiency, competition and innovation', fuelling increased levels of investment which in turn lead to growth (Levitt 2002). According to this model the lowering of regulatory barriers leads to increased price competition as both investors (foreign and increasingly domestic) and companies (foreign and domestic) turn to capital markets for reduced cost funding (Barrell *et al.* 2001). In other words cross-country studies suggest openness is positively related to per capita income (Pain 2002).

This in turn reduces the risk of the misallocation of capital as increased competition leads to more efficient use of resources in 'intensive' rather than 'extensive' development (Barrell and Choy 2003: 5; Barrell *et al.* 2004: 8). The benefits accrued lead to enhanced productivity (Barrell and Pain 1997), greater job opportunities and increased per capita income (Pain 2002). The NIESR even goes so far as to estimate the benefits of enhanced European integration to amount to a 3 per cent increase on GDP (Barrell and Choy 2003: 4). The essence of neoliberal competitiveness thus involves *rescaled* competition. In addition, the departure from the historical pro-Keynesian focus of the NIESR emphasizes the hegemonic status of neoliberal common sense within the UK.

Nonetheless, these claims will be largely unsurprising to scholars of Comparative or International Political Economy; the language and logic of neo-liberalization has fuelled a formidable analytical tradition. Of greater import are the dynamics of confronting competing ideologies and securing the universal plane in both France and Germany. Gramsci depicted this moment as one in which,

> Corporate interests, in their present and future development, transcend the corporate limits of the purely economic class, and can and must become the interests of other subordinate groups too . . . [I]t is the phase in which previously germinated ideologies . . . come into confrontation and conflict, until only one of them, or at least a single combination of them, tends to prevail, to gain the upper hand, to propagate itself throughout society – bringing about not only unison of economic and political aims, but also intellectual and moral unity, posing all the questions around which the struggle rages not on a corporate but a 'universal' plane and thus creating the hegemony of a fundamental social group over a series of subordinate groups.
>
> (Gramsci 1971: 181)

We noted in earlier chapters that Germany and France had experienced varying degrees of neoliberalization, effected by – for example – the degree of interconnectivity between finance and production, nationally and transnationally oriented fractions. Yet we noted that neoliberalization cannot be attributed solely to the agency of our fractions but from the impulsions–agency–common sense nexus. Hence, we now turn our attention to these struggles over the hegemony of neoliberal common sense.

CESifo

In keeping with our heartland–contender state thesis the struggles with existing alternative common senses is most visible in France and Germany. Within the CESifo research a similar causal link is also propagated: the institute again claims that openness to global trade and finance promotes growth. Importantly though, here the intellectuals attempt to confront and overcome various contending arguments and anomalies in the data. These attempts are symptomatic of the institutes' social function in incorporating, marginalizing or countering alternative ideologies.

In a comparative study of two periods of liberalization and globally integrated markets (late nineteenth and late twentieth centuries) one piece of research adopts as its *problématique* the question 'Do financially more open economies grow faster

than closed ones, precisely because of their openness to the global capital market?'
(Schularick and Steger 2006: 1). They proceed to explain that:

> In a perfect neoclassical textbook world, there are good arguments for a
> positive growth impact of integration with the international capital market . . .
> Closer financial integration could also strengthen domestic financial systems
> leading to more investment, more efficient capital allocation and higher
> growth . . . However, arguments against the economic wisdom of openness
> to global capital flows have also been put forward.
>
> (Schularick and Steger 2006: 1)

In so doing the intellectuals both acknowledge and consider an alternative pathway
to growth other than that of integration and liberalization. Further they proceed to
admit that,

> Theoretical models have identified a number of channels through which
> international financial integration can promote economic growth . . . however
> there is as yet no clear and robust empirical proof that the effect is
> quantitatively significant.
>
> (Schularick and Steger 2006: 1)

They note various reasons for the lack of agreement on the relation between
openness and growth, including the measurements of openness, the absence or
presence of legal requirements and the measurements of integration itself. They
conclude though by noting that, their research, 'demonstrates that international
financial integration can [indeed] contribute to higher growth' (Schularick and
Steger 2006: 2) and 'support[s] *all these* economists who believe in the virtues of
international capital mobility' (ibid., emphasis added).

The significance of this tension and concluding statement might be lost, given
the almost unquestioning acceptance of this so-called 'received wisdom'. Our aim,
however, is not only to emphasize this as a historically contingent truth claim
rather than a transhistorical axiom, but to highlight the struggles to construct this
truth claim as analytically important. Evidently the CESifo seeks to reconcile a
pre-established body of research – on financial openness – with sediments of prior
common senses within the German economy. This process involves considering,
confronting and countering alternative economic 'paradigms' for economic
growth. Economic growth – an indicator which typically conceals the unequal
distribution of wealth effects – functions as a measure of the 'public good' implied
in a policy paradigm, providing the pre-requisite ' "fixed" or fixable yardstick' as
universal and ahistorical benchmark (Gramsci 1971: 357). Yet – and this is worth
noting – the very consideration of alternative paradigms is given leverage precisely
because of both perceived successes in other national political economies and the
crises of domestic models. The two form part of a dynamic whole.

This assertion – concerning struggles between common senses – is supported
by the findings of other CESifo research. One such piece attempts to reconcile
the logic of the free market with the 'political' difficulties of organizing the

ideal-typical. Referring again to an established body of economic research, the economist asserts that 'we have a solid understanding from economic theory and experience of the benefits of multilateral free trade' (Deardorff 2004). At the same time however, he acknowledges the apparent contradiction between the 'theory' of liberalization and its distortions in 'reality'. He explains that,

> Free trade increases the ability for large corporations to operate across national borders, thus – the sceptics would say – increasing their power over the economy and over peoples and governments around the world. Because corporations pursue only their self interest and not the social good, they exploit the world for their own profit. Thus Globalization = Corporate Power = Everybody Else Loses!
>
> (Deardorff 2004)

Returning to one big puzzle which concerns us, we begin to perceive the social function of the intellectual in securing consent amongst member states with alternative common senses. He notes that globalization might appear to be against Germany's 'best interests', emphasizing that 'the influence of . . . large corporations has dominated the drafting of the texts of international economic agreements and has done so, understandably, so as to promote the interests of those producers'. He concludes however that 'Their interests are *not necessarily harmful* to society' (Deardorff 2004, emphasis added). He engages with the sceptic on his own terrain, acknowledging the contradiction in globalization yet suggesting that public goods – in the form of economic growth and employment – can be derived precisely because of self-interested firms.

This pattern is recurrent (see, for example, Loayza and Ranciere 2002). Elsewhere the institute engages with further criticisms of liberalization: the apparent correlation between financial openness and financial crises – albeit in spite of increased economic growth. In fact, our first and second chapters (i) questioned the *type* of growth propagated through financial expansion and (ii) highlighted the *necessary* and *inherent* linkages between neoliberalization and crises. Nonetheless, the CESifo economists argue that, 'there is no agreement regarding the growth-enhancing effects of financial liberalization, mainly because it is associated with risky international bank flows, lending booms, and crises' (Tornell and Westermann 2004: 1); according to this reading crises are engendered through perversities in cross-border investment flows. Having outlined such a conjunctural explanation they make a sustained 'case for liberalization despite the occurrence of crises' (ibid.). In their own words the occurrence of crises are a necessary, if regrettable, consequence of financial liberalization and one which can be minimized through effective regulation (ibid.). I strongly reject this reading of financial expansion.

In brief, two interwoven skeins are evident in the CESifo: on the one hand contending for a causal link between liberalization/integration and growth; whilst on the other hand, attempting to counter alternative ideological criticisms and contending pathways to economic growth. The scepticism of certain German social groups is palpable; both political and societal hegemony remain highly contested. It must be recalled however, that the efficacy of a common sense does not simply depend on the powers of persuasion of the intellectual. Ostensibly he acts as an independent observer of exogenous conditions which – in fact – he simultaneously mediates and provokes. As we shall see then, this exogenous and irresistible characterization of neoliberalism is highly significant. For Germany, the relative successes of neoliberalization are – in part – dependent upon the narration of crises of the German model.

The spatio-temporal dimension of common sense production is thus hugely significant. We have already noted the 'materiality' of variegated neoliberalism, manifested in the commonalities and differences of neoliberalization. Here we begin to see the commonalities and differences – or convergence within divergence – of neoliberal common sense. Significantly though, these processes – expressed materially and ideologically – are coterminous and co-dependent rather than autonomous (see McMichael 1990). This last point requires clarification: in effect, these processes cannot be understood in the singular since 'interrelated instances are integral to, and define, the general historical process' (ibid.: 389). As the next chapter explains, for example, although beginning from different historical starting points – represented in the departure from the post-war British model in the 1970s and the social market economy (Germany) in the early 1980s – an ongoing interrelationship has continued to shape not only the 'material' reforms of both models but the dynamics of emergent (Rhenish) neoliberal common sense and thus the global reconstitution of capitalism. Thus our understanding of neoliberalization must take on board – at an abstract level – both the expansionary impulses of the capitalist system and the internally related impulses of common sense production; and these more specifically given the particularities of the neoliberal mode of accumulation.

CEPII

Returning to our immediate concern, we perceive similar dynamics within the CEPII: the linkages between openness and growth; and attempts to confront alternative paradigms. In the first instance CEPII research affirms that, 'openness . . . is potentially a source of dramatic gains, in other words, a long-term rise in the rate of growth' (Fouquin and Gaulier 1999), whilst simultaneously showing traces of struggles with previously germinated common senses.

As with the NIESR (UK) and the CESifo (Germany) the CEPII addresses the most deeply embedded common sense in their national context (see Schmidt 1996): here 'protectionism' is discussed in negative (normative) terms. In outlining the 'costs' of protectionism the institute emphasizes its detrimental social effects, contending that only a 'limited few' benefit from resisting the competitive imperative. The institute states that

> [our] conclusions go against the received wisdom concerning protectionism and liberalization in continental Europe, where protectionism is commonly

depicted and even justified as serving a certain '*public interest*' . . . and the freedom of exchange is generally viewed as a process favouring narrowly defined, *private interests*. The results of our research present a very different perspective, in fact one which is didactically opposed to European protectionism: accordingly, only a 'happy few' benefit from large private 'rents' extracted as a result of protectionism, whereas the most significant resulting costs are borne by the majority of European consumers.

(Messerlin 2002: 31, emphasis added)

Given the French tendency towards so-called 'protectionism', the above research is highly significant (see Steil 1995; Underhill 1997). Not only does the intellectual construct a connection between openness and economic growth but cogently emphasizes the 'public interest' intrinsic to this economic policy. Here he speaks implicitly to the transnational–national contradiction – for example, as confronting the Gallic fraction – and thereby supporting their transnationalization concern; yet he also seeks to neutralize formerly hegemonic common senses, connecting French economic failure to material condensations of these previous common senses. So the intellectual sits as mediator *between* international and domestic social processes (Chapter 7), as well as *within* national–domestic configurations.

Arguably the most prominent characteristic of the *dirigiste* model however, was the degree of both macro- and micro-economic management by the French interventionist state (again, see Schmidt 1996, 2002). Traces of struggles with this common sense are therefore abundant. The neoliberal claims of the CEPII are twofold: on the one hand public procurement and extensive state involvement are condemned. For example, in research concerning the effects of public procurement policies the institute asserts that 'empirical investigation' has decisively demonstrated their negative impact on cross-border trade flows, hence advocating the extension of market freedoms (Crozet and Trionfetti 2002). On the other hand, CEPII draws attention to the need for public involvement in the market in a supervisory or market-enabling capacity. It highlights: the need for public involvement to accompany liberalization attempts, removing barriers within and between markets (Fouquin and Gaulier 1999); specific instances of French regulators' problematic reticence to engage in competitive restructuring (Aglietta 1997); and the specific benefits of state-initiated liberalization. For example, examining the French experience of liberalization, the institute states that:

The active promotion of capital markets and financial innovation led to structural changes in the financing of the French economy and in bank activities. In the financial innovation process, there were winners and losers even if it was not a zero-sum game. In contrast with the experience of Anglo-Saxon countries, [however] the Ministry of Finance played the main role as regards the timing and the content of the financial innovation process.

(de Boissieu and Pisani-Ferry 1995: 15)

This role is more significant in 'contender' states, following the first-mover advantage of the Atlantic heartland (van der Pijl 1998). Importantly though, it again reinforces the argument that neoliberalization is neither simply the 'spontaneous, automatic expression of economic facts' nor solely derived from the strategic agency of hegemonic social forces, but is constructed and enforced by state regulation building on more fundamental material–ideological transformations (Gramsci 1971: 159).

The logic of no alternative

As Colin Hay and Matthew Watson noted, the production of neoliberal common sense is intrinsically bound up in the construction of the 'logic of no alternative'. As such, neoliberal economic research serves to conceal remaining contingent elements by rendering processes of neoliberalization 'necessary' (Hay and Watson 2003: 290). Three facets of neoliberal economic research buttress this premise: one is the repeated (discursive) reference to exogenous pressures for structural reform, commonly referred to as globalization (Hay and Watson 2003: 291). The second is the inference that previous post-war economic policies with burgeoning welfare programmes and subsidized or 'championed' domestic industries, are unsuitable, given the international mobility of capital and market actors (Esping-Andersen 1999). The third is the widely accepted understanding that the compromise between capital and labour at the heart of post-war policy was also at the heart of the crises throughout the 1970s (Holloway 1996: 25–27). This 'fact' has been tactically deployed to engender the increased subjugation of labour to capital under neoliberalization. In conclusion, and to (mis)quote Paul Krugman, 'People believe certain [ideas] because everybody important believes them. Indeed, when a conventional wisdom is at its fullest strength, one's agreement with that conventional wisdom becomes almost a litmus test of one's suitability to be taken seriously' (Krugman 1995: 36, cited in Hay and Watson 2003: 191).

Here I focus on the specific example of the CESifo. For reasons outlined earlier, the CESifo is more prominently engaged in struggles to secure neoliberal common sense than either the NIESR or the CEPII. Whilst neoliberal common sense is already hegemonic within the UK, French experiences of crises and acquiescence to variegated neoliberalism have been offset by specific historical conditions within the French system, namely: the obvious tensions between *dirigiste* common senses and more economic liberal skeins; the less extensive role of French research centres; and features of Gallic accumulation strategies, including the fusion of nationally and transnationally oriented, production and finance fractions. In contradistinction, Germany has been in the process of undertaking dramatic structural reforms (see Chapter 8) symptomatic of hegemonic struggles and the reluctant acceptance of neoliberal common sense – at both political and societal levels – where both of these developments are connected to the proximity of Germanic financial systems and *ordo-liberal* common sense to neoliberalism.

As before, the intellectual tackles objections to neoliberalism head on. In effect though, this constitutes a second stage: the first is establishing causal linkages between neoliberal reform and public goods; the second requires emphasizing neoliberal reform as necessity. This assertion is evident in the interactions between CESifo and the German public. Here the institute considers it a primary objective to shape public understandings on 'economic' issues. In its 2005 Annual Report it explains that, 'as an essential part of its services, the ... institute provides data, information, and other service products to the public' (CESifo 2005: 7). This serves a particular social function as the CESifo aims to 'inform the general public on ... economic issues *with the goal of increasing acceptance for necessary economic reforms*' (ibid.: 11, emphasis added).

Interestingly, the CESifo acknowledges that neoliberalization inherently over-privileges capital at the expense of labour. For example, in his opening speech to the 2006 CESifo Forum, the head of the institute, Professor Hans-Werner Sinn acknowledged explicitly what has been implicit throughout our case studies; namely the conflict between the interests of the transnationally oriented fraction (the liberalization project) and wider social interests. He noted the following:

> There are, of course, gains from trade that economists ... are eager to stress. But ... it does not state that everybody gains but only that the winners of this process gain more than the losers lose. This is no trivial qualification as the losers might encompass a major part of the working population. If I, as an economist, tell them 'don't worry, there are winners – the capitalists – they will win even more than you lose', that is no help for them at all. On the contrary, I am afraid they might find this even worse than a situation where everyone loses proportionally.
>
> (Sinn 2006)[8]

Underlying this monologue is the neoliberal contradiction highlighted by this book.

It is here that struggles for the universal plane are waged: whilst objections and strong traces of formerly hegemonic common senses remain, the construction of economic 'necessity' acquires a disciplining function. Spontaneous consent again gives way to reluctant acquiescence. Two final components are apparent: one is the prerogative of economic research to 'increase acceptance' for reforms which, as Sinn admitted, tend to exploit non-capitalists; the other is that the pro-competitive structural reforms outlined in this economic research are presented as 'necessary' to (a historically defined notion of) German progress. Neoliberal common sense is intrinsically founded upon its articulation as the 'only alternative' under the contemporary conditions of capitalism.

Summary: Organic economists

This chapter picked up where Part I left off, arguing that variegated neoliberalism, the spread of neoliberalization and recent EU financial market reform were embedded in three more fundamental processes: crises of accumulation; the transnationalization of capital and the agency of emergent fractions; and changes in common sense. As a result, the agency of our three fractions was possible only because of their positioning at the apex of these changes. Specifically, here it was argued that the neoliberal consensus which had underpinned EU policy reform was a constituent of a nascent neoliberal common sense. As a dominant conception of the world, or worldview, neoliberal common sense has been articulated and organized by what I argue are 'organic economists' in policy research centres, comprising a state–capital–intellectual formation at the national level, yet already displaying international components (see Chapter 7). Herein their economic research has two fundamental elements: the first is the construction of causal linkages between competition and public goods such as economic growth – and this was common across all three case studies. The second feature, however, relates to spatio-temporal variegation and reveals the traces of struggles with historically and geographically specific common senses. Finally, this chapter considered the construction of the logic of no alternative.

In Germany, there was evidence of engagement in pro-competitive restructuring and, significantly, the more incremental integration in global competition. These relate to the hegemonic struggles between a previously germinated common sense – often depicted as ordo-liberalism, with relatively free market principles embedded in strong institutions – and a greater degree of 'openness' or, in our terms, a *neoliberal* common sense.[9] Further, the extensive role and funding of German research institutes, coupled with the specific prominence of the CESifo in state–capital forums, are both conditions for and products of the extent of neoliberalization in Germany.

Comparatively speaking, this also throws light on the French case. Here there was evidence of a specific engagement with the common senses of protectionism and, more broadly, *dirigisme*. Nonetheless, the transition or, more accurately, molecular emergence of neoliberal common sense stands in sharp contradistinction to elements of previously hegemonic common senses in the French system; the result, as later chapters conclude, is a less economic liberal variant (so to speak) of variegated neoliberalism. Further, the less extensive role of economic research centres in France, coupled with the less overtly 'ideological' tradition of the CEPII, have both contributed to and resulted from the less emphatic changes within the French model. Locating both the content and the 'efficacy' of the hegemonic projects of our three fractions thus becomes more evident.

The next chapter considers the spatial dimensions of neoliberal common sense through a look at the centrality of the Atlantic heartland and the scientific committees in our three research centres.

7 Scientific committees and the Atlantic heartland

This chapter aims to elucidate the role of the Atlantic heartland. Where the previous chapter considered the socially constructed causal relations between competition and growth, the traces of struggles with competing common senses, and the logic of no alternative, this chapter concludes Part III on the production of neoliberal common sense. Through examining the Atlantic heartland, the importance of positivist – 'scientific' – standards underpinning the knowledge claims of these intellectuals becomes even starker; the unique influence of Anglo-American economists and processes of socialization within this international community of intellectuals are now placed under the spotlight. This again contributes to understanding why previously averse states – for example, France and Germany – have begun to undergo neoliberalization and further reinforces the origins of the intellectual consensus underpinning recent EU reform.

Within neoliberalization, crises provide unique historical junctures for struggles over the 'universal plane' (Gramsci 1971: 181). In effect, crises inherently foster fertile conditions for the dissemination of alternative common senses since 'solutions' or 'alternatives' must engage with some general aspects of crises themselves (Gramsci 1971: 184). Herein those specialized in the elaboration of ideas fulfil a specific social function precisely because of their 'logical rigour', their 'coherence' and their ability to contextualize their ideas within the 'entire history of thought', giving the appearance that the solution they present to this particular 'problem' has been reached after consideration of 'every previous attempt at a solution' (ibid.: 347). Their social function in 'the cultural battle to transform the popular mentality' is therefore enabled by their 'scientific' abilities (ibid.: 348). Where this process operates through multiple avenues for the dissemination of similar ideas, particular conceptions of the world become increasingly dominant, since 'repetition is the best didactic means for working on the popular mentality' (ibid.: 340).

International intellectual communities

There is now a vast literature on so-called 'intellectual' or 'epistemic' communities. Holzner explains that 'epistemic communities' are 'those knowledge-oriented work communities in which cultural standards and social arrangements interpenetrate around a primary commitment to epistemic criteria in knowledge production and application' (Holzner, cited in Haas 1991: 40). In effect, and as Haas proceeds to explain, these communities coalesce around 'a commitment to a causal model and a common set of political values' (ibid.: 41). By implication therefore, the knowledge claims produced by such communities necessarily have a pragmatic or political agenda (ibid.); so far, so good. Interestingly however, Haas also emphasizes – largely unwittingly, I would argue – the positivist criteria for adjudicating between these truth claims: he notes, for example, that 'The ultimate test of truth is the collective decision by the users of knowledge as to which claim is more successful in solving a problem agreed by all as requiring solution' (ibid.). As a result, not only are knowledge claims judged against an apparently independent social reality in a manner reminiscent of the natural sciences, but a collective or community logic contributes to this final decision. These elements are worth noting.

Much of the contemporary literature on epistemic communities itself displays features of soft-positivism. For example, certain accounts have attempted to measure the impact of economic ideas by establishing formal linkages between economist and politician, economic research and political policy (Chwieroth 2007: 444–45). Though interesting, this assumes that the only or primary relationship between 'economic' ideas and 'economic' policy is when economists 'become policymakers' through 'persuasion', 'negotiation' and their 'interpretation' of material trends (ibid.: 446). Already the apparent separation of ideas from material trends posits a false distinction. Examining these intellectual communities through Gramscian lenses therefore enables the following: first, building on the previous chapter's conception of common sense as dominant worldview, we now examine the international aspect of this common sense; and second, it allows us to focus on the diffusion of this common sense through the commitment of organic economists to so-called *scientific* standards and the disciplining strategies which this permits. These two elements are crucial in explaining why, at least in part, heterodox and often antagonistically opposed 'models of capitalism' have pursued similar neoliberal trajectories. Obviously, the nature of competition under global capitalism and the impulsions under crises condition and shape these processes, yet neither these phenomena nor the way agents perceive and respond to them are detached from particular – in this case neoliberal – worldviews.

The Atlantic heartland

In his analysis, Kees van der Pijl employed the concept of a Lockean heartland to account for the progressively expanding core of the state system (see Chapter 3) (2006: 13). Here the concept is used to convey the following, outlined at length: first, the fact that processes of capital market liberalization began (in the contemporary era) in this 'Atlantic' heartland of the UK and US financial markets. This reinvigorated patterns of capitalist development with an extensive history. Second, these initial developments in the heartland compounded crises in other EU member states (France and Germany for example) throughout the late 1980s and early 1990s. The result was that where *Modell Deutschland* had been the exemplar for socio-economic prosperity in the early 1980s the heartland re-assumed this role during the 1990s; a fact much resented by continental Europe. Third, these 'material' or visible elements were accompanied by the increasing prominence of economic research configured around a relatively homogeneous body of economic ideas (Rees 2009). Within this it should be noted that, among the social sciences, economics is a uniquely internationalized discipline, in which English has emerged as the entirely dominant scientific language. Further, the international economics community is dominated, both in numbers and intellectual prestige, by Anglo-American economists.

The purpose of what follows then is to demonstrate the emergence of (i) an international community within which (ii) Atlantic intellectuals occupy a privileged position. All three of the institutes, for example, are members of international research communities: the CESifo Research Network consists of more than 500 economists from all over the world (2005: 8) whilst the CEPII is involved in a conglomeration of research centres entitled the European Forecasting Network with members from the Universities of Bocconi, Madrid, Florence, Cambridge and Barcelona. Further, this international community is evidenced in more formal enterprises. One such body is the European Economic Advisory Group (EEAG), where all eight of its members (originating from seven European countries) have strong ties with the Institute and the Group is formally connected with the Institute's research network.

The significance of the international community lies in the ability to produce and diffuse knowledge claims. The previous chapter highlighted the connection between the three research centres and their respective states and business communities. Seeking to secure popular consent for neoliberal common sense however, our organic economists have developed strategies for targeting subaltern social groups in the three countries. Hence, the EEAG has representatives from the Universities of Helsinki, Stockholm, Florence, Oxford, Toulouse, Zurich, Barcelona and Munich, the Group collaborating to produce an annual report on the state of the European economy and its prospects. In essence, the report 'analyses the growth performance of different European countries, focusing on two key driving factors, namely education and competition policy' (CESifo 2007). In so doing it aims to provide both economic forecasts and discussion of topical issues for policymakers, academics, business and, significantly, the public (ibid.). Here research is not only confined to esoteric policy-relevant discourses but specifically aims to inform and delimit popular understandings of the possible and sensible.

Again, *function* veils *social function* as, on the one hand, the Group disseminates an 'empirically verified' account of European economic developments which, on the other hand, presents a relatively coherent yet implicit worldview embodied in a series of assumptions about social reality and economic growth. In turn, this report is broadcast through a series of high-profile annual press conferences. For example, in 2006 these lasted six weeks and were located in the major European cities of Osnabruck, Stockholm, Rome, Barcelona, Madrid, Munich, London and

Brussels. The intention was clear: to reach a wide audience with a single, formal assessment of the 'state of the European economy' and its 'necessary' structural reforms. The CESifo is clearly a member of this intellectual community, thereby engaged in the *international* production of neoliberal common sense.

Similarly, the CEPII is interconnected with other research centres in the European Forecasting Network (ostensibly) established to consider the practical workings of the European single market. In its view, it aims to 'provide a critical analysis of the current economic situation in the Euro area . . . casts of the main macroeconomic and financial variables, policy advice and in-depth study of topics of particular relevance for the working of the EMU' (EFN 2007).

As with the EEAG, the EFN has an internationally diverse membership emanating from the University of Bocconi, the University of Madrid, the European University Institute in Florence, the University of Cambridge, the Department of Statistics at the University of Barcelona and Erasmus University and the CEPII and the Halle Institute for Economic Research. Significantly, the common sense it produces draws together more diverse and less coherent economic research findings with more pragmatic, policy-oriented claims from institutes like the CEPII and the Halle. The result? The knowledge claims produced by the EFN are unequivocally pro-competitive, neoliberal claims, concerning the socio-economic benefits of deeper and more extensive integration of EU markets (see for example EFN 2004). The point thus far is simple: not only are our research institutes organically situated in their respective member states but they are engaged in an international community of economists. The tension therein should also be apparent: articulating worldviews seeking to secure spontaneous consent for the particularistic interests of our fractions, yet – and because of the international elements – infusing this common sense with sediments 'alien' to the domestic context. Though organic to the (ruling) class fractions they therefore simultaneously shape their worldviews and perceptions of interests.

Research standards in historical perspective

The analytical crux of this chapter lies then in our examination of the Atlantic heartland. The claim is this: within the production of neoliberal common sense, the heartland plays a formative role. There are, so to speak, material elements (*inter alia*, crises, transnationalization, pro-competitive regulation) which were considered earlier; here, I argue that the socialization of the international intellectual community is defined or conditioned by the heartland. This is more subtle than a stark, coercive disciplining of economic ideas. Instead – in the first instance – the intellectual culture, 'scientific standards' and modes of dissemination originate within and are subsequently conditioned by the heartland. Further, these characteristics (or what might be termed behavioural norms) are institutionalized within councils responsible, in the final analysis, for their enforcement. Herein the dynamics of hegemony are replicated within the intellectual community: econo-mists consent to these behavioural norms because – *inter alia* – opportunity structures and career progression are weighted in favour of these approaches (Rees

2009); nonetheless, more coercive apparatuses also exist for disciplining renegade knowledge claims. The reasons for the immanence of neoliberal common sense thus become clearer.

A brief analysis of the economics profession supports this claim. Rees (2009) cites two contributory factors: one is the recruitment process for economists; the other is publication filters. On the first, he argues that

> the major graduate schools, from which most academic economists are recruited, impose significant homogeneity of approach and subject matter. Success here means being good at passing exams in the institutions' chosen subjects and writing dissertations of which they approve; this is a powerful filter.

(Rees 2009)

On the second, Rees notes that 'likewise career success requires publishing in a relatively small number of major journals which also enforce quite a bit of conformity in approach and subject matter' (ibid.). We will return to the issue of academic disciplines in the concluding chapter.

Historically it is easy to understand the Atlantic dominance of the economics profession. In short, the ideas and theorems which have shaped economic policy in the post-war era originate in Atlantic academic circles; this is both condition for and outcome of the proximity and extent of intellectual and state cooperation considered in Chapter 6. As a result, these ideas have had ongoing significance in shaping US and UK state policy, and a particular significance – as this book would suggest – during times of crisis.[1]

So, in four key texts, John Maynard Keynes was to set out his treatise on managing the instabilities at the heart of the capitalist system. In his view, prices, credit and employment were of utmost importance; as a result he challenged the premise – in our terms the *liberal* premise – that internationally mobile investors and investments are fundamental requirements. Instead, so he argued, they produce exogenous interference with national macroeconomic planning (1933: 760–63). In the immediate post-war era and, specifically, following the crisis surrounding the gold standard, his ideas were intrinsic to the distinctive national 'models' outlined in previous chapters.

Subsequently, a group of economists fittingly labelled the 'neoclassical synthesists' formed 'a particular hybrid of Keynesian and neoclassical economic principles' (Best 2005: 90). These economists, including Samuelson and Solow,[2] developed theorems which (i) demonstrated a Keynesian faith in the capacity of government to intervene in financial markets with considerable technical sophistication, yet (ii) also reflected a far more neo-classical faith in the rationality of the market (ibid.: 106). Though challenged by monetarist ideas focused on state management of the money supply, these North American and UK-based synthesists were fundamental to 1960s/70s attempts to construct an international financial system facilitating freer movements of investments and financial instruments. In light of the emerging crises facing the Bretton Woods system these ideas re-emphasized the global circulation of capital as prerequisite for sustained national 'prosperity'; the seeds for neoliberal common sense were being sown.

Finally, a more complex amalgam of new classical, monetarist and rational expectation theories were formulated and systematically reformulated to produce the (variegated) neoliberal common sense currently under scrutiny. These ideas revolved around 'the neoclassical tenets of the fundamental theorem of welfare economics and the efficient markets hypothesis, together with the new classical theories of rational expectations and market credibility' (Best 2005: 123). Here, previously 'opposing' thinkers, such as Milton Friedman, Friedrich von Hayek and the 'synthesists', experienced a rapprochement as political–economic ambiguities inherent in earlier theories were progressively replaced by underlying assumptions of technical rationality. These thinkers simply reinforced the belief that all government intervention in markets would create, in the long run, devastating distortions. As earlier chapters have noted however, the schism between theory and practice should now be evident (Crouch 2009: 396–97); neoliberalism employs discourses of free markets as ideological tools when, in reality, state intervention and monopolistic tendencies are the norm. Nonetheless, the rescaling and restructuring of governance are therefore bound up within this Atlantic-originating neoliberal common sense.

Three interrelated points therefore emerge: first, neoliberal common sense is, as our introductory chapter suggested, a complex, often seemingly contradictory blend of economic ideas and undisclosed assumptions about the world, based on the premise that liberalizing and integrating markets is *the* best method of socio-economic provision. Second, though, this means that whilst, to an outsider, differences within the economics profession between – *inter alia* – neo-classical, monetarist and new classical economics may appear significant and divisive, the key assumptions highlighted above provide a sufficiently inclusive belief system to unify these intellectuals. For example, Ray Rees again notes that,

> The international economics profession is fairly homogeneous. The bulk of it . . . subscribe to the same body of economic ideas. By and large there is a great deal of overall homogeneity in the approach and *belief systems* and the *views* of economists. That may sound a bit paradoxical because we have this reputation of always disagreeing with each other, but in fact, the disagreements are by and large within a paradigm. So we subscribe to very similar things.
>
> (Interview CESifo 2006)

Later he notes that,

> The *dominant view* among economists of the German economy [for example] . . . is rather close to Thatcherism actually. They see the problems of the German economy . . . low growth rates and high unemployment, as being in the labour market and the need for reform is to loosen up the labour

market, reduce the power of the unions, roll-back the welfare state . . . [So] the economics profession is dominated by the Anglo-Saxon tradition.

(Interview CESifo 2006)

And these ideas are echoed amongst French intellectuals. In the words of a Director from the CEPII:

The idea is now . . . we need to know the price of public policy. What is the price? What do you pay for? What is the result? You have to have results. You decide a policy, the objective is such and such, we need to know if the tool we use is efficient or not . . . we need to make the cost appear. [So] that is . . . a kind of liberalism . . . Don't discuss the social objective, you want poor people to have social security, and so on and so on. Instead, is it efficient? How much does it cost?

(Interview CEPII 2006)

In his view this is again 'the influence of the Anglo-Saxons' (ibid.). The result is that the nascent hegemony of neoliberal common sense, manifested in material social processes such as career progression and publication, reinforces the privileged position of the Atlantic heartland.

Finally, it is apparent that the complex amalgam of economic ideas comprising neoliberal common sense is tacitly united by their acceptance of so-called 'scientific–rational assumptions'. As Best (2005: 89) emphasizes, post-Keynesian economics was predicated on a 'faith in the neutrality of technique', which itself 'rested on a further assumption that the market is essentially rational'. It remains to be seen whether these assumptions have been fatally marred by the 2007–09 crisis. Nonetheless, historically they have engendered research standards and norms which are fundamental to the disciplining processes, both consensual (in the first instance) and coercive (in the last instance), within the dissemination of neoliberal common sense.

Scientific councils and the heartland

Focusing on the German and French cases we find further evidence of these claims. For example, a brief sociological analysis of the scientific councils within the CESifo and the CEPII is revealing. As Chapter 2 contended, the legacy of positivism is complex. Suffice it to note that the purported separation of subject from object underpins the activities of our organic intellectuals. Simply, the 'scientific standards' applied by our three research institutes refer to the, albeit often implicit, assumption that knowledge claims can be empirically tested through processes of conjecture and refutation against 'pre-existing facts' (see, for example, Popper 1963).

For our purposes, a watertight definition is less immediately important than an investigation of the application of these scientific criteria.[3] In short, the immanence of these standards within international economics has fuelled the rise in scientific councils; councils whose function it is to ensure rigorous compliance with these criteria (Interview CEPII). These councils are both a feature of the international intellectual community and a disciplining mechanism of the Atlantic heartland.

The CESifo council

The scientific councils of the CESifo and the CEPII are composed of twelve members of various nationalities whose role is threefold: they meet 'to provide independent, external quality control'; to 'advise the Executive Board and the Administrative Council in the long-term planning of research and development'; and to advise on 'future appointment proceedings for Executive Board members of the ifo Institute' (CESifo 2005).

Whilst meaningful differences between the research agendas of these members should not be overlooked, this chapter argues that these differences are now, by and large, *within* a neoliberal paradigm (Bosanquet 1982). This is, of course, no small claim. Nonetheless: first, the above analysis has outlined the similar worldviews and rational assumptions of what might be termed Atlantic economics; second, the fact that, on the one hand, there is an obvious dominance of Atlantic economics – epitomized by the numerical supremacy of North American economists in the scientific councils – whilst, on the other, the CESifo and CEPII produce neoliberal claims, is itself an intriguing feature if the two are entirely disconnected.

The Scientific Council of the CESifo is headed by Assaf Razin, who received his PhD at Chicago, was professor at Cornell and visiting professor in the International Monetary Fund. As Bosanquet (1982: 8) has argued, the University of Chicago is the statistical and empirical home of the Atlantic intellectual tradition. It was here that Friedman developed a form of monetary economics for example; his representation argued that the all-important private sector would develop a long-run equilibrium if government intervention is limited to certain 'automatic rules' (ibid.: 55). Both he and George Stigler were subsequently at the heart of the 'post-war Chicago academic and policy revolution', fundamentally shaping Reagan and Thatcherite economic policy (Leeson 2000: 46–47). Further, and as Stigler (1988: 211) later noted, the Chicago school engaged in a fervent process of proselytizing and reproduction: he wrote that 'a scholar is an evangelist seeking to convert his learner brethren to the new enlightenment he is preaching' (cited in Leeson 2000: 71; see also van Overtveldt 2007). The result was that a plethora of highly intelligent graduate students, such as Razin, were socialized within the Atlantic intellectual tradition.

Returning to the CESifo council members it is also worth noting that Razin has European connections, through the Council of the European Economic Institute, and worked with economists such as Charles Wyplosz (himself linked to the CEPII). A relatively cogent network of intellectuals begins to emerge. Of the other eleven economists on the council, seven were prominent scholars at North American universities such as Cornell, Harvard and MIT, with four also having received their PhDs at North American institutions. One of the most prominent of these is Robert Solow who, alongside Samuelson at MIT, developed the neo-classical model in the post-war era, conducted research for the McKinsey Institute and is often perceived to be responsible for the 'orthodoxy' in economic thought (Solow 1956).

Similarly two others were involved with the Brookings Institute and Hoover Institution, both renowned for their roles in the 'eclipse' of Keynesian economics (Leeson 2000: 142).[4] In addition, several of the Council members were members of either the American Economic Association or the European Economic Association. Of particular import, however, is Professor Olivier Blanchard (also present on the Scientific Council of the CEPII) from MIT. His background and influence will be outlined below yet his presence in the CESifo is noteworthy, not least for his former supervision of another Council member (Guiseppe Bertola). Given the rapprochement of neo-classical/new classical, monetarist and rational expectations models, the network of economists is both understandable and analytically significant. Suffice it to note that the prominence of Atlantic intellectuals or those socialized within Anglo-American economic circles is already evident.

The CEPII council

In Paris, the CEPII scientific council meets annually and has two roles: first, to validate the work of the Centre and, second, to examine its research methods, its publication strategies and its collaborative work alongside other centres (CEPII 2007). As above, the consensual elements of neoliberal common sense are again apparent. In essence the council meets to assess the 'scientific quality of the different programs' (Blanchard 2006) in respect to both the 'methods as well as the means of diffusing the research' (Fouquin 2006). Ostensibly, this so-called 'validation' relies upon the expertise of its members who consider 'publications in French and Anglo-Saxon journals' as a proxy for the quality, pertinence and validity of the CEPII research (Blanchard 2006). The criteria and assessment methods tend towards a conservative approach, reproducing knowledge claims firmly rooted in the Atlantic tradition.

The council is comprised of ten members convened under the auspices of Professor Olivier Blanchard. The chairman since 2004, Blanchard is a Professor of Economics at the MIT and was appointed Chief Economist at the IMF in 2008. Analytically, he epitomizes the emergent shift and struggles within both French capitalism and common sense. Though a French national by birth, Blanchard earned his PhD in economics at MIT; again there is evidence of his socialization within the Atlantic tradition. In the USA he remains closely linked to American economic circles, being formerly vice-president of the American Economic Association and a member of the American Academy of Sciences; in France he was also a member of the French Economic Advisory Council to the French Prime Minister since 1997 (Blanchard 2007).

As he is a prominent figure in both CEPII and CESifo case studies, a brief examination of his economic research is informative. In particular, Professor

Blanchard was involved in the production of the *Rapport Camdessus* (2004) for the French government. Entitled *'Le sursaut – vers une nouvelle croissance pour la France'* or 'The jolt towards a new era of French growth' the report addressed the recent slow growth of the French economy and the rise in unemployment (ibid.: 9) symptomatic of the intellectuals' ability to shape perceptions of (purportedly objective) conditions of crisis. The report concluded that France is in need of transforming its model for economic growth (ibid.).[5] Moreover, a further four of the ten CEPII council members were involved in producing the report.

The Report appears to reveal several significant indicators of the economic direction promoted by the scientific council. Unsurprisingly though, whilst there are obvious neoliberal undertones, historical tendencies of the French system are also evident; traces of the struggles between previously germinated and emergent common senses are apparent. The report focused on the following four elements: first, whilst the French 'model' must be adapted it must retain the particular 'values' which France has historically prioritized (ibid.: 49); 'not all forms of growth are necessarily desirable; economic growth must also be beneficial to social progress and increasing the well-beings of individuals' (ibid.: 52). Second, it noted the need for 'improving the efficiency of markets in goods and services by the liberalization from ineffective rules' within the French economy (ibid.: 56), emphasizing that 'strong growth is synonymous with a dynamic market for goods and services . . . [and] to achieve this it is necessary for the market to be as extensive as possible and that it may function freely' (ibid.: 109, 118).[6] The report emphatically stated that the benefits of more liberal market regulations are already evident in other countries and that France needs to imitate their example (ibid.: 110).[7] Third, the report argued for 'public authorities to assist in the improvement of competition, and the rise in investment' (ibid.); it noted that former, competition-limiting interventionism had more *negative* long-term effects on the economy than any benefits it might have brought (ibid.: 123). Fourth and finally, it noted that there is a need to implement EU regulations more swiftly to overcome the insufficient levels of competition which characterize French markets (ibid.). Insofar as the report reveals the common sense assumptions of Blanchard and connected Council members, it emphasizes both the embeddedness of neoliberal knowledge claims within traditional (Gallic) common sense whilst also emphasizing – rhetorically at least – the liberal imperative at the expense of previous protectionist measures.

Finally, a brief look at the remaining members of the council confirms the institutionalized importance of the Atlantic heartland. Of the ten members, two are of particular note. Both are Professors at the Graduate Institute of International Studies in Geneva. Charles Wyplosz (also involved with the Camdessus report) received his PhD from Harvard and has been involved with both the global integration of financial markets and the restructuring process in France. Though a graduate of the *grands écoles* in Paris (1972) he subsequently taught at a series of North American universities, including the University of California at Berkeley, Harvard, MIT and the University of Pennsylvania (Wyplosz 2007). Further, his acceptance within Atlantic economic circles is also emphasized by his position on the editorial board of several journals, including the prominent *International Journal of Finance and Economics*. Here a group of scholars from British (Warwick, LSE, Belfast) and American (California, Princeton, Harvard, Columbia) institutions dominate – numerically – the board. Again, through processes of both socialization and career-shaping the Atlantic heartland tends to occupy a privileged position.

If further evidence were required, Wyplosz's research supports his acceptance of neoliberal common sense. For example, in a paper (1998) delivered to the Forum on Debt and Development, he addressed the concern that 'financial markets are prone to failures'. What is illuminating is that he is at the more 'radical' end of the neoliberal paradigm – so to speak – on the one hand broadly subscribing to the amalgam of new classical and monetarist theories whilst, on the other hand, emphasizing inherent informational asymmetries within financial markets (ibid.: 3–5). This latter point sits uncomfortably with the efficient markets thesis and undermines the dominant tendency within neoliberal common sense to depoliticize markets (ibid.: 5, 10). Nonetheless, it sits comfortably with our conception of variegated neoliberal common sense as embodying heterodox and often contradictory economic ideas utilized or reframed (at a more concrete level) in the interests of securing class rule. As earlier chapters noted, degrees of emphasis on depoliticization and repoliticization tend to vary, yet Wyplosz sits firmly within the neoliberal 'paradigm' (ibid.: 10–11).

There are distinct parallels between Wyplosz and his colleague at the Geneva Institute, Professor Richard Baldwin. He also received his PhD at MIT under Paul Krugman, the former IMF chief economist, before becoming a member of the US President's Council of Economic Advisors and consulting for the EU, the OECD and the World Bank (Baldwin 2007). Firmly rooted in Atlantic intellectual circles, he was a professor at the University of Columbia (1986–91) and is Policy Director for the Centre for Economic Policy Research in London.

Concerning his knowledge claims he emphasizes several features outlined in Chapter 6. For example, in a paper (2004) presented at a workshop in Seoul on 'Economic Cooperation in East Asia', Baldwin considered 'European Economic Integration and [its] Implications for East Asia'. He argued that the primary lesson from 'European regional trade liberalization was the foundation of regional peace, prosperity and stability' (ibid.: 1). Interestingly, he explicitly takes his lead from classical liberal thinkers such as Smith and Bastiat (ibid.) yet perceives liberalization as a means to goals even 'more important' than economic prosperity, arguing that:

> Trade is good for peace because it boosts 'social interdependence' by increasing communication, a convergence of economic interests, and the establishment of cultural ties that promote relationships of trust and respect between trading partners that will prevent them from resorting to forceful means to resolve disputes.

(Baldwin 2004: 2)

Moreover, he also argues that 'Free trade simultaneously makes peace more economically attractive and makes war most economically costly. It does this by making nations more economically interdependent'. In this and other respects he acknowledges an intellectual debt to Paul Krugman and his work on regional trade. The pro-neoliberal emphasis of Wyplosz and Baldwin, accompanied by their socialization within Atlantic circles, emphasizes the conditions within which the CEPII operates.

The evidence from the CEPII scientific council presents a convincing case: the immanence of 'scientific' research standards underpins the consensual – in the first instance – and disciplining – in the last instance – role of scientific councils; these councils are dominated by 'Atlantic' economists or economists socialized within Anglo-American circles. As we shall see, this allows for a very limited set of ideas to be considered rational and sensible within these economic research institutes.

Molecular emergence

Underlying these two chapters on neoliberal common sense is the premise that processes of neoliberalization are neither simply *inevitable responses* to the 'exogenous' pressures of so-called global market forces, nor *imposed* by dominant Anglo-Saxon agents. Instead the book has repeatedly argued that the tendencies under capitalism, exacerbated and affording unique junctures for change under crises, have precipitated neoliberalization. The agency of a nascent Atlantic fraction and the US and UK power blocs, embedded in the embryonic neoliberal common sense of the 1970s shaped both the Keynesian crisis itself and the direction of responses. Having examined the contemporary agency of our three fractions (Chapters 3, 4 and 5) it was argued that the content and efficacy of their hegemonic projects required an understanding of neoliberal common sense. We have examined the three research centres as agents – though not the only agents – of this production process.

The argument of this chapter builds upon the notions that (i) certain hegemonic ideas are effective because of the purported *solutions* or *threats* which appear to 'fit' with material–social conditions and (ii) consensual, hegemonic rule relies on the socially constructed assumption that the provision of public goods through neoliberalism is the *only* logical alternative. This chapter argues that (iii) scientific research standards provide historically specific conditions for processes of socialization and opportunities for disciplining renegade knowledge claims; these are evidenced in scientific research councils and suggest the privileged position of the Atlantic heartland. Though at different stages of path-dependent trajectories, the UK, France and Germany are therefore engaged in producing and reproducing the variegated neoliberal consensus.

Summary: Atlantic heartland

Chapters 6 and 7 have argued that processes of neoliberalization and the recent period of EU integration can only be understood within the context of changes in common sense. As we have seen, this common sense has emerged historically in the post-war era, with an intellectual heritage in earlier classical political economy, and has been spurred on by and simultaneously fuelled post-war crises and the global restructuring of capitalism. Financial expansion, at the heart of neoliberalization, is clearly rooted in the amalgam of new classical, monetarist and rational expectations theorems; the hegemony of these ideas, coupled with the dominance of the Atlantic heartland, have contributed to the seemingly ubiquitous conception of 'neoliberalism as the only alternative'. It remains unclear whether this will change following the 2007–09 crisis although – as the concluding chapter explains – indications suggest otherwise. Concerning our case studies, the rationale for elements of variegated neoliberal convergence is now more apparent. Crises and the nature of global competition are necessary but insufficient conditions for competing national capitalisms to pursue neoliberalization; given the immanence of neoliberal common sense conditioning notions of the rational and the sensible this is more understandable.

Having outlined in Parts II and III the dynamics and agents of neoliberalization the final Part (IV) now turns to the more overtly normative question of counter-hegemony and demystifying the transnational capitalist class (TCC) myth. My concern here is that, given the seemingly incessant spread of variegated neoliberalism, academic endeavour has tended – or so I argue – to further compound this through the reification of the TCC. I argue that, in considering questions of counter-hegemonic resistance, a more nuanced account of the fragility of transnational unity offers potentially fruitful insight. In the concluding chapter I then turn to examine the role of International Political Economy (IPE) in contesting neoliberalization; and this is incredibly timely, given its obvious failures to provide alternatives at the outset of the 2007–09 crisis.

Part IV

The transnational capitalist class and resisting neoliberalization

8 De-reifying the transnational capitalist class

This chapter aims to de-reify the notion of a transnational capitalist class (TCC). The concept of variegated neoliberalism, whilst enabling the conceptualization of convergence and divergence as dialectically interwoven moments in capitalist development, also allows for an understanding of the differential 'projects' of transnationally oriented fractions *within* a contingent neoliberal consensus (Chapter 5). This chapter returns to this argument in an attempt to highlight the fragility of this consensus; by implication it also aims to provide a more nuanced understanding of opportunities for resisting neoliberalization. In effect, by emphasizing the explanatory power of the impulsions–agency–common sense nexus and then moving to highlight contingent elements therein we aim to circumvent two criticisms: one concerns the overestimation of the coherence of neoliberalism (Drainville 1994); a second critiques *neo*-Gramscian analysis for their agent-centrism (Bonefeld 2006). Yet prospects for counter-hegemony still derive from this more nuanced account.

Obviously, this chapter's argument is not without precedent. The 'hyper-globalization' thesis, centred on a 'borderless world' (Ohmae 1990) and accounts of 'footloose capital' (Garrett 1998) and – with certain parallels – the 'retreat of the state' (Strange 1996) are examples; the common thread here was the seemingly irresistible pressure of cross-border price signals (Cerny 1994), actors or capital flows (Webb 1994), and markets in goods and services. Attempts to 'demystify globalization' (Hay and Marsh 2000) have therefore emphasized – *inter alia* – ongoing national path dependencies (Hall and Soskice 2001), and the discursive construction of exogenous threats (Wendt 2001), and have provided critiques of impersonal, agent-less accounts of globalization (Hay 1999). These critiques bear similarities to that of this book.

Moreover, these debates are echoed within historical materialism. For example, an experiential understanding of class, coupled with an exponential rise in the linkages between capitalists with cross-border operations, has underpinned some accounts of the 'transnational capitalist class' (Sklair 2001). Elsewhere the ideological pertinence of 'transnational' material–economic operations has purportedly propagated a common 'project' amongst 'transnational capital' (van Apeldoorn 2002), whilst yet others have argued that this transnational capitalist class now possesses interests and an identity disembedded from national context (Robinson and Harris 2000).

It is important to recall, however, that the hallmarks of critical endeavour are: historically grounded enquiry into conditions of capitalist unfreedom and exploitation (Morton 2006: 63); the rejection of fetishized 'forms' in favour of the underlying social content (Bonefeld 2006: 46–48); and the de-reification of apparently (at worst) disconnected or (at best) externally related phenomena in favour of the internal complexity of various elements as part of an organic whole (Marx 1993 [1858]: 108). In essence, accounts positing a disembedded TCC or overstating the transnational unity of capital have serious political consequences. As André Drainville noted, these accounts suffer because the

> theorization of the articulation between accumulation and politics in the world economy is underdeveloped, and leads to *an exaggerated view of the coherence of neoliberalism*. The politics of open Marxism [read neo-Gramscianism], constrained by assumptions of an organic unity of global elites, and the political cogency of transnational concepts of control, leaves few possibilities for political organization.
>
> (Drainville 1994: 111, emphasis added)

This chapter argues that an account emphasizing the national–domestic embeddedness of transnationally oriented fractions rejects the notion of a transnational capitalist class as conceptually misleading, and suggests that this has potentially significant consequences for counter-hegemonic efforts.

I begin by outlining several prominent accounts of the TCC before (re-)examining the national–domestic embeddedness of our fractions. Beginning with their responses to the Markets in Financial Instruments Directive (MiFID) (see also Chapters 4 and 5) I argue that this embeddedness continues to formatively shape their interests within EU integration, making them *transnationally oriented* as distinct from *transnational* fractions. I then extend this argument to outline three competing hegemonic projects, within a variegated neoliberal framework, which are firmly rooted in the conflicting accumulation strategies of the three fractions. This concludes the earlier analysis of Chapters 3 and 5 and will be discussed further in Chapter 9.

A transnational capitalist class?

Robinson on the TCC

An innovative and provocative account of the transnational capitalist class is provided by William Robinson. He argues that we are entering a quantitatively new epoch in global capitalism (2004: 2). He rejects the notion that capitalism be understood solely as the series of *market* relations between buyers and sellers of commodities, opting for, in his terms, 'Marx's definition' of capitalism as a social relation of *production* (ibid.: 8). For his argument this assertion is fundamental; it enables him to claim that the new epoch which emerged in the 1970s centres on the *transnationalization* of production (ibid.: 9). He proceeds to differentiate this transnationalization from processes of internationalization insofar as internationalization refers to the 'geographical extension across national borders' whilst transnationalization refers to the 'functional integration of such internationally dispersed activities' (ibid.: 14).

He explains this claim with an example from the automobile industry, highlighting that both the production and the assembly of an automobile, (essentially a 'single' commodity), now occur in diverse international locations (ibid.: 10–11). Not only this, but the transnational dispersal of production has been accompanied by a centralization of command in the hands of a relatively smaller series of capitalists (ibid.: 11). He then presents his *coup de grâce*: that this global capitalism is entirely different from previous epochs of capitalism. Whereas former periods of capitalism were characterized by international trade of nationally produced commodities and international integration of national capitalists, this is now a 'transnational world'. By this he means that the 'whole world is now integrated . . . into a globalized circuit of production and accumulation in a single global market' (ibid.: 11).

This chapter focuses though on his treatment of the transnational capitalist class. For Robinson the fact that production rarely occurs in one single national context suggests that production and accumulation are now inherently 'transnational'. Transnational space therefore replaces national space in a highly problematic dichotomy. Whilst this is almost certainly *not* Robinson's aim, it is seemingly reinforced by his claims regarding the 'transnational' capitalist class.

The underlying difficulty is that to convincingly argue for a new epoch in global capitalism Robinson is continuously forced to reassert a division between the transnational and the national. Through the functional diversification of production locations 'people all around the world have become swept up into transnational class relations' (2004: 34). He is keen to emphasize that the TCC then, is not simply the coagulation of *national* capitalist classes. He explains that a *national* bourgeoisie develops from a shared 'history, politics and culture' all of which are *nationally* based; on the contrary 'globalization . . . is establishing the material conditions for the rise of a bourgeoisie whose coordinates are no longer national' (ibid.: 36–37). Hence a new 'fractionation or axis' is emerging, dividing 'national and transnational fractions of classes' (ibid.: 37). Crudely, transnational 'space' becomes a 'level' *on top of* the national, at once functionally integrating diverse national 'spaces' and yet reducible to none (see ibid.: 20, 33, 41). Simultaneously, territories inadvertently provide a geographic basis for capitalism yet the material basis determinant to the development of the capitalist class is no longer dependent on these territorial spaces (ibid.: 44).

Transnationally oriented

Put simply, I argue for a conception of the transnational as both relational and scalar (Chapter 2). As a result, it is not only accumulation which has a material basis in 'national' – so to speak – territories, but the interests and identities of capital as a collective social force are tied to territoriality. Here the contradictions within capital are expressed through the tacit distinction between a positional and an experiential understanding of class. In positional terms all three fractions share a common transnational orientation in their accumulation strategies, contributing to the highlighted neoliberal consensus. Simultaneously, the fractions engage, to varying degrees, in collective enterprises such as pan-European trade associations (Financial Services Roundtable, European Banking Federation) which lend themselves to the consolidation of this neoliberal consensus – an experiential phenomena contributing to common interest formation. As we shall see, however, these fractions remain (positionally) embedded within circuits of capital and social configurations – including regulatory and state infrastructures – which, so the evidence of EU financial integration suggests, fundamentally condition interests. Further, as this book has highlighted, the very coalescence of transnationally oriented fractions remains deeply rooted in a national–domestic context; also driving relational elements. It is for this reason that scale, function *and* socio-institutional configuration are emphasized in shaping interests. I argue that these national–domestic factors remain significantly more important to interest and identity formation for the three fractions. I therefore propose the rejection – certainly at this historical juncture – of the TCC.

These details obviously have a bearing on our discussion of convergence and divergence. They suggest that whilst certain structural or macro-convergences are apparent in terms of models of capital market finance, micro-patterns of market organization continue to differ dramatically. Beyond this however, I argue that these organizational differences are symptomatic of underlying accumulation strategies and interconnected, distinct common senses embodied in, though not confined to, divergent hegemonic projects. In one respect then, accounts emphasizing coterminous convergence and divergence accurately recognize the material forms of variegated neoliberalism. My aim, however, is to transcend this *form*-al analysis to examine the social content of financial expansion within neoliberalization. In arguing that recent financial expansion represents an attempt to offset crises of accumulation originating in the 1970s I have aimed to (i) problematize the dominant assumption that (financial) neoliberalization is driven by a public interest and (ii) contribute to counter-hegemonic notions of resistance.

MiFID: Price transparency and patterns of market organization

I begin by examining these claims in light of EU legislation. Essentially, post–2000 EU financial market integration provides a unique empirical case study of variegated neoliberalism: on the one hand the crises, agents and common sense we bring to light in this book culminated in the construction of a more extensive and deeply integrated system, structured around capital market finance; on the other hand the ferocity and longevity of conflicts in this period highlight the resilience of path dependencies both because and in spite of neoliberalization. Here these dynamics provide an entry point to our discussions of the transnational capitalist class.

As we saw in Chapter 3, the Markets in Financial Instrument Directive (MiFID) has been both the most significant and most controversial EU directive in post–2000 financial market efforts (McCreevy 2006). Essentially it reignited conflicts over different financial systems experienced during the 1990s (see Underhill 1997; Steil 1995; Brown 1997; Moloney 2003). Whilst the UK and German systems were historically dominated by investment firms and universal banks trading on account, France operated under a stock exchange-based model. In the UK and Germany then, similar regulations existed, delaying price disclosure and avoiding undue risk to the firm. This is because, unlike a 'regulated market', an investment firm/bank enters into a 'risk position' whereby it is not simply a trading platform for third parties.

Early MiFID drafts however, required that regulated markets (stock exchanges) and systematic internalizers (investment banks and firms) declare firm 'bid-offer spreads'[1] immediately *prior* to execution. The Rhenish and Atlantic fractions therefore contended that this requirement risked 'the market turning against' them as other participants raised or lowered prices too rapidly for the internalizer to benefit from its own negotiated price (ZKA August 2005). For this reason, both Rhenish and Atlantic fractions were extremely cautious about the wording of the price transparency clauses.[2] The diametrically opposed policy positions of the Atlantic and Gallic fractions are therefore most informative to the argument presented in this chapter.

Atlantic misgivings

Whilst stock exchanges (whether quote- or order-driven) necessarily operate under publicly known prices, the City of London has historically operated a system whereby bloc (large) trades were allowed an extended period prior to the disclosure of execution prices. This allowed for the bloc trades to be 'unwound' over a given period. Whilst exchanges and investment firms compete within the City of London, allowing for both patterns of price disclosure, French stock exchanges depended upon transparency requirements for their monopoly on trading in the French system; the French application of the 'concentration principle' also ensured that foreign firms could only operate *through* the 'regulated market' itself, reinforcing the dominance of stock exchanges (Chapter 5).

In a bid to increase cross-border competition between firms/banks and exchanges in European capital markets, early MiFID drafts therefore abolished this concentration principle (Casey and Lanoo 2006: 6). Of course, this move threatened the exchanges ability to compete, risking a migration of transactions to the more liberal regulatory climate of the City. Understandably, the Atlantic fraction favoured this move. In the words of the BBA:

> We support the proposed abolition of the concentration requirements imposed in certain Member States. We consider that if genuine pan-European capital markets are to be developed it is not logical to sustain concentration requirements which effectively result in a particular Stock Exchange in a particular

Member State having a monopoly over the trading of the shares of the issuers from that jurisdiction.

(BBA January 2002)

That certain countries had formerly operated with concentration (and publicly known prices) prompted the issue of price transparency when concentration was removed; once again, the disjuncture between rhetoric and practice in levelling the playing field is apparent. Thus, when the Level 1 directive was adopted by the European Council (21 April 2004) articles 4, 25, 26, 27, 29 and 44 included provisions for a degree of price transparency (Directive 2004/39/EC).

At Level 2 however – where the Committee of European Securities Regulators (CESR) 'flesh out' the framework directives – the conflicts which interest us came to the fore.[3] Early Level 2 proposals aroused the concern of the Atlantic and Rhenish fractions in two ways: one regarded the real-time disclosure of prices, that is, at time of execution; the other concerned the wide definition of systematic internalization, that is, the operations conducted by firms/banks intended to be categorized as internalization and subject to transparency requirements. For reasons which will become clear, I examine these details at some length.

In brief, the Atlantic fraction immediately lobbied for exemptions and less excessive obligations. The shared concern of the Atlantic and Rhenish fractions was that the transparency requirements might skew competition towards regulated markets, thereby mirroring the now obsolete concentration principle. In the words of the BBA:

Commercial pressures and market forces achieve greater choice and flexibility of execution without a need for intrusive regulatory intervention. Any proposals by CESR need to avoid skewed incentives towards concentration of trades on the main stock exchange and allow the possibility of genuine competition and better prices elsewhere.

(BBA October 2004)

Similarly, within the CESR market participants' consultative panel, Dr Rolf Breuer of Deutsche Bank contended that:

The proposed pre-trade transparency regime harms both investment firms offering internalization and clients seeking off-exchange execution . . . market efficiency cannot be improved by forcing a concentration of liquidity, since disregarding client needs would decrease trading activity.

(CESR June 2003)

Both Atlantic and Rhenish fractions recognized that, rather than allowing competition between exchange and firm/bank, the transparency clauses, as they stood, might favour the exchange. The expansion of their market operations would thus be threatened.

As we saw in Chapter 4, the fractions again sought to reinforce their policy position through the construction of strategic threats. For example, the BBA reminded the CESR of the global/pan-European operations of their firms:

> There are many jurisdictions around the world where there are still no [such] regulatory obligations to safeguard client assets and the only way in which to hold securities for clients is through a local custodian. *The global basis on which banks in Europe operate must be taken into account.*
>
> (BBA September 2004, emphasis added)

Elsewhere they noted the potentially damaging effects for the EU:

> CESR's proposals for pre-trade transparency obligations for RMs (regulated markets) and MTFs (multi-trading facilities) seem to be based on a particular perception of how equity markets should operate, and do not allow for the diversity of means by which such markets do, or may choose to, advertise trading interests. The proposals are likely to be inflexible, and damage the competitiveness of European markets
>
> (LIBA *et al.* October 2004)

Further, they argued that European consumers would ultimately bear the brunt of these extraneous costs:

> We (the BBA) believe that the current proposals are too wide ranging and specific and are likely to result in heavy systems and implementation *costs which will ultimately be passed on to investors.* For example the requirement to make public all information for every trade may actually result in reduced pre-trade transparency as electronic order books must be temporarily frozen in order to change the information contained in them.
>
> (BBA October 2004, emphasis added)

Evidently 'the attractiveness of *European* markets for European and international investors' was a major concern for the Atlantic fraction (LIBA *et al.* October 2004, emphasis added). Interestingly, again, the Atlantic hegemonic project sought to transcend their particularistic interests (excessive cost burdens) by suggesting a universal impact (greater investor costs). Here however, we are concerned with the significance of their national–domestic market systems.

The difference between the capital adequacy directives and the MiFID is thus significant. Though the multi-regulatory tensions engendered by conflicting Basel, EU and UK requirements highlighted the transnational-global scale of the Atlantic fraction (Chapter 5), the pan-EU scope of the MiFID highlights the importance of the City of London. During the MiFID negotiations the fundamental concern to protect the City's regulatory structure rose to the surface. Accumulation strategies are tacitly united by a similar emphasis or dependence on particular socio-political configurations, circuits of capital, and spatial scales. These elements remain necessarily embedded within national (so to speak) economies and function as shaping factors for the interests and identity of the fractions. For the Atlantic fraction it means that, within the European context, the City of London operates as their 'domestic' home market. Though Chapter 3 touched upon this, here the policy positions of the Atlantic fraction clearly reflect their rooted-ness in the financial market arrangements within the City of London. To demonstrate this we will consider the specifics of their objections with the original CESR draft text; namely, systematic internalization and the threshold requirements.

The issue of internalization is summed up in the following quote by the BBA who, immediately following the Level 2 drafting, stated that,

> Logically a firm can be a systematic internalizer and a non-systematic internalizer at the same time in different areas of business. All that should be necessary is that a firm makes it clear when it is dealing as a systematic internalizer and when it is not.
>
> (BBA January 2005)

In effect, an investment firm or a bank trading securities could, on occasion, trade in a category defined by the EU directive as 'systematic internalization'[4], whereas, at other times, the same firm might be exempt from this classification.

In view of the additional cost burdens and the potential competitive disadvantage vis-à-vis regulated markets the Atlantic fraction sought to limit the definition of an internalizer to avoid indiscriminate price-disclosure requirements. This objective informed several other elements of the MiFID but was clearly at the heart of the price-transparency and internalization requirements. In the words of the LIBA,

> The treatment of internalizers in paragraph 99 is inconsistent with the treatment of on-exchange market makers in paragraphs 79 and 80. It also fails to take account of the different commercial position of RMs and SIs[5]. The regulation of SIs should not be based on the commercial judgements of their competitors. The primary motivation of an RM is to keep a share trading, because it does not want to harm its market makers.
>
> (LIBA *et al.* April 2005)

In this example the MiFID text allowed market makers within a regulated market to withdraw quotes because, by definition, all of their prices are necessarily publicly available. On the other hand, in attempting to apply obligations for internalizers to publish firm bid-offer prices, the CESR text had suggested that once published, such quotes could not be withdrawn. This stipulation would have harmed firms which cater for a different cross-section of the market suited to their ability to constantly re-negotiate prices (ibid.). Details aside, the importance is that the Atlantic fraction sought to ensure an equal footing with financial markets dominated by regulated markets; markets such as the French one. We are starting to see the significance of the City's market systems.

Similarly, the Atlantic fraction also sought to limit the proportion of shares required to adhere to the transparency clauses. Outlining their concern, the Atlantic fraction stated that, 'orders that would be damaged by being displayed to the exchange . . . should not come under the scope' of transparency requirements (BBA January 2005). Two amendments were therefore proposed by the Atlantic fraction: the exemption of bloc trades from the requirements; and a high threshold for measuring which shares ought to fall under the transparency obligations (ibid.). The exemption of bloc trades was clearly a product of London's niche in unwinding large orders (see above) and this is, of course, central to our argument.[6] The criteria for measuring thresholds warrant a brief explanation, however, shedding further light on this issue.

The CESR had initially contended that price transparency should be applied to liquid shares, to which the British Bankers Association responded that 'liquidity is always a relative and subjective concept' (ibid.). Towards the beginning of 2005 the Atlantic fraction elaborated, arguing that,

> In the view of our members the pre-trade quoting obligation should apply in relation to those shares which are most frequently traded and which represent the major part of the volume of shares traded across Europe as a whole. Consequently we consider that the two most important elements in a definition for the pre-trade quote obligation are (1) average number of daily trades in a share and (2) average total daily turnover in a share.
>
> (BBA January 2005)

The above definition had the advantage of taking into account the role of internalizers in the overall scope of shares traded. The BBA explained that:

> The focus should be on applying the obligation to the most liquid stocks in Europe by daily number of transactions and daily turnover. If the figures for daily number of transactions and daily turnover are set too low this may ensure that a larger number of shares are captured from a wider range of member states but in the process it risks damaging liquidity because systematic internalizers stop internalizing either in part or in whole because it does not commercially make sense.
>
> (BBA January 2005)

In brief, the Gallic fraction were concerned that systematic internalizers should not undermine the profit-related potential of their dominant regulated markets, whereas the Atlantic fraction were keen to note that excessive demands (and costs) would reduce the attractiveness of a particular security for an internalizer and hence negatively impact liquidity. A compromise needed to be achieved between the two sets of embedded market arrangements. As the negotiations unfolded, then, the Atlantic fraction clearly revealed their concern to protect the favourable regulatory climate in the City.

The BBA lobbied for a low threshold of an average number of 500 daily trades in a given share and for an average daily turnover of €2 million. What matters, for our purposes, is that the BBA's proposals incorporated a sufficiently large proportion of shares traded on a pan-European basis but with two all-important caveats: first, the figure was not sufficiently high as to invoke excessive costs on internalizers and therefore discourage their operations; second, however, by virtue of London's high trading volumes, its propensity for bloc trades (largely exempted from the clauses) and the fact that the aforementioned calculations were conducted on a pan-European basis, the City markets would be able to maintain their competitive advantage in already established niches.

In effect, this was the *coup de grâce*: the Atlantic fraction were *primarily* concerned to protect their competitive advantage within the City of London. Aside from – or arguably a constituent of – wider MiFID conflicts over embedded market traditions and the transnational-global scale of the Atlantic fraction, they *also* fundamentally revolved around the Atlantic fraction's embedded-ness in the City's financial system. This claim potentially sits uneasily with a false protectionist–neoliberal dichotomy, yet it supports our variegated neoliberal thesis and also reinforces the argument that neoliberalism is underpinned and legitimized by active, albeit often depoliticized, state policy.[7]

Champions of transparency

In essence, the Gallic fraction were diametrically opposed to the Atlantic fraction in price transparency negotiations. This opposition obviously stemmed from the differing market traditions in the City and Paris. Nonetheless, in protecting the privileged position of French regulated markets we again see attempts to sustain the regulatory environment and social configurations upon which their accumulation strategies are based. As above, the protectionism–neoliberalism binary must be abandoned since Chapter 5 has already explored the, albeit distinctive, neoliberal interests of the Gallic fraction. Though the French system has undergone radical transformation from its previously competition-limiting past, attempts to partition the new from the old – thereby relegating the *dirigiste* model to the past – are misleading. In reality, the molecular emergence of neoliberalism means both *dirigisme* and social protection are inherent features of Gallic neoliberalism.

The price transparency clauses, however, are indicative of the intra-fractional struggles, ostensibly over organizational details, within the contingent neoliberal consensus. The Gallic position is already apparent: they sought to ensure that their (more dominant) regulated markets would not lose out to internalizers. Given the abolition of the concentration principle, the Gallic fraction earnestly sought for the inclusion of price transparency requirements throughout 2002–04 (AFEI 2002). Their primary concern was that, without transparency obligations, even the comparative advantage of the regulated markets within the French system would be lost to Atlantic and Rhenish internalizers. Concerning transparency, they claimed that:

Anything other than this would create pockets of liquidity known to only a privileged few with information not available to other investors. Not only would this interfere with equal access to information . . . but it would probably create a vicious circle whereby order internalization contributes to wider spreads on regulated markets and Multi-lateral Trading Facilities (MTFs). This in turn would make internalization *easier and more advantageous*.

(AFEI 2002, emphasis added)

Underlying the rhetoric was an obvious concern to preserve the domestic comparative advantage of the regulated market.

Though they agreed that measuring liquidity – central to the Atlantic proposals – is 'a complex issue which, in any case, can never be dealt with entirely satisfactorily' the Association Française des Entreprises d'Investissements (AFEI) also recommended 'adopting a criterion that is simple and easy to check, namely the trading volume in a particular security' (AFEI April 2004). Ensuing negotiations involved dense minutiae; suffice it to note that a compromise was reached which reflected the concerns of both market systems (Interview AFEI). In their Annual Report, the AFEI noted that the

energetic joint effort by AFEI and others was instrumental in changing the orientation of the draft directive shortly before its official adoption by the European Commission. Throughout the ensuing discussions between the Parliament and the Council, AFEI and its counterparts underscored the importance of this issue from the viewpoint of functional market efficiency. The point of view championed by AFEI and its counterparts has *partially* prevailed.

(AFEI 2003, emphasis added)

They later noted that:

The language finally adopted by the Parliament and Council at the end of the first quarter of 2004 clearly reflects a willingness to seek a *compromise*. Article 27 of the directive delivers a balance achieved by *extracting concessions from both sides*. Compared with the general objective that AFEI had sought, it cannot be considered entirely satisfactory, at least as regards market clearing by internalizers. On the other hand, compared with the original draft, the directive as adopted marks a major step forward towards genuine market transparency.

(AFEI 2003, emphasis added)

The final compromise determined a liquidity threshold based on an established standard market size (SMS) according to which transparency obligations for internalizers would be assigned.

Two points should be noted, both of which are relevant to questions of competitive and comparative advantages: the first is that, in lowering the SMS threshold, the Gallic fraction missed the opportunity to adversely impact the City's market niche. The AFEI voiced their disappointment, stating, 'This approach, which lowers the SMS threshold, runs counter to the spirit of compromise achieved in adopting the directive, which was aimed at increasing market transparency in the interest of investors' (AFEI March 2005). What they meant was that they had failed to impose Gallic standards on UK markets. The second point though reveals the Gallic success in protecting key elements of the French system. The AFEI noted:

> We have a tradition of a centralized market . . . but the original MiFID document left completely aside the question of transparency . . . and for us it was difficult to imagine completely abandoning it. One of the 'aces' of the French market is to have provided a strong element of transparency, [and] we have fought hard for transparency [and] tried to find a balance between what the English and the French wanted.
>
> (Interview AFEI 2006)

Retaining sufficient transparency suggests regulated markets will remain dominant within the French system.

Three hegemonic projects

The first part of this chapter effectively completed our analysis of the distinctive accumulation strategies of the three fractions: where Chapter 3 outlined their respective scales this chapter has reinforced the national–domestic embeddedness of these fractions in the UK, French and German systems. The second part of this chapter now explores their respective hegemonic projects, further emphasizing that within the contingent consensus these fractions remain highly distinct. The corollary argument is that these projects reflect, to a significant degree, the accumulation strategies previously noted.

In his analysis of Transnational Capitalism and the European Roundtable of Industrialists, Bastiaan van Apeldoorn (2002) also identified three competing projects shaping the progress of the single market. He labelled these projects 'supranational social democracy', the 'neo-mercantalist project' and the 'neoliberal project' (van Apeldoorn 2002: 79–80). In his view 'embedded neoliberalism' was the solution to the conflict between neoliberalism and neo-mercantilism insofar as it provided a 'hegemonic articulation of the now dominant neoliberal perspective with remaining elements of the neo-mercantilist discourse' (ibid.: 158). In seeking to highlight the contingency of the neoliberal consensus I argue, however, that the concept of *variegated* neoliberalism is more adept at conveying the similarities and yet (even more significant) *differences* within neoliberalism. Rather than merging to form a coherent single project (ibid.: 160)[8], I argue that there remain three competing projects which share a common interest in integration but remain significantly distinctive. This argument is important for the potentialities of resistance.

The Atlantic project: 'liberal neoliberalism'

The particularities of the Atlantic project were noted in Chapter 3. Its more classically liberal traits are a feature of the transnational-*global* scale of the Atlantic fraction, their more apparent integration in circuits of finance capital, as well as their historic role in shaping the British form of state and the particularities of its regulatory regime. For now though, a brief review of the Atlantic project presents the Gallic and Rhenish projects in sharp relief.

The Atlantic rhetoric is therefore pregnant with the reification of markets and their apparent competitive rationality. In relation to the conflicts between execution venues examined earlier, the LIBA contends that 'markets have a *natural tendency*' (LIBA *et al.* October 2004, emphasis added) to resolve such matters. They assert that, 'regulation should not seek to create or favour new venues artificially where no investor demand for them exists. Such an attempt would fail anyway *if it did not correspond to a market need*' (ibid., emphasis added).

The claim that (so-called) 'market pressures' will resolve competition between execution venues without regulatory intervention reveals a feature of their accumulation strategies: namely, the less interventionist role of the UK state (BBA October 2004; LIBA *et al.* December 2004; Barclays February 2004). It is both genuine concern – rooted in material condensations in the British system – and yet simultaneously ideological construct – concealing a willingness to allow protectionism and monopolies as necessary to their own particularistic interests. They further explain this contention, stating:

> We believe that the role of regulation should not be to pre-empt or second guess market developments, particularly those of an innovative nature, but *to follow* and act *only* where there is a perceived threat to the stability of markets and institutions, and to the position of consumers.
>
> (BBA January 2005, emphasis added)

The more typically liberal and expansionary concerns are interwoven with a geographically specific one; namely maintaining the competitive advantages established in the City which underpin their accumulation strategies.

This apparent contradiction gives rise to the misleading binaries of international/transnational and national highlighted in certain academic accounts. Our concepts of variegated neoliberalism and a relational, scalar transnational therefore merely restate the obvious tendencies under capitalism. On the one hand, capital operates under an incessant and necessarily expansionary impulsion, in geographically distinct patterns and with temporally contingent phases; on the other hand, the compression of space through time is premised on infrastructures – regulatory and other. The *transnationally* oriented–*nationally* embedded nexus is thus simply contradiction, precondition, product and outcome of the accumulation of capital itself.

For the Atlantic fraction this tendency manifested itself in the City's markets. 'London has long been Europe's biggest financial centre, and indeed, in terms of international business, the world's. Investment banks from both Europe and the rest of the world chose to have their European base there' (Economist 1998). For example, almost 75 per cent of the BBA membership are non-UK banks and firms (BBA April 2004), yet the majority of these actors have operations within other member states but consider their primary base for operations to be the City of London; generally for historical reasons (cf. RBS February 2004). In effect, this is the *liberal* neoliberal project of the Atlantic fraction.

The Gallic project: 'social neoliberalism'

With the Gallic fraction, the transparency concerns were symptomatic of attempts to retain accumulation strategies infused with 'social' components. 'Social' should not be read as socially equitable, however. Instead, underlying the price-transparency disagreements was a Gallic project based on preserving 'long-term relationships' between finance and industry in contradistinction to the perceived threat of Atlanticist profit-seeking, 'short-termism' (FBF June 2003). As Chapters 2–5 argued, the Gallic fraction represent social forces more closely integrated both in circuits of finance and production capital, and accompanying nationally based social linkages.

Given this distinction, the Gallic project tactically employed its terminology to contrast with the Atlantic, more classically liberal project. The French Banking Federation stated, for example, that 'Europe must develop its *own* model, based on its *own* values' (FBF 2003, emphasis added). They explained that Europe must preserve the relations between financial service providers and industry, and avoid reducing financial services to the imperatives of short-termism. The FBF emphatically stated that the Gallic project

> has combined a performance focus with stringent requirements in terms of individual consumer recognition and protection, seeks to establish *long-term relationships* between companies, their employees, customers and suppliers, and has developed a time-tested system for *social dialogue and consensus-building*.
>
> (FBF June 2003, emphasis added)

The FBF asserted that the Gallic values 'seek in particular to strike a *lasting balance between the interests* of their shareholders, employees, customers and suppliers' (FBF 2003, emphasis added), asserting that 'economic and social life cannot be reduced to a simple consideration of shareholder returns' (FBF June 2003). These positions portray traces of the financial network economy, in part a product of the French system of cross-shareholdings and *noyaux durs* yet (and perhaps somewhat ironically) with sediments of the German social market economy transposed during the 1980s (see Chapter 2; see also Morin 2000; Clift 2004).

Price transparency was therefore merely a constituent part of a wider Gallic project. As the FBF explain,

One of the fundamental principles of the European model conceived by French banks is the need to ensure equal treatment of all players (producers and consumers) in a given market. When an investor places an order to buy or sell a security, comparison with bid and ask prices must be possible to ensure that the transaction price is determined in total transparency. French banks, and 'Continental' banks in general, which attach great importance to the transparency provided by regulated financial markets, cannot accept the idea that a non-transparent intermediary could prevent an investor . . . from knowing how and at what price his order was placed.

(FBF June 2003)

The importance French banks attach to transparency reveals their preference for on-exchange trading. Complete rejection of transparency threatens *all* on-exchange transactions, with French banks forced to compete under market practices familiar to Atlantic firms. Profit margins would suffer and linkages between French production and French finance would weaken (ibid.). In every respect, transparency and Gallic accumulation strategies go hand in hand. As a result – of course – the overriding Gallic concern is to secure and retain class rule, rather than a puritanical devotion to social values.

Finally then, an important – albeit obvious – clarification must be made. Though Gallic rhetoric emphasizes 'values', employee and consumer interests, and longer-term concerns – in other words, social protection – this is merely a distinctive feature of Gallic accumulation strategies vis-à-vis the Atlantic focus on circulating capital, speculation and finance-led accumulation. The Gallic fraction still retains *social* linkages with production capitals, hence the primacy of production in generating surplus value remains relatively obvious (Marx 1978 [1885]: 271–80); profits from financial activities are, on balance, less important in the French system. In comparison, the relatively weaker linkages of Atlantic fraction and production, coupled with profits from financial expansion and speculative investments, presents an illusion in the minds of the Atlantic fraction; namely, of the irrelevance of sustaining the expansion of the forces of production. For the Gallic fraction though, this rhetoric signifies two elements: first, it reinforces the social function of a hegemonic project as corporate interests (profit incentives) presented on a universal plane (purportedly beneficial to shareholders and consumers alike); second, though, such 'values' – whether in the form of genuine concessions or otherwise – are only sustainable in so far as they fail to exacerbate the contradiction between wage demands and accumulation (Marx 1990 [1867]: 771). As noted, the ongoing crisis of the French accumulation regime threatens these values. Nonetheless, the Gallic project can be characterized as *social* neoliberalism if only to differentiate it from the Atlantic project; both alike capture the expansionary–embedded contradiction.

The Rhenish project: 'socio-liberal neoliberalism'

Under MiFID negotiations the Rhenish fraction often shared policy positions with the Atlantic fraction. This is predominantly because banks in the German system tend to match buy and sell orders of professional investors in off-exchange transactions, much as they do in the City. The influence of similar embedded patterns of market organization lends itself to similar interests, on an issue-specific basis, between Rhenish and Atlantic fractions (BVR January 2005; BVI April 2005).

These patterns of market organization are necessary but insufficient elements in understanding the projects of the transnationally oriented fractions; their accumulation strategies provide a more nuanced account of factors shaping their interests (Bieler and Morton 2001b: 17). In this respect, the Rhenish fraction bear similarities to *both* the Atlantic and the Gallic fractions. Certain Rhenish members operate globally whilst the majority operate on a transnational-*European* scale; predictably the Rhenish project therefore displays more classical liberal tendencies. On the other hand, the Rhenish fraction are also similarly rooted in the German market and linked with localized circuits of production capital resembling the Gallic fraction (Interview Deutsche Bank).

As a result, the Rhenish project is a product, at least in part, of the state of the German economy. There has been a decline in traditional forms of credit provision and a greater dependence on both capital market and foreign investment as less costly sources of finance. In 2002 the BdB remarked that, 'the bank loan has declined in importance. Companies are increasingly turning to the capital market and to foreign affiliates to finance their activities' (BdB 2002). Similarly Dr Manfred Weber commented in a review of the banking sector that:

> Loans from domestic banks, along with trade credit, traditionally used to dominate. The reasons for this were, among other things, the long-underdeveloped capital market in Germany, the reluctance of savers to put their money in shares and the widespread 'own master' mentality of many entrepreneurs, who wanted to avoid any interference by outside investors . . . the most serious change in the pattern of corporate financing as far as banks are concerned is that *growing tendency on the part of German enterprises since the mid–1990s to obtain funds through affiliates abroad.*
>
> (Weber 2002, emphasis added)

This has, in effect, fuelled a complete restructuring of German finance. Between the end of 1995 and the end of 2001, domestic enterprises' debt with foreign affiliates grew by around €270 billion (ibid.). The pattern is clear: crises of accumulation manifested in a faltering economy have fuelled restructuring and rescaling of accumulation strategies. German banks have been compelled towards a greater reliance on securities instruments as German companies turned their attentions to foreign sources of investment.

The result has again produced a seemingly contradictory dual character to the Rhenish hegemonic project. The first skein seeks to promote greater reliance of capital market innovation, global/European[9] competitiveness and more classically liberal reform. The second skein is fundamentally concerned to preserve historical linkages with nationally based social forces and the integration with production capital upon which their strategies have been constructed. Transnationalization has been accompanied by a renewed emphasis on domestic–national embeddedness; liberalization by a deepening protectionism; convergence by an embedded path dependency.

This is apparent in the rhetoric of the Initiativ Finanzstandort Deutschland and the Bundesverband deutscher Banken; on the one hand, the IFD emphatically states that, 'Considering these strengths of Finanzstandort Deutschland, it is clear that a greater focus on the capital market, while ringing in a new era for Germany as a financial centre, *does not represent a radical break with the past*' (IFD 2005, emphasis added). Whilst, simultaneously, the BdB asserts that:

> Persistent economic stagnation, the seemingly inexorable rise in unemployment, the critical state of the nation's public finances, as well as the financial problems besetting the social security system have led to the realisation that Germany's current economic and social problems *cannot be solved by a traditional approach*.
>
> (BdB 2004, emphasis added)

Rather than reflecting two *different* views on the same problem or a strategically employed rhetoric, they are *both* interconnected elements of the Rhenish project. Simultaneously they pursue: domestic structural reform whilst preserving traditional German configurations of social forces; and an interest in transnational global/European liberalization. For example, the IFD states that the proposed reforms pose, 'tremendous opportunities by enabling better use of the benefits of the capital market *while preserving traditionally intensive client relationships*' (IFD 2005, emphasis added). They explain that credit institutions will be able to securitize much of their debt whilst retaining formal linkages with industry; a means of 'combining credit and capital markets':

> But even businesses not seeking direct access to the capital market will have to address its requirements at least indirectly, as banks place more of their counterparty risk in the capital market through loan securitization or derivatives. In this symbiosis with the capital market, *classic credit financing will gain fresh appeal – and with it the traditional 'house bank' relationship*.
>
> (IFD 2005, emphasis added)

In sum, business 'will continue to rest on close customer relationships' (ibid.).

They suggest 'pro-active . . . strategic decisions' to remove state guarantees and privatize public credit institutions (DZ Bank 2004). The 'levelling' of the capital market playing field for financial service providers would therefore be sufficient to promote this kind of symbiotic capital-credit relationships. The BdB explains that:

> The high level of state ownership in the German banking industry is an anachronism . . . Only the withdrawal of the state and the privatisation of

public-sector banks will ensure that the German economy is provided with financial services in an efficient and market-driven manner.

(BdB 2004)

They explain that around 45 per cent of the banking market is covered by state-owned financial institutions (ibid.) with the following implications for capital market competition:

> These state guarantees (known as *Anstaltslast* and *Gewährträgerhaftung*) represent a massive competitive advantage for state-owned financial institutions. Germany's Landesbanken in particular are able to raise money far more cheaply on the capital market because the state, and in the final analysis the taxpayer, is responsible for these banks' viability and accepts liability for their debts. Private sector competitors have to pay considerably more for their issues of debt securities.

(BdB 2004)

Clearly these neoliberal reforms – removing restrictions on competition – are coupled with a desire to retain domestic configurations and circuits upon which their strategies are established.

Simultaneously they desire to expand their transnationally oriented operations (primarily within the EU). The Rhenish project therefore highlights the removal of cross-national obstacles to the operations of foreign banks and firms. The BdB explains that, 'it is essential, in the interests of consumers and banks alike, to eliminate the existing "artificial obstacles" to cross-border business and apply consistent, EU-wide solutions' (BdB March 2004). The IFD further notes that, 'Many EU member states discriminate in tax terms against foreign investment service providers' (IFD June 2004). Again, competition-limiting regulations or tariffs – whether within Germany or other member states – simply present themselves as another barrier to the accumulation imperative and it is this imperative – again, as opposed to a puritanical devotion – which underpins their attempts to secure class rule at the political level. Suffice it to note that the Rhenish project is both distinctive and that its particularities are substantively rooted in the national–domestic embeddedness of the Rhenish fraction. Bearing similarities to both Gallic and Atlantic projects, this is effectively a *socio-liberal* neoliberalism.

Summary: De-reifying the TCC

In sum, there are clear differences between the three projects: the Atlantic fraction's concerns are more classically liberal, arguing for flexible, market-driven reform and arms-length regulation; the Gallic fraction propose preserving 'longer-term' consensual relations as opposed to short-termist, shareholder incentives, yet simultaneously require liberalization to expand their accumulation strategies; and the Rhenish aim, simultaneously, for more liberal market integration and yet domestic restructuring which retains close production-finance linkages. All three reveal the transnational–national, expansionary–embedded contradiction, at once elucidating the variegated neoliberal consensus and – in this chapter – the national–domestic rootedness of the fractions (Macartney 2009a).

Moreover, these differences are significant, given the overarching contingent neoliberal consensus; the concept of variegation thus offers an alternative to the problematic impasse of convergence-path dependency accounts. Instead, we can more accurately speak of convergent divergence. Our impulsions–agency–common sense nexus suggests that processes of neoliberalization are necessarily accompanied by renewed emphasis on the national–domestic embeddedness of transnationally oriented capital. So convergent divergence is – as noted – the very condition and product of capitalist accumulation; in expanding operations and breaking down barriers across borders, capital does not abandon its national–domestic basis. Instead, it seeks to reinforce these relations and configurations as the very foundation for ongoing accumulation and expansion. Moreover, the liberalizing and restructuring imperative is also reflected in the national–domestic context; an element of class struggle captured by the sub- and supra-national character of the term 'transnational'. This is as true for patterns of finance-led accumulation – more closely associated with the Atlantic fraction – as it is for the strategies more closely connected to production – as in the case of the Gallic fraction. This embeddedness is therefore significant in demystifying the transnational capitalist class as agents of neoliberalism.

Further – and in contrast with mainstream accounts of integration – a Gramscian historical materialist account reveals (i) the class struggles shaping regulatory policy and yet (ii) the overall trajectory of neoliberal EU integration. Put simply, though our focus is on so-called 'elite agency' in this chapter, we disclose the social content of the regulatory policy and policy positions embodied in their discourses and, more importantly, the social content of neoliberalization for European working classes. Unlike certain accounts, this is neither attributed solely to the agents themselves (see Coen 2008) nor to 'a certain idea of Europe' (see Parsons 2003) in the hands of epistemic communities. Instead, whilst de-reifying the TCC contributes to counter-hegemonic potentialities we also now note the seemingly ubiquitous tide of an impulsions–agency–common sense nexus. The accumulation of sediments and condensations of class struggle and common sense further contribute to the 'material force' of capitalisms' dynamisms, creating a form of lock-in or transnational – that is, on multiple scales – path dependency. This tide – stemmed and channelled by elite agents – leaves European working classes in a permanently asymmetrical relationship to ruling classes – manifest most acutely at the level of the state (see Chapter 4). Crises provide the necessary moment to disrupt the flow of neoliberalization, and thus our concluding chapter now returns to this issue.

9   Conclusions

Summary of the book

This book set out to contribute to the literature on demystifying globalization. I began by arguing that – given the relative opaqueness of globalization as a concept – neoliberalization is its driving motor. I raised three conceptual puzzles: one was to explore the dynamics and internal workings of neoliberalization; the second was to question why previously averse EU member states have engaged in neoliberalization; the third was to ask what the recent spate of EU financial market integration can tell us about the former two. These questions were related to the 2007–09 financial crisis, as both indicative of underlying trends in neo-liberalism and potentially a window of opportunity for counter-hegemonic change. This final chapter therefore also questions why – employing arguments from this book – such dramatic change seems not to have occurred.

In essence, the nature and epicentre of the crisis of Keynesianism – manifested in falling profit rates, high inflation and rising wage demands, coupled with the historical importance of both London and New York as financial centres – fuelled a new period of capitalist development, reinvigorating the heartland–contender state dynamic. A nascent Atlantic fraction in London and the immanent critique provided by the new classical, monetarist and rational expectations models' faith in markets provided the shape of the response to the crisis. By the end of the 1990s a combination of burgeoning contradictions in the post-war models of – in particular – France and Germany, the diffusion of a (variegated) neoliberal intellectual consensus and the imperatives generated through transnationalization – both exogenously in the form of lower costs of capital market finance and endogenously through the emergence of transnationally oriented fractions – reached breaking point. The Lisbon and Lamfalussy agendas heralded a new spatial fix.

The book deliberately focused on the period immediately following these developments in order to chart the dynamics of these processes whilst examining whether these former national models were irrevocably set on a course towards neoliberal convergence. My concern was thus: to what extent are we witnessing the emergence of a hegemonic transnational capitalist class; and – similarly – to what extent is this the death knell for previously distinctive national models? The book has aimed to refute both these assertions. Rather than revisit the individual chapter arguments, then, I focus this final chapter on a discussion of these concerns. In the final section I consider the implications of this study for Gramscian historical materialism in relation to the 2007–09 financial crisis.

Another Europe is possible?[1]

Variegated neoliberalism and convergent divergence

In essence, this book set out to provide an alternative to the binary tendencies, the state centrism, and the formal analysis of the Varieties of Capitalism literature. As I argued in Chapter 2, this literature has tended to obfuscate the underlying class struggles and asymmetrical social relations embodied in the global restructuring of capitalism, characterized here as neoliberalization. At the heart of neoliberalization lie two analytical keys: one is the argument that although the overall process was rooted in burgeoning contradictions in the capital–labour relation in the 1970s and 1980s, it was displaced by a form of finance-led accumulation and prolonged financial expansion; the second is that, at a more concrete level, this process has centred on attempts to secure and/or restore class rule by emergent transnationally oriented fractions of capital.

Our argument concerning convergent divergence is therefore both condition and outcome of the accumulation of capital itself, epitomized in the notion of the transnational as – at once – a transnationally oriented–nationally embedded scalar relation. It therefore seeks to expand upon the concepts of the space–time compression and spatial fixes, highlighting that the transnationalization of capital involves both attempts to break down cross-border barriers to accumulation, whilst retaining – and, somewhat paradoxically, attempting to restructure – domestic–national configurations to avoid forfeiting competitive advantages; this therefore presents itself as a simultaneously expanded (on supranational scales) and deepened (on localized scales) impulsion. It is thus understandable that to the *formal* analysis of the Varieties of Capitalism, limited by notions of state centrism and soft positivism, this would appear as the binaries of (i) either liberalization or protectionism, and (ii) either convergence or path dependency. As a result, though neoliberalization is reshaping global capitalism, it is founded upon the above contradiction such that we witness *variegated* neoliberalism.

Crises as unique opportunities

The book has also focused on questions of change. One key resource of Gramscian historical materialism is that Gramsci's writings are infused with a philosophy of praxis. Gramsci's concern was to demonstrate that the seemingly abstract, objective and exogenous are indeed mutable precisely because 'reality' is 'the totality of historically determined social relations' (1971: 133). As he noted 'one cannot expect an individual or a book to change reality but only to interpret and indicate the possible lines of action' (cited in Bieler and Morton 2001b: v).

Throughout the book I have therefore made repeated references to Gramsci's notion of counter-hegemony. In particular, these have focused on (i) the significance of crises and (ii) the role of the so-called 'transnational capitalist class'. In highlighting the impulsions–agency–common sense nexus, however, an obvious tension arises between revealing openings for counter-hegemony and simultaneously closing them off.

Again, let me explain. In the first instance, the book has sought to emphatically de-reify the notion of a disembedded transnational capitalist class often assumed to be the key protagonists of neoliberalization. I have emphasized, through an analysis of their accumulation strategies and hegemonic projects, that these capitalists remain fundamentally embedded in specific national–domestic contexts. As a result, I have rejected the notion of a transnational capitalist class in favour of *transnationally oriented fractions* of capital. At the same time, I also emphasized the fragility of the contingent neoliberal consensus which has underpinned EU policy. So I have demystified both the agents and the projects behind neoliberalization, simultaneously problematizing accounts of exogenous, agentless, unstoppable forces, and those which attribute too great a degree of organizational capacity to its agents.

Whilst the conclusions of this book are more informative than prescriptive, these first two conclusions offer hope for resistance efforts: the suggestion is that, given the fragility of this consensus and the ongoing conflicts between European capitalists, attempts by European working classes to foster forms of solidarity – whether at the national or European level – are potentially fruitful avenues for resistance. In this respect, the conclusions of the book contribute to those accounts analysing the different forms of organizing this resistance (Amoore 2005; Bieler 2006).

The tension arises, however, because – having demystified the agents and projects – I risk replacing them with another ubiquitous and irresistible force in the shape of the impulsions–agency–common sense nexus. Put simply, disempowering the agents doesn't reduce the scale of the problem if the agents are themselves only conditions and products of a more encompassing process. It is here that I have sought to depart from earlier neo-Gramscian accounts; as noted, to emphasize particular agents detached from their relation to the movement of capital and the dynamics of accumulation (in general) and of neoliberalism (in particular) is to subscribe to a form of political pluralism. Yet, in establishing the above nexus we also find the resolution to the above tension: specifically, crises provide unique ruptures in the dynamics of these underlying social processes, whereupon the above conclusions (concerning contingent elements) could be usefully employed for both agent and common sense to capitalize on these moments.

To clarify, in the book I have sought to emphasize the unique importance of crises as both symptomatic of the burgeoning contradictions of (i) a particular mode of accumulation and (ii) material condensations of a hegemonic common sense. Moreover, they are moments for (iii) the reconfiguration of power relations, institutions and patterns of socio-economic development, *provided* the counter-hegemonic agents and common senses are sufficiently prepared. To justify this argument I have attempted – in transcending multiple levels of abstraction – to draw upon a variety of readings of historical materialism. So the tension between opening and closing political space for resistance is resolved in our conception of crises. These conclusions are therefore perhaps best examined in light of the 2007–09 crisis, which provides an informative – if somewhat disappointing – illustration.

2007–09 crisis?

In essence, a profound crisis of capitalism provided the preconditions for the shift to neoliberalism which suggests that a fundamental crisis can provide the preconditions for a move away from the neoliberal mode. My concern however, is that the financial crisis of 2007–09 did not provide such an opportunity. I highlight three reasons for this assertion: the relative lack of an organized working-class movement; the ubiquity of the neoliberal consensus; and the institutionalization of neoliberalism.

The state of labour under the 2007–09 crisis is – in light of the analysis of this book – sharply juxtaposed against the strategic agency of our fractions of capital, particularly in the Keynesian crisis. During the 1970s and at subsequent junctures in alternative geographical locations rallying points have formed because of capitalists' relative awareness of shared interests, embedded in similar accumulation strategies. They have sought – fairly successfully it must be said – to capture the common sense of the era and manipulate unfolding impulsions. The same cannot be said for labour at this historical juncture. This is, in part, a feature of the transnationalization of production and the accompanying fragmentation of the working class.

It is also linked to the success of neoliberalism being perceived as the only alternative; so much so that a German finance minister responded to the UK's temporary bail-out packages of 2008 as a return to 'crass Keynesianism'. In truth, the crisis came at exactly the right stage of neoliberal common senses' development – when it had reached relative maturity across the political economies of the West – in order for capital to survive and reinforce its hold through state aid. The crisis came at a particularly anti-utopian moment, when no alternative common senses were sufficiently gestated. Further, alternatives had progressively been derided and marginalized – almost to the point of extinction.

As we have emphasized throughout, though, hegemonic common senses become institutionalized in material social processes. The final point then is that the emphasis on depoliticization – as *appearance* of removal of state control (Burnham 2001) – has become deeply embedded in forms of Madisonian governance, coupled with almost corporatist connections with nascent hegemonic, transnationally oriented fractions. This book has highlighted these tendencies in the form of the Lamfalussy Process. The efficacy and crystallization of these social processes and formations have enabled neoliberalism to survive the haemorrhage relatively unscathed.

To my mind, the contradictions of financial expansion – outlined in Chapter 1 – as offsetting crises in production through financial profiteering, go some way to explain the occurrence and shape of the current crisis, yet fail to account for the lack of a fitting alternative. Nonetheless, there is cause for hope and the need for counter-hegemonic efforts. The contradictions of the neoliberal system – predicated on an exponential financial expansion to compensate for failure to secure the necessary expansion of surplus value – suggest that the system itself is unsustainable.

This is reinforced through the crisis management efforts. At present, huge state bailouts, the purchasing of so-called 'toxic assets', and the reconfiguration of regulatory architectures mask – or perhaps highlight – the fact that Western states believe the neoliberal financial system can and should be saved. Whether this is simply pragmatism or an ideological attachment to the neoliberal growth-stimulus promise, these states appear locked in to a new period of path dependency: neoliberal path dependency. On our reading, however, these immediate efforts simply patch up a system which will subsequently – in the near or more distant future – unravel with worse consequences (Macartney 2009b); neoliberalization was rooted in burgeoning contradictions in the capital–labour relation, yet was displaced through prolonged and untenable financial expansion. The lesson from the crisis then is that – whilst state managers and capitalists appear intent on emphasizing the opposite – wider social groups must recognize that neoliberalism fuels inherently and necessarily unequal social relations and is *not* the only alternative. Genuine alternative common senses must emerge from the alternative organic intellectuals, and the working classes must find ways to foster forms of solidarity. Perhaps the obvious conclusion – though unsatisfactory for some – is that an organic or cataclysmic crisis is required for a complete collapse of neoliberalism whilst, in the meantime, pragmatism dictates that – by generating political momentum through collective working-class agency and alternative common senses – more socially equitable reform of neoliberalism remains a viable demand (see Gramsci 1971: 276). Nonetheless, crises will re-occur. We must be ready when they do.

Whence organic intellectuals?

This raises profound and timely questions on the relationship between academia and the 'real world'; questions which reach beyond the immediate analysis of this book. At the time of writing, scholars of international studies (broadly conceived) are engaged in examining the transatlantic divide between British and American International Political Economy (Cohen 2007; Higgott and Watson 2008; Phillips 2009; etc.). The obvious, understandable and yet nonetheless ironic fact is that the foremost contributions to 'real-world' politics by political scholars tend to sit within a rationalist/institutionalist paradigm, simply reinforcing elements of the microeconomic transaction-cost approach to policymaking evidenced in Chapters 6 and 7. The dearth of critical engagement should therefore surely be added to causal accounts of the crisis.

Moreover, the glut of scholarship in the aftermath of the crisis demands pause for reflection. Since 2007–09, countless musings on the crisis have been written in top-ranked journals.[2] Yet a cursory glance at their content supports an obvious conclusion: the majority simply emphasize – *inter alia* – that this is a repackaging of neoliberalism and that, with the right regulation, repeat occurrences can be avoided. Doubtless this will be echoed in numerous edited volumes and monographs to come. This is, however, a comment on the discipline itself. For reasons both superficially obvious and yet too complex to do justice to here, the academic profession has come to thrive on quick-fire publications; more significantly, this creates a culture of journalistic sensationalism, chasing the immediate fad, driven by the imperative to 'publish or perish'. Surely Castree is right then to note that 'there is clearly a deep connection between the forces now structuring academic labour in countries like the UK and US and the very possibility – never mind the practical details – of reaching beyond the academy [itself]' (Castree 2002: 104). It would seem that many of the same incentive structures and disciplinary boundaries witnessed in Chapter 7 contribute to neutering academic critique and separating theory from practice. Nonetheless, we must begin by acknowledging that the discipline we shape – whether proactively or passively – in turn reshapes the 'outside world'; this begins with self-reflection in order to establish how our conception of the world remakes it in our own image. As Gramsci (1971: 324) noted, 'The starting point of critical elaboration is the consciousness of what one really is, and is "knowing thyself" as a product of the historical process to date which has deposited in you an infinity of traces, without leaving an inventory'.

Another Gramscianism is possible

The challenge for critical IPE

Finally then, I direct these concerns specifically at historical materialism. As Ian Bruff (2008) noted in his concluding chapter, historical materialist perspectives continue to be marginalized as either dogmatic or economistic within the study of International Political Economy. In one respect this is both ironic and a severe misrecognition. In a seminal 1983 article entitled 'Three Modes of Economism' Richard Ashley questioned the validity of what he called 'taboo terms' like economism. Such terms are typically beyond critical reflection and used to enforce disciplinary boundaries (1983: 464). In his words, 'when taboo terms are used . . . the terms themselves and the relations and practices they connote are typically undefined and suspended beyond the reach of critical analysis' (ibid.). He notes then that,

> As a taboo term . . . 'economism' has to have this vague quality. Since its role is to affirm the domain of 'that which must not be said', the term must exclude questions and arguments from political discourse without saying that which it excludes.
>
> (Ashley 1983)

The irony is that in attempting to maintain certain parameters for the study of the international political economy – however implicit and poorly defined – political science engages in unscientific, political disciplining – 'policing' the field in a manner reminiscent of the American positivist social sciences from which British 'heterodox' approaches have repeatedly sought to depart (see Weber 1994).

More significantly though, Ashley notes (ibid.: 467) that those who label historical materialism 'economistic' do so 'By reading Marx as if he were referring to modes of production as specific economic variables existing independently of social, political, legal and other relations – an interpretation sharply at variance with Marx's own claims'. Upon this (mis)reading, critics suggest that historical materialism attempts to explain political and social life through reference to underlying economic impulsions – taking the economic sphere to be a distinct realm with overwhelming causal powers over political and social aspects. Of course, this kind of autonomistic reductionism misses the very essence of Marx's critique.

Since 1983 however, various straw men of historical materialism have been constructed only to be dismissed. Either historical materialism is written out of the canon of international theory or it is presented as mere economism. On the first reading, Hobson and Lawson (2008: 431), for example, refer to historical materialism within the second wave of Historical Sociology in International Relations, four pages from the end of their summary of theories of history. Here historical materialism is subsumed within a wider framework which renders it just another approach (ibid.: 430–33). On the second reading, more justice is done to the particularities of historical materialism as distinct from other social theories, yet the complexities of Marx's analysis are ignored in favour of allegations of an economic determinism or economism. Perhaps the most obvious example here is Marieke de Goede's (2002: 80) critique of historical materialism as embodying a prediscursive economic materiality. Again – as in Ashley's critique – de Goede assumes that historical materialism reproduces the false distinction between discourses and materiality (Laffey 2004: 460). Given this straw man, Marxist economism is easily dismissed.

It must be said however, that certain Gramscian variants of historical materialism have made themselves a hostage to fortune. Building on Robert Cox's (1981) notion of the triangular relations of ideas, material capabilities and institutions, a series of neo-Gramscian renditions of historical materialism have simply mapped these triangles on to empirical case studies. One obvious problem therein is the overemphasis on contingency embedded within Cox's triangles: changing ideas change institutions, much as changing institutions change ideas, whilst changing material capabilities also change institutions and/or ideas, and changing ideas and/or institutions change material capabilities (Macartney 2008). Everything and nothing is explained (Burnham 2006: 32). Moreover, the inclusion of ideas as bearers of explanatory power immediately encroaches on the stamping ground of social constructivists and post-structuralists who perceive the embedded materialism of these neo-Gramscian perspectives as evidence of economism; on the other hand, the categories of class, capital and labour arouse the attentions of

Marxists who subsequently respond to the prominence of ideas and the under-theorization of formal categories with an alternative taboo term, namely 'pluralist-idealism'. In effect, such neo-Gramscian accounts get hit hard from either side.

This book has therefore sought to build upon a reading of Marxism which highlights the unavoidable role of ideas and discourses through a conception of contested common senses. This has involved jettisoning certain formal categories of neo-Gramscian analysis in favour of a re-reading of Marx and Gramsci – centred on the conjuncture provided by their writings on crises. In so doing it has aimed to walk the fine line between over-contingency and over-determinism through a more nuanced theorization of 'the articulation between accumulation and politics in the world economy' (Drainville 1994: 111). I argue that – from Marx and subsequent non-Gramscian Marxists – we obtain a more abstract understanding of the expansionary impulsions which tend to generate crises, the requirement to shift the burden of crises through devaluation, and the shift to expand finance and credit as means to offset crises in surplus value production. The stillborn mode called neoliberalism derives from this analysis. I argue, however, that these 'tendencies' can be best understood historically – that is, at a more concrete level of analysis – given the fractation of capital and Gramsci's concept of common sense. Here, the historically specific conditions for accumulation and expansion are embedded within common sense frames of reference. Further, the struggles between competing common senses are manifested in conflicting hegemonic projects at the level of the state. Understandably then, crises provide unique conditions for struggles over future paths of development represented in alternative common senses. As this book repeatedly emphasized therefore, the nuanced material–ideological dialectic is fundamental to an understanding of potentialities for counter-hegemonic resistance to neoliberalization.

Returning to the assertion that crises are windows of opportunity, it must be noted that Marxism has done a particularly poor job. Where few – if any – other theories even have the counter-hegemonic potential to offer an alternative, Marxists have tended to devote more time to introspective dialogue than to either outward-focused agency or establishing the conditions – rooted in the burgeoning contradictions under neoliberalism – to predict and prepare for the 2007–09 global crisis (Wolfe 1996: 25, cited in Castree 2002: 103). Too much ink has been spilt determining which avenue to pursue; too little energy devoted to promoting change. Similarly – and with an eye to the future – where neo-Gramscianism perhaps lacks the theoretical apparatus to explain how and why another such crisis will occur, exclusively materialist readings of Marxism lack the pragmatic apparatus to explain the significance of projects embedded in alternative versions of common sense. This is of course, an area for further research.

In conclusion, the impulsions–agency–common sense nexus has one modest aim: to avoid the criticisms of agent-centrism in neo-Gramscianism and the totalizing, seemingly debilitating extremes of a more economic deterministic reading of Marx, suggesting that crises *only* provide *utile* windows if collective agency and alternative common sense are sufficiently mature in their development. The 2007–09 crisis was a missed opportunity; the next time round ought not to be so.

Notes

1 Globalization and financial market integration

1 Bucking Bronco was a child's game which involved loading items on to the back of a horse until the horse inevitably 'bucked'. The analogy is that contemporary neoliberal capitalism pushes the contradictions of a fictitious, finance-led accumulation to the limits until the system finally 'bucks'.
2 In April 2005 the Chairman of the German Social Democratic Party, Franz Müntefering, famously likened private equity firms and foreign investors to locusts sucking out the lifeblood of firms and threatening the livelihoods of employees.
3 As Chapter 4 explains, these ruling classes are connected to state managers through the *power bloc*, operating under the hegemonic leadership of a particular class fraction or coalition thereof.
4 See below for some significant examples.
5 The term 'level playing field' is frequently used as a euphemism for the single market.
6 For a more in-depth study of the details of Lisbon and the FSAP, see Commission (2005): 5; Young (2005): 109.
7 See Figure 1.5.

2 Conceptualizing changing capitalisms and Gramscian historical materialism

1 Significantly, Marx too, took issue with the assumptions of the 'free market' that social provision was a natural product of a fully developed market.
2 This account builds on certain neo-Gramscian concepts whilst incorporating a wider reading of historical materialism. I return in the conclusion to explaining why I jettison a more traditional neo-Gramscian account.
3 Already this claim elucidates the social content of financial market expansion, to which we will return.
4 Of course, 'neoliberal' worldviews contributed to the crisis conditions, though I examine this below.
5 That is, a 'living dead' system.
6 The term 'accumulation regime' has similarities with a particular 'model' of capitalism. It encompasses the particular state form, dominant class configurations alongside their respective accumulation strategies, and the common senses attached to this social formation.
7 This is not to be read in the Althusserian sense of over-determinism, but instead is a critique of an economistic reading of Marx.
8 For the time being, the terms 'finance' and 'productive fractions' will be used to describe different constituents of the overall circuit of capital. As Chapter 3 will argue, these

fractions are best referred to as Atlantic, Gallic and Rhenish fractions, since the distinction between – for example – finance and production is, at best, blurred under neoliberalism.
9 For an excellent critique, see Hay (2001): 203–04.

3 Transnationally oriented fractions of capital

1 Admittedly, this misquotes Vogel who was referring to the uneasy relationship of business and politics.
2 By focusing on national associations however, the chapter begins to tease out the ongoing prevalence of distinct projects within neoliberalization and the further entrenchment of these interests, not just through national channels but in EU processes.
3 Within the Rhenish fraction I include universal banking institutions such as Commerzbank and, because – up until their merger in May 2009 – of its separate status, Dresdner Bank.
4 Again, it must be recalled, however, that credit institutions may well, and in the French case almost certainly do, securitize debt through established regulated markets yet they still (in France) maintain quantitatively different accumulation strategies to those investment banks which characterize the Atlantic fraction and trade, substantially, on their own account.

4 Political agency of transnationally oriented fractions

1 Clearly this is not to suggest that the hegemonic project of one of our fractions is not without internally conflicting interests; competition between capitalists ensures this is not the case. Nonetheless, as the book is arguing, with interests formatively shaped by commonalities in accumulation strategies (scale, function and social configurations) the national–domestic embeddedness of the fractions engenders a degree of internal cohesion.
2 Nonetheless, as with our explanation of the nexus, this does not imply a causal chain which begins with impulsions and ends with state policy, although this may often be the case. Instead there are many examples and instances of discontinuities, ruptures and contradictions creating multi-causal processes of continuity and change both within the state and the wider social formation and political economy. As noted in Chapter 2, for example, the very conditions of state activity both past and present are themselves constituted by sediments of past and present modes of accumulation and common sense in each of the three case studies. Similarly, neoliberalization emerged from particular social formations embedded in particular crystallizations of common sense which in turn engendered new/nascent formations based broadly around the hegemony of transnationally oriented capital. Here Poulantzas' (1978: 129) insight that the relations of power manifested within struggles – for example, over particular common senses – are inscribed into the institutional structure of the state as a material condensation of social processes is useful (see Bruff 2008: 61–63). Similar arguments also apply to the EU.
3 The terms '*liberal* neoliberal', '*social* neoliberal' and '*socio-liberal* neoliberal' are simply analytical devices providing a stylized caricature of the three fractions' projects. In essence, they seek to capture the neoliberal and yet distinctive elements incorporated within variegated neoliberalism.
4 Obviously the rhetoric he employs to describe this crisis aims to depict the crisis as all-pervasive (Hay and Rosamond 2002). This is a component in the production of common sense; everyone is affected and there is only one alternative, says the common sense (see Chapters 5 and 6).

5 It should therefore be apparent that the implicit assumption that the trajectory of EU integration can be derived from the policy outcomes of 'strategic' interactions between its agents (be it states or firms) is simply misguided.
6 See the Lamfalussy diagram (Figure 1.5). See also Quaglia (2007).
7 The methodological decision to focus on national trade associations rather than European ones is a component in the argument that neoliberalization displays national specificities as well as an attempt to examine the national embeddedness of capital often obscured by a focus on 'transnational' forms of class agency (cf. van Apeldoorn 2002).
8 This is a panel which attempts to incorporate relevant market actors in the Lamfalussy Process.
9 Another term for trades executed outside of the regulated market (stock exchange).

5 A contingent neoliberal consensus

1 That is, related to the CRD negotiations.
2 A term used to describe 'gold-plating' or adding to already complex legislation.
3 The traditional distinction here is between US 'prescriptive' and UK 'principles-based' regulation (cf. Moran 1991). Its usage by the Atlantic fraction here reflects their connection to market arrangements in the City of London.
4 This is a reference to the role of market actors and market mechanisms in determining market outcomes.
5 In order to provide an accurate contextualization of neoliberalism in the Rhenish project it is necessary to look beyond policy responses to an analysis of annual reports and similar material.
6 On this, see Geoffrey Underhill (1997), Benn Steil (1995) and Philip Brown (1997).
7 Chapter 8 will explain, however, that immediately following the removal of concentration the Gallic fraction countered by seeking domestic-national protection through price transparency.

6 Organic economists as producers of neoliberal common sense

1 This statistic is produced by Media Tenor (a media research company) (CESifo 2005).
2 The didactic separation of finance and production capital here is merely a stylized reference to firms involved primarily in financial services and those involved primarily in production.
3 On the intellectual–political distinction, see Nelson Polsby (1983).
4 The Groupe d'Economie Mondiale (GEM), itself a faculty of the Sciences-Po, is one such example. What is noteworthy at the outset is that the GEM is linked to both the Service d'Etude de l'Activitè Economique (SEAE) and the AEI-Brookings Joint Centre, meaning that it is essentially a hybrid of a traditional, mainstream French policy unit within the Sciences-Po and a collaboration between the American Enterprise Institute and the Brookings Institution, two leading Washington-based units. For this reason the CEPII is preferred as 'organic' to the Gallic fraction.
5 Since the subject matter of the 2005 Summit is relevant to our problem area the question of whether or not the list of participants is typical of other years is largely secondary.
6 These being Holland, Germany, Spain, Poland, Latvia, Belgium, Ireland, Hungary, Iceland, Sweden, France, the Slovak Republic, Luxembourg, Lithuania, England, Bulgaria, Croatia, Estonia, the USA, Austria, Finland, Canada.
7 This is a relatively unoriginal claim; nonetheless it must be empirically established before the argument can proceed.

8 It is also worth noting that Professors Sinn and Olivier Blanchard (below) were formatively involved in neoliberal reform in Central and Eastern Europe (Shields 2001).
9 Of course, this 'openness' has more to do with dismantling barriers to the accumulation strategy of our fractions that a genuine 'level' and integrated playing field (see Chapter 5).

7 Scientific committees and the Atlantic heartland

1 For an outstanding overview of the significance of 'Atlantic' economists, see Best (2005).
2 These names are significant in the ensuing analysis of scientific councils.
3 This is all the more apparent, given that no definition, at least explicitly emphasized, is apparent within the economics profession.
4 The Hoover Institution, for example, became the home department of Milton Friedman in the late 1970s.
5 'Cette situation reflète certes les aléas de la conjoncture, mais j'ai la conviction qu'elle révèle aussi les limites de notre modèle de croissance' (Camdessus 2004 : 9).
6 Recall, of course, that neoliberalization employs concepts of 'free markets', the 'level playing field' and improved competition as rhetorical devices (see Chapter 6).
7 This seems to confirm the conception of France as a contender state, engaged in later development.

8 De-reifying the transnational capitalist class

1 The term 'bid-offer spread' refers to the difference between the buy (bid) and sell (offer) price of a financial instrument.
2 Similar arguments have also been raised concerning post-trade transparency clauses, as the original draft text stipulated that prices of securities should be declared within a minute following the execution of the trade (Directive 2004/39/EC). Academics have explained the especially devastating effect these clauses would have on London and Frankfurt which specialize in 'order-driven' systems, whereby block trades are 'unwound' over long periods; sometimes up to several days (Steil 1995: 36). Immediate price disclosure threatens this practice.
3 See Chapter 1 for an explanation of Level 1 and Level 2 in the Lamfalussy Process.
4 Defined as 'approved intermediaries who, on an organised, frequent and systematic basis, execute equity orders from their clients in-house (these intermediaries generally hold cash and securities accounts for these clients), by acting as a counterparty, that is by taking the transaction on their own trading position' (Directive 2004/39/EC).
5 Regulated markets (RM) and systematic internalizers (SI).
6 This is obviously also indicative of wider dynamics within the UK and US financial systems, revealed in the aftermath of the 2007–09 financial crisis. The regulation of the entire shadow banking system and special purpose vehicles (SPVs) was arguably lax precisely because of strategic Atlantic demands to UK and US regulators. It emphasizes however, the significance of these particular market systems to the Atlantic fraction.
7 This is, of course, not universally the case but reflects the tendency – under the second phase of neoliberalism – to, purportedly, remove 'important functions from centralized state control and [be] placed in the remit of "objective" institutions, technocrats, or juridical frameworks' (Shields 2008: 460).
8 As van Apeldoorn obviously notes, the single project comprises conflicting, contradictory tendencies not negated here by the term 'coherent'.
9 Essentially, the extent to which the operations of the Rhenish fraction are global or European in scale varies according to the member firm/bank being considered.

9 Conclusions

1 See Bieler and Morton (2004).
2 For example, see the *British Journal of Politics and International Relations* (2009) 11(3); *Journal of Common Market Studies* (2009) 47(0) and 47(3); *Review of International Political Economy* (2009) 16(3).

Bibliography

AFEI (2002) *Annual Report*, <http://www.afei.com/pj/GB/D0000060.pdf> (accessed 1 June 2005).

—— (2003) *Annual Report*, <http://www.afei.com/pj/FR/D0000773.pdf> (accessed 31 May 2005).

—— (2004) *Annual Report*, (personal correspondence with Julie Ansidei, Head of European Affairs, 1 July 2005).

—— (February 2004) *Response of AFEI: Implementing Financial Instruments Markets*, <http://www.cesr-eu.org/> (accessed 4 May 2005).

—— (April 2004) 'Implementing measures for the Financial Markets Instruments Directive', available at <http://www.cesr-eu.org/>.

—— (June 2004) *The role of CESR at 'Level 3' under the Lamfalussy process*, <http://www.cesr-eu.org/> (accessed 4 May 2005).

—— (October 2004) *Implementing Measures for the Markets in Financial Instruments Directive First CESR Mandate: Observations of the French Association of Investment Firms (AFEI) on Best Execution and Market Transparency*, <http://www.cesr-eu.org/> (accessed 5 May 2005).

—— (December 2004) *Implementing Measures for the Directive In Markets In Financial Instruments (MiFiD) First Mandate of CESR: Second Consultation Round Observations of AFEI*, <http://www.cesr-eu.org/> (accessed 5 May 2005).

—— (March 2005) *Memorandum: Application of capital requirements directive to investment firms* (personal correspondence Emmanuel de Fournoux, Director AFEI, 1 July 2005).

Aglietta, M. (1997) 'La crise bancaire en France et dans le monde': *La Lettre du CEPII* No. 155. <http://www.cepii.fr/francgraph/publications/lettre/pdf/1997/ let155.pdf> (accessed 1st May 2006).

Albert, M. (1993) *Capitalism against Capitalism*, London: Whurr.

Allianz Group (2005) *Annual Report*, <http://www.allianz.com/migration/images/pdf/ saobj_1104673_06_03_16_annual_report_allianz_group_2005___englisch.pdf> (accessed 18 January 2007).

Amable, B. (2003) *The Diversity of Modern Capitalism*, Oxford: Oxford University Press.

Amoore, L. (2005) *The Global Resistance Reader*, London: Routledge.

Arrowsmith, (1998) *Thinking the Unthinkable about EMU: Coping with Turbulence Between 1998 and 2002*, London: NIESR.

Ashley, R. (1983) 'Three Modes of Economism', *International Studies Quarterly* 27(4): 463–96.

Baldwin, R. (2004) 'European Economic Integration and Implications for East Asia', presented at a workshop in Seoul, *Economic Cooperation in East Asia*, by KIEP and Korean Customs Service.

—— (2007) *Professor Richard Baldwin homepage.* <http://hei.unige.ch/sections/ec/faculty/profile/baldwin.html> (accessed 8 August 2007).

—— (2009) *homepage* (various links). <http://graduateinstitute.ch/ctei/baldwin_home.html> (accessed 30 March 2009).

Barclays (February 2004) *Barclays Response to CESR's Call for Evidence on the FIMD Mandates.* <http://www.cesr-eu.org/> (accessed 20 April 2005).

—— (December 2004) *Second Consultation Paper on the First Set of Mandates Regarding Possible Implementing Measures for the Market in Financial Instruments Directive*, <http://www.cesr-eu.org/> (accessed 15 April 2005).

Barrell, R. and Choy, A. (2003) *Economic Integration and Openness in Europe and East Asia*, London: NIESR.

Barrell, R. and Pain, N. (1997) 'Foreign direct investment, technological change, and economic growth within Europe', *The Economic Journal*, 107: 1770–86.

Barrell, R., Holland, D. and Pain, N. (2001) 'Openness, integration and transition: prospects and policies for economies in transition', prepared for International Economics Study Group 25th Annual Conference, Isle of Thorns, Sussex, September 2000. *NIESR Discussion Paper*, 177.

Barrell, R., Holland, D. and Pomerantz, O. (2004) 'Integration, accession and expansion.' *NIESR Occasional Paper*, 57.

BBA (January 2002) *Revision of the ISD: Market Structure, Transparency and Liquidity*, <http://www.bba.org.uk/bba/jsp/polopoly.jsp?d=155anda=609> (accessed 3 January 2007).

—— (April 2004) *BBA Response to CESR Consultative Concept Paper on Transaction Reporting*, <http://www.cesr-eu.org/> (accessed 13 April 2005).

—— (July 2004) *BBA response to CESR Call for Evidence re 2nd MIFID Mandate*, <http://www.cesr-eu.org/> (accessed 13 April 2005).

—— (September 2004) *BBA Response to CESR advice on possible implementing measures of the Directive on Markets in Financial Instruments*, <http://www.bba.org.uk/bba/jsp/polopoly.jsp?d=155anda=4483> (accessed 16 March 2005).

—— (October 2004) *Response to CESR advice on possible implementing measures of the Directive on Markets in Financial Instruments (2nd part of response – Best Execution and Transparency)*, <http://www.bba.org.uk/bba/jsp/polopoly. jsp?d=155anda=4535> (accessed 17 March 2005).

—— (January 2005) *Response to CESR advice on possible implementing measures of the Directive on Markets in Financial Instruments (1st Consultation on 2ndSet of Mandates)*, <http://www.bba.org.uk/content/1/c4/50/95/BBA_MIFID_Response_2nd_mandate_%2821_Jan_05%29.pdf> (accessed 15 March 2005).

BBA and LIBA (December 2002) *Commentary on QIS 3 Technical Guidance*, <http://www.liba.org.uk/issues/2003%20papers/QI3%20Response.PDF> (accessed 16 February 2005).

—— (June 2003a) *A Response to Consultation Paper 155*, <http://www.liba.org.uk/issues/2003%20papers/Tier%201%20Capital.PDF> (accessed 15 February 2005).

—— (June 2003b) *Response to CP 136: Individual Capital Adequacy Standards*, <http://www.liba.org.uk/issues/2003%20papers/Individual%20Capital%20Adequacy%20Standards.PDF> (accessed 14 February 2005).

—— (December 2003) 'CP 189: Implementation of new Basel and EU Capital Adequacy Standards', <http://www.jmlsg.org.uk/bba/jsp/polopoly.jsp?d=155anda=1566> (accessed 17 February 2005).

BdB (2002) *Annual Report*, <http://www.bankenbericht.de/banken2002 /pdf/SUMMARY. pdf> (accessed 22 August 2005).

—— (2004) *Banking Survey*, <http://www.bankenbericht.de/pdf/Bb_2004_%20en.pdf> (accessed 19 August 2005).

—— (January 2004) *Response of the Association of German Banks to the CESR Call for Evidence in connection with the future Financial Instruments Markets Directive (FIMD)*, <http://www.cesr-eu.org/> (accessed 2 August 2005).

—— (March 2004) *Continuing the Integration of European Markets for Financial Services*, <http://www.bankenverband.de/download/ broschueren/br0403_vw_azf_eudl_en.pdf> (accessed 18 August 2005).

—— (June 2005) *Towards More Growth With the Lisbon Strategy*, <http://www. bankenverband.de/pic/artikelpic/062005/vo0506_pr_lisbon-english-summary.pdf> (accessed 18 August 2005).

Beise, M. and Stahl, H. (1999) 'Public research and industrial innovations in Germany', Research Policy 28(4): 397–422.

Best, J. (2005) *The Limits of Transparency: Ambiguity and the History of International Finance*, Ithaca, NY: Cornell University Press.

Bieler, A. (2000) *Globalisation and Enlargement of the European Union: Austria and Swedish social forces in the struggle over membership*, London: Routledge.

—— (2002) 'The struggle over EU enlargement: a historical materialist analysis of European integration', *Journal of European Public Policy* 9(4): 575–97.

—— (2006) *The Struggle for a Social Europe: Trade unions and EMU in times of global restructuring*, Manchester: Manchester University Press.

Bieler, A. and Morton, A.D. (eds) (2001a) *Social Forces in the Making of the New Europe*, London: Palgrave.

—— (2001b) 'Introduction: Neo-Gramscian perspectives in international political economy and the relevance to European integration', in Bieler, A. and Morton, A.D. (eds) *Social Forces in the Making of the New Europe*, London: Palgrave, pp. 3–24.

—— (2003) 'Globalisation, the state and class struggle: a "Critical Economy" engagement with Open Marxism', *British Journal of Politics and International Relations* 5(4): 467–99.

—— (2004) 'Another Europe is possible'? Labour and social movements at the European Social Forum. *Globalizations* 1(2): 305–27.

—— (2006) 'A critical theory route to hegemony, world order and historical change: neo-Gramscian perspectives in international relations', in Bieler, A., Bonefeld, W., Burnham, P. and Morton, A.D (2006) *Globalization, the State and Class Struggle*. Basingstoke: Palgrave, pp. 9–27.

—— (2008) 'The deficits of discourse in IPE: turning base metal into gold?', *International Studies Quarterly* 52(1): 103–28.

Blanchard, O. (2006) Personal correspondence with Olivier Blanchard (Director Scientific Committee CEPII).

—— (2007) *Olivier Blanchard Homepage*, <http://econ-www.mit.edu/faculty/index. htm?prof_id=blancharand type=shortbio>

Blyth, M. (2002) *Great Transformations: Economic ideas and institutional change in the twentieth century*, Cambridge: Cambridge University Press.

—— (2001) 'The transformation of the Swedish model: economic ideas, distributional conflict, and institutional change', *World Politics* 54(1): 1–26.

—— (2003) 'Same as it never was: temporality and typology in the Varieties of Capitalism,' *Comparative European Politics* 1: 215–25.

—— (2007) 'Powering, puzzling, or persuading? The mechanisms of building institutional orders', *International Studies Quarterly* 51(4): 761–77.

Blyth, M., Seabrooke, L. and Widmaier, W. (2007) 'Exogenous shocks or endogenous constructions? The meanings of wars and crises', *International Studies Quarterly*, 51(4): 747–59.

BNP Paribas (2005) *Annual Report* (various links), <http://invest.bnpparibas.com/en/financial-reports/documents/annual-report–2005-PART1.pdf> (accessed 16 January 2007).

Bonefeld, W. (1996) 'Monetarism and Crisis', in Bonefeld, W. and Holloway, J. (eds) *Global Capital, National State and the Politics of Money*, Basingstoke: Macmillan, pp. 35–68.

—— (2006) 'Social constitution and critical economy', in Bieler, A., Bonefeld, W., Burnham, P. and Morton, A.D., *Globalization, the State and Class Struggle*, Basingstoke: Palgrave, 176–86.

Bosanquet, N. (1982) *After the New Right*, London: Heinemann.

Bouwen, P. (2002) 'Corporate lobbying in the European Union: the logic of access', *Journal of European Public Policy* 9(3): 365–90.

Brenner, N. (1998) 'Between fixity and motion: accumulation, territorial organization and the historical geography of spatial scales', *Environment and Planning D: Society and Space* 16(4): 459–81.

—— (1999a) 'Beyond state-centrism? Space, territoriality, and geographical scale in globalization studies', *Theory and Society* 28(1): 39–78.

—— (1999b) 'Globalisation as Reterritorialisation: the re-scaling of urban governance in the European Union', *Urban Studies* 36(3): 431–51.

Brown, P. (1997) 'The making of the European Financial Area: Global market integration and the EU Single Market for financial services,' in Underhill, G. (ed.) *The New World Order in International Finance*, Basingstoke: Macmillan, pp. 124–43.

Bruff, I. (2008) *Culture and Consensus in European Varieties of Capitalism: A 'common sense' analysis*, Basingstoke: Palgrave.

Burnham, P. (1991) 'Neo-Gramscian hegemony and the international order', *Capital and Class* 45: 73–93.

—— (1994) 'Open Marxism and vulgar political economy', *Review of International Political Economy* 1(2): 221–31.

—— (1995) 'State and market in international political economy: towards a Marxian alternative', *Studies in Marxism* 2: 135–59.

—— (2001) 'New Labour and the politics of depoliticisation', *British Journal of Politics and International Relations* 3(2): 127–49.

—— (2006) 'Neo-Gramscian hegemony and the international order', in Bieler, A., Bonefeld, W., Burnham, P. and Morton A.D. (eds) *Globalization, the State and Class Struggle*, Basingstoke: Palgrave, pp. 28–44.

BVI (April 2005) *CESR's Draft Technical Advice on Possible Implementing Measures of the Directive 2004/39/EC on Markets in Financial Instruments (aspects of the definition of investment advice and of the general obligation to act fairly, honestly and professionally in the best interests of clients; best execution; market transparency) – Second Consultation Paper (Ref.: CESR/05–164)*, <http://www.cesr-eu.org/> (accessed 18 August 2005).

BVR (January 2005) *Consultation on CESR's Draft Technical Advice on Possible Implementing Measures of the Directive 2004/ 39/ EC on Markets in Financial Instruments, 2nd Set of Mandates – Ref.: CESR 04/ 562 October 2004 here: Response to Section III Markets*, <http://www.cesr-eu.org/> (accessed 2 August 2005).

Camdessus, M. (2004) *Rapport Camdessus : Le sursaut vers une nouvelle croissance pour la France*, <http://lesrapports.ladocumentationfrancaise.fr/BRP /044000498 /0000.pdf> (accessed 21 April 2006).

Casey, J.P. and Lanoo, K. (2006) 'The MiFID Implementing Measures : Excessive detail or level playing field?', *ECMI Policy Brief*, 1: 1–8.

Castree, N. (2002) 'Border Geography', *Area* 34(1): 103–12.

—— (2005) 'The epistemology of particulars: Human geography, case studies and "context" (Editorial),' *Geoforum* 36: 541–44.

Cecchini, P. (1988) *The European Challenge: 1992*. London: Wildwood House.

CEPII (2007) *CEPII website*. <www.cepii.org> (accessed 1 June 2008).

Cerny, P. (1989) 'The "Little Big Bang" in Paris: Financial Market Regulation in a Dirigiste System,' *European Journal of Political Research* 17: 169–192.

—— (1994) 'The dynamics of financial globalization: Technology, market structure, and policy response,' *Policy Sciences* 27(4): 319–342.

—— (2000) 'Political globalization and the competition state', in Richard Stubbs and Geoffrey Underhill (eds) *Political Economy and the Changing Global Order*, Second edition, Oxford: Oxford University Press, pp. 300–07.

CESifo (2005) *Annual Report* (pdf), (accessed 4 July 2006).

—— (2007) *CESIfo website*. <http://www.cesifo-group.de/portal/page?_pageid=36,34586 and dad=portaland_schema= PORTAL> (accessed 7 June 2006).

CESR (June 2003) *Public Statement of the Third Meeting of the Market Participants Consultative Panel*. <http://www.cesr-eu.org/> (accessed 14 April 2005).

Chwieroth, J. (2007) 'Neoliberal economists and capital account liberalization in emerging markets', *International Organization* 61(2): 443–63.

Citibank (2007) *Citibank website* (various links). <http://www.citibank.co.uk/personal /banking/info/aboutcitibank/index.htm>; <http://www.citibank.co.uk/personal/banking/ info/aboutcitibank/background.htm> (accessed 12 January 2007).

Citigroup (2003) *Response to CP 189*, (personal correspondence with Mr Simon Hills, BBA, Director).

Clarke, S. (1988) *Keynesianism, Monetarism and the Crisis of the State*, Aldershot: Edward Elgar.

—— (1993) *Marx's Theory of Crisis*. London: St Martin's Press.

—— (2001) 'The globalisation of capital, crisis and class struggle', *Capital and Class* 75: 93–101

Clift, B. (2004) 'The French model of capitalism: still exceptional?,' in Perrino, J. and Clift, B. (eds) *Where Are National Capitalisms Now?* London: Palgrave, pp. 91–110.

Coates, D. (2000) *Models of Capitalism: Growth and stagnation in the modern era*, London: Polity Press.

Coen, D. (1997) 'The evolution of the large firm as a political actor in the European Union', *Journal of European Public Policy* 4(1): 91–108.

—— (1998) 'The European business interest and the nation state: large-firm lobbying in the European Union and member states', *Journal of Public Policy* 18(1): 75–100.

—— (2007) Empirical and theoretical studies in EU lobbying', *Journal of European Public Policy* 14(3): 333–45.

Cohen, E. (1995) 'France: national champions in search of a mission', in Hayward, J. (ed.), *Industrial Enterprise and European Integration: From national to international champions in Western Europe*. Oxford: Oxford University Press.

Cohen, B. (2007) 'The Transatlantic Divide: why are American and British IPE so different?', *Review of International Political Economy* 14(2): 197–219.

Coleman, W.D. and Perl, A. (1999) 'Internationalized policy environments and policy network analysis', *Political Studies* 47(4): 691–709.

Commerzbank (2005) *Annual Report*. <https://www.commerzbank.com/aktionaere/service/archive/konzern/2005/gb2005/download/commerz_gb_e_2005.pdf> (accessed 18 January 2007).

—— (2007) Commerzbank website (various links) https://www.commerzbank.com/konzern/geschichte/download/cb_history.pdf (accessed 18 January 2007).

Commission Bancaire (CB) (2004) www.banque-france.fr/gb/supervi/telechar/presracb04.pdf (accessed 20 August 2006).

Commission of European Communities (1988) *The European Challenge 1992* (Cecchini Report), Brussels: EC Commission.

—— (1997) *Single Market Review Subseries 3: Dismantling of Barriers, Volume 5: Capital Market Liberalization*, London: Kogan Page.

—— (1999) *Implementing the Framework for Financial Markets: Action plan* (Com(1999)232). <http://europa.eu/ scadplus/leg/en/lvb/l24210.htm> (accessed 5 October 2006).

—— (2001) *The Final Report of the Committee of Wise Men* (Lamfalussy Report). Brussels: Commission.

—— (2005) *FSAP Evaluation – Part I: Process and Implementation* (October). Brussels. <http://ec.europa.eu/internal_market/finances/docs/actionplan/index/051028_fsap_evaluation_part_i_en.pdf> (accessed 21 April 2008).

Council (2000) *Regulation of European Securities Markets – Terms of Reference for the Committee of Wise Men* (July 17), Brussels. <http://ec.europa.eu/internal_market/securities/docs/lamfalussy/wisemen/mandate_en.pdf> (accessed 23 March 2007).

Cox, R. (1981) 'Social forces, states and world orders: beyond international relations theory', *Millennium: Journal of International Studies* 10(2): 126–55.

Crédit Agricole (2005) *Annual Report* (various links) <http://www.credit-agricole-sa.fr/ca_clean/medias_casa/documents/ra2005uk/index.htm> (accessed 17 January 2007).

Credit Suisse (2005) *Annual Report* <http://www.credit-suisse.com/investors /doc/csg_ar_2005_en.pdf> (accessed 12 January 2007).

Crouch, C (2009) 'Privatized Keynesianism: an unacknowledged policy regime', *British Journal of Politics and International Relations* 11(3): 382–99.

Crouch, C. and Streeck, W. (eds) (1997) *Political Economy of Modern Capitalism: Mapping convergence and diversity*. London: Sage.

Crozet, M. and Trionfetti, F. (2002) 'Effets-frontières entre les pays de l'union Européenne: le poids des politiques d'achats publics,' *Économie internationale* 89–90: 189–208. <http://www.cepii.fr/francgraph/publications/ecointern /rev8990/rev8990crozet.pdf> (accessed 8 February 2006).

Deardorff, A.V. (2004) 'Who makes the rules of globalization?', *Venice Summer Institute 2004 Workshop on 'Dissecting Globalization'* 21–22 July 2004 Venice International University, San Servolo. <http://www.cesifo-group.de/pls/portal/docs/PAGE/IFOCONTENT/BISHERIGESEITEN/CESIFO_INHALTE/EVENTS/SUMMER_INSTITUTE/VENICE_2004/WHALLEY_PAPERS/VSI04-DEARDORFF.PDF> (accessed 3 July 2006).

De Boissieu, C. and Pisani-Ferry, J. (1995) 'The political economy of French economic policy and the transition to EMU,' *Working Paper CEPII* 95(09): 1–44. <http://www.cepii.fr/anglaisgraph/workpap/pdf/1995/wp95–09.pdf (accessed 9 February 2006).

De Goede, M. (2002) 'Beyond economism in international political economy', *Review of International Studies* 29(1): 79–97.

Deeg, R. (1999) *Finance Capitalism Unveiled: Banks and the German political economy.* Michigan: University of Michigan.

—— (2005) 'The comeback of Modell Deutschland? The New German Political Economy in the EU', *German Politics* 14(3): 332–53.

Denham, A. and Garnett, M. (1998) 'Think tanks, British politics and the "climate of opinion", in Stone, D., Denham, A. and Garnett, M. (eds) *Think Tanks Across Nations: A comparative approach*, Manchester: Manchester University Press, pp. 21–41.

—— (2004) 'A "hollowed out" tradition? British think tanks in the twenty-first century', in Stone, D. and Denham, A. (eds) *Think Tank Traditions: Policy research and the politics of ideas*, Manchester: Manchester University Press, pp. 232–46.

Deutsche Bank (2004) *Annual Report.* <http://annualreport.deutsche-bank.com/2004/ar/deutschebankgroup/groupexecutivecommittee.php> (accessed 1 September 2005).

—— (2005) 'Which supervisory tools for the EU securities markets?', (Himalaya report) *Response by Deutsche Bank to CESR report Ref. CESR / 04–333f*, (3rd February). <http://www.cesr-eu.org/> (accessed 17 August 2005).

Dexia (2005) *Annual Report* <http://www.dexia.com/docs/2006/20060510_AG/VoletA_UK/20060510_VoletA_UK.pdf> (accessed 17 January 2007).

Drainville, A. (1994) 'International political economy in the age of open Marxism', *Review of International Political Economy* 1(1): 105–31.

Duménil, G. and Lévy, D. (2001) 'Costs and benefits of neoliberalism: a class analysis', *Review of International Political Economy* 8(4): 578–607.

Dunn, J. and Perl, A. (1994) 'Policy networks and industrial revitalization: high speed rail initiatives in France and Germany', *Journal of Public Policy* 14(3): 311–43.

Dyson, K. (2002) 'Germany and the Euro: Redefining EMU, handling paradox, and managing uncertainty and contingency', in Dyson, K. (ed.) *European States and the Euro: Europeanization, variation, and convergence.* Oxford: Oxford University Press, pp. 173–211.

—— (2008) 'Germany: a crisis of leadership in the Euro area', in Dyson, K. (ed.) *The Euro at Ten: Europeanization, Power, and Convergence*, Oxford: Oxford University Press, pp. 132–64.

DZ Bank (2004) *Annual Report.* <http://www.dzbank.de/internet_en/index.jsp;jsessionid=0000KHsgedFycx-bDdZ_wyIcroK:10mv51hct?fname=index.htmlandpath=%2Fprofile%2Fdzbank%2Finvestor_relations_englandrname=internet_en_profileandflagSite=falseandmEE=profileandmZE=dzbankandmDE=investor_relations_englandm4E=andm5E=andm6E=andflagNav=trueandisExternal=trueanddownload=%2Finternet_gr%2F_profil%2F_downloads%2Fannual_report_2004.pdf> (accessed 14 September 2005).

ECB (2009) *Monthly Bulletin* (August). <http://www.ecb.int/pub/pdf/mobu/mb200908 en.pdf> (accessed 10 September 2009).

Economist, The (1998) *London Under Threat*, November 21 1998, p. 72.

EFN (2004) *Autumn Report.* <http://www.efn.uni-bocconi.it/EFN%20AUTUMN %202004.pdf> (accessed 16 September 2005).

—— (2007) EFN website, www.efn.uni-bocconi.it/ (accessed 8 August 2007).

Eichel, H. (2004) *Statement by the Federal Minister of Finance Hans Eichel on 'Agenda 2010 – Structural reforms for more growth' at the conference 'Advancing Enterprise – Britain in a Global Economy*' in London. <http://www.bundesfinanzministerium. de/cln_03/nn_12996/EN/News/Speeches/1000173.html> (accessed 1 September 2005).

—— (2005) Federal Minister of Finance Hans Eichel, on occasion of the Euromoney German Capital Markets Forum 28 May in Berlin http://www.bundesfinanz ministerium.de/cln_04/nn_18760/EN/News/Speeches/003.html (accessed 31 August 2005).

Engels, F. (1978 [1884]) *The Origin of the Family, Private Property and the State*, Peking: Foreign Language Press.

Esping-Andersen, G. (1999) *Social Foundations of Postindustrial Societies*, Oxford: Oxford University Press.

FBF (2002a) *Assemblee Generale* <http://www.fbf.fr/web/internet/content_fbf.nsf/ (WebPageList)/FBF+an+I/$File/FBFan1.pdf (accessed 28 April 2005).

—— (2002b) *Management Report* <http://www.fbf.fr/Web/Internet/content_europe.nsf/ PictureList/Chap1+Europe++Mgmt+report/$file/fbf_chap1_europe.pdf> (accessed 28 April 2005).

—— (2003) *Five Principles for a Unified European Banking and Financial Services Market: Conclusions by French bankers* <http://www.fbf.fr/Web/internet/content_ europe.nsf/(WebPageList)/5+principles+for+a+unified+european+banking+and+financi al+services+market++conclusions+by+French+bankers/$File/Five+principles.pdf> (accessed 25 April 2005).

—— (April 2003) *La future directive européenne sur l'adéquation des fonds propres* <http://www.fbf.fr/web/internet/content_presse.nsf/(WebPageList)/992F51B03AAB8C 4DC1256D9100507E8E> (accessed 26th April 2005).

—— (June 2003) *French bankers rally in Brussels and propose five principles for a unified European banking and financial services market* <http://www.fbf.fr/Web/internet/ content_europe.nsf/(WebPageList)/French+bankers+rally+in+Brussels+and+propose+ five+principles+for+a+unified+European+banking+and+financial+services+market? Open> (accessed 29 April 2005).

—— (October 2003*) Press release – Solvency ratio: Basel II and the European Directive must be consistent* <http://www.fbf.fr/web/internet/content_europe.nsf/(WebPageList)/ 71F88DB9D2891B80C1256DCC004A90C3> (accessed 25 April 2005).

—— (2004) *Annual Report.* <http://www.fbf.fr/web/internet/content_fbf.nsf/ (WebPageList)/Rapport+d+activite/$File/RAPPORT-ACTIVITE_FBF_2004.pdf> (accessed 29 April 2005).

Fieschi, C. and Gaffney, J. (1998) 'French think tanks in comparative perspective', in Stone, D., Denham, A. and Garnett, M. (eds) *Think Tanks Across Nations: A comparative approach*, Manchester: Manchester University Press, pp. 42–58.

—— (2004) 'French think tanks in comparative perspective', in Stone, D. and Denham, A. (eds) *Think Tank Traditions: Policy research and the politics of ideas*, Manchester: Manchester University Press, pp. 105–20.

Financial Times (FT) (23 October 2008), '*The big myth of taxpayer cost*' <http://www.ft.com/cms/s/a0595798-a131–11dd–82fd–000077b07658,Authorised= false.html?_i_location=http%3A%2F%2Fwww.ft.com%2Fcms%2Fs%2F0%2Fa05957 98-a131–11dd–82fd–000077b07658.htmland_i_referer=http%3A%2F%2F www.ft.com%2Fcomment%2Fcolumnists%2Fsamuelbrittan> (accessed 11 November 2008).

Fine, B. and Milonakis, D. (2009) *From Economics Imperialism to Freakonomics: The shifting boundaries between economics and other social sciences*, London: Routledge.

Fontagné, L. (2006) *Personal Correspondence with Lionel Fontagne* (Director CEPII).

Fouquin, M. (2006) *Personal correspondence with Michel Fouquin* (Director CEPII).

Fouquin, M. and Gaulier, G. (1999) 'Ouverture, concurrence et multilateralisme', *La Lettre du CEPII*. No. 184.

Froud, J., Johal, S., Haslam, C. and Williams, K. (2001) 'Accumulation under conditions of inequality', *Review of International Political Economy* 8(1): 66–95.

FSA (June 2000) *Minutes of the 7th Meeting.* <http://www.fsa.gov.uk/pubs/international/meeting7.pdf> (accessed 7 March 2005).

—— (September 2000) *Minutes of the 8th meeting of the advisory group on the review of the capital adequacy framework* (28 September 2000). <http://www.fsa.gov.uk/pubs/international/meeting8.pdf> (accessed 7 March 2005).

—— (January 2001) *Minutes of the 10th Meeting of the Advisory Group on the Review of the Capital Adequacy Framework*, (30 January 2001). <http://www.fsa.gov.uk/pubs/international/meeting10.pdf> (accessed 8 March 2005)

—— (2002) *Financial Services Authority – Individual Capital Adequacy Standards – Feedback on CP 136*. <http://www.fsa.gov.uk/pubs/policy/ps136.pdf> (accessed 16 February 2005).

—— (December 2004*) Minutes of the meeting of the Basel2/CRD implementation Advisory Group.* <http://www.fsa.gov.uk/ pubs/international/basel_minutes3.pdf> (accessed 7 March 2005).

Gallas, A. (2009) 'Offensive completed: a neo-Poulantzasian analysis of the Thatcherite era, 1977–1999. Unpublished PhD thesis, Lancaster University.

Gamble, A. (2001) 'Neo-liberalism', *Capital and Class* 75: 127–34.

Garrett, G. (1998) *Partisan Politics in the Global Economy*, New York: Cambridge University Press.

Gellner, W. (1998) 'Think tanks in Germany', in Stone, D., Denham, A. and Garnett, M. (eds) *Think Tanks Across Nations: A comparative approach*, Manchester: Manchester University Press, pp. 82–106.

Gill, Stephen (1995) Globalisation, market civilisation, and disciplinary neoliberalism, *Millennium – Journal of International Studies* 24(3): 399–423.

Gramsci, A. (1971) *Selections from the Prison Notebooks of Antonio Gramsci*, translated and edited by Hoare, Q. and Nowell-Smith, G., London: Lawrence & Wishart.

—— (1985) *Selections from Cultural Writings*, edited by Forgacs, D. and Nowell-Smith, G., translated by Boelhower, W., London: Lawrence & Wishart.

—— (1995) *Further Selections from the Prison Notebooks*, translated and edited by Boothman, D., London: Lawrence & Wishart.

—— (1996) *Prison Notebooks. Vol. II*, translated and edited by Buttigieg, J.A., New York: Columbia University Press.

Grande, E. (1996) 'The state and interest groups in a framework of multi-level decision-making: the case of the European Union', *Journal of European Public Policy* 3(3): 318–38.

Grisham, G. (2005) Personal correspondence, 15 February, with Gill Grisham, Secretary, NIESR (London).

Guardian (1 November 2008), 'Lenders rushing to seek repossessions' <http://www.guardian.co.uk/money/2008/nov/01/repossessions-mortgages-credit-recession-crunch> (accessed 11 November 2008).

Haas, E.B. (1991) *When Knowledge is Power*, Berkeley: University of California Press.

Hall, S. (1988) *The Hard Road to Renewal: Thatcherism and the crisis of the Left*. London: Verso.

—— (1991) 'Gramsci and us', in: Simon, R. (ed.) *Gramsci's Political Thought: An Introduction*, revised edition, London: Lawrence & Wishart, pp. 114–30.

Hall, P. and Soskice D. (eds) (2001) *Varieties of Capitalism: The institutional foundations of comparative advantage*, Oxford: Oxford University Press.

Harvey, D. (1982) *The Limits to Capital*. Oxford: Basil Blackwell.

—— (1985) 'The geopolitics of capitalism', in Gregory, D. and Urry, J. (eds) *Social Relations and Spatial Structures*. New York: St. Martins Press, pp. 128–63.

—— (2006 [1982]) *The Limits to Capital*, London: Verso.

—— (2007) *A Brief History of Neoliberalism*, Oxford: Oxford University Press.

Hausman, D. (1992) *The Inexact and Separate Science of Economics*, Cambridge: Cambridge University Press.

Hay, C. (1999) 'What place for ideas in the structure-agency debate: Globalisation as a "Process without a subject" ', paper delivered at annual conference for the British International Studies Association, University of Manchester, 20–22 December.

—— (2001) 'The "crisis" of Keynesianism and the rise of neoliberalism in Britain', in Campbell, J.L. and Pedersen, O.K. (eds) *The Rise of Neoliberalism and Institutional Analysis*. Princeton, NJ: Princeton University Press, pp. 193–218.

—— (2002) *Political Analysis*, Basingstoke: Palgrave.

Hay, C. and Marsh, D. (2000) 'Introduction: demystifying globalization', in Colin Hay and David Marsh (eds) *Demystifying Globalization*, Basingstoke: Macmillan, pp. 1–20.

Hay, C. and Rosamond, B. (2002) 'Globalization, European integration and the discursive construction of economic imperatives,' *Journal of European Public Policy* 9 (2): pp. 147–67.

Hay, C. and Watson, M. (2003) 'The discourse of globalisation and the logic of no alternative: rendering the contingent necessary in the political economy of New Labour', *Policy and Politics*, 31 (3): 289–305.

Heritier, A. (1996) 'The accommodation of diversity in European policy-making and its outcomes: regulatory policy as a patchwork', *Journal of European Public Policy* 3(2): 149–67.

Hickel, R. (1975) 'Kapitalfraktionen: Thesen zur Analyse der herrschenden Klasse', *Kursbuch* 42.

Higgott, R. and Watson, M. (2008) 'All at sea in a barbed wire canoe', *Review of International Political Economy* 15(1): 1–17.

Hobson, J. and Seabrooke, L. (2006) *Everyday Politics of the World Economy*, Cambridge: Cambridge University Press.

Hobson, J. and Lawson, G. (2008) 'What is history in International Relations?', *Millennium* 37(2): 415–35.

Hodges and Woolcock (1993) 'Atlantic capitalism versus Rhine capitalism', *West European Politics* 16(3): 329–44.

Holloway, J. (1992) 'Crisis, fetishism, class decomposition', in Bonefeld, W., Gunn, R. and Psychopedis, K. (eds) *Open Marxism, Vol 1: History and Dialectics; Vol 2: Theory and Practice*. London: Pluto Press.

—— (1996) 'The abyss opens: the rise and fall of Keynesianism', in Bonefeld, W. and Holloway, J. (eds) *Global Capital, National State and the Politics of Money*, Basingstoke: Macmillan, pp. 7–34.

HVB (2004) *Annual Report* <http://www.hvbgroup.com/-snm–0134963952–1126663331–0000009459–0000000510–1126694385-enm-system/galleries/download/en/ir/Reports/2005–03–17_gb_2004_konzern.pdf> (accessed 14 September 2005).

IFD (June 2004) *The future of European financial market integration.* <http://www.finanzstandort.de/download/IFD_June_2004_European_Financial_market_en.pdf> (accessed 30 August 2005).

—— (2005) *Report on Finanzstandort Deutschland No. 1.* <http://www.finanzstandort.de/download/IFD_Finanzstandort_Bericht_Nr–1_Teil–1_en.pdf> (accessed 30th August 2005).

Interview AFEI (2006) with Julie Ansidei, Head of European Affairs, 7 September 2006, Paris.

Interview BdB (2006) with anonymous Senior Official, 13 September 2006, Berlin.

Interview CEPII (2006) with Professor Michel Fouquin, Director, 8 September 2006, Paris.

Interview CESifo (2006) with Professor Ray Rees, Director, 15 September 2006.

Interview Deutsche Bank (2006) with Dr Bernhard Speyer, Head of Deutsche Research, 12 September 2006, Frankfurt.

Jessop, B. (1997) 'A neo-Gramscian approach to the regulation of urban regimes', in Lauria, M. (ed.) *Reconstructing Urban Regime Theory*, London: Sage, pp. 51–73.

Jones, (1998) *Sixty Years of Economic Research: A brief history of the National Institute of Economic and Social Research 1938–98*, NIESR.

Josselin, D. (1996) 'Domestic policy networks and European negotiations: evidence from British and French financial services', *Journal of European Public Policy* 3(3): 297–317.

JPMorgan Chase (2007) JPMorgan Chase website (various links). <http://www.jpmorganchase.com/cm/cs?pagename=Chase/Hrefandurlname=jpmc/about>; <http://www.jpmorganchase.com/cm/cs?pagename=Chase/Hrefandurlname=jpmc/about/history> (accessed 12 January 2007).

Kapstein, E. (1992) *Governing the Global Economy: International finance and the state.* Cambridge, MA: Harvard University Press.

Kellawan, K. (2006) (9 January) Personal correspondence with Keira Kellawan (secretary NIESR).

Keynes, J.M. (1933) 'National self-sufficiency', *Yale Review* 22: 755–69.

Kitschelt, H., Lange, P., Marks, G. and Stephens, J.D. (1999) *Continuity and Change in Contemporary Capitalism*, Cambridge: Cambridge University Press.

Koch-Weser (2005) 'Financial sector as an engine for growth and employment', speech by the State Secretary as part of the Parliamentary Evening on the Initiative Finanzstandort Deutschland (IFD) in Brüssels. <http://www.bundesfinanzministerium.de/cln_04/nn_6512/sid_DA97B6429F6E01CD4AF8E77642DF30F9/nsc_true/EN/News/Speeches/002.html> (accessed 29 August 2005).

Krasner, S. (1996) 'The accomplishments of international political economy,' in Smith, S., Booth, K. and Zalewski, M. (eds) *International Theory: Positivism and beyond*, Cambridge: Cambridge University Press, pp. 108–27.

Lacher, H. (2003) 'Putting the state in its place: the critique of state-centrism and its limits', *Review of International Studies* 29(4): 521–41.

Laffey, M. (2004) 'The red herring of economism', *Review of International Studies* 30(3): 459–68.

Lamfalussy (2001) *Committee of Wise Men on the Regulation of European Securities Markets (Lamfalussy), Final Report* (February 15), Brussels: Commission of the European Communities. <http://ec.europa.eu/internal_market/securities/docs/lamfalussy/ wisemen/final-report-wise-men_en.pdf>.

Leeson, R. (2000) *The Eclipse of Keynesianism: The political economy of the Chicago counter-revolution*. Basingstoke: Palgrave.

Lefebvre, H. (1978) *The Survival of Capitalism: Reproduction of the relations of production*. London: Allison & Busby.

Levitt, M. (2002) 'British Business and the Euro: EMU and the financial sectors', speech by Malcolm Levitt (Senior European Advisor, Price Waterhouse Coopers) <http://www.niesr.ac.uk/event/6feb02/6feb02.htm> (accessed 18 November 2005).

LIBA (December 2004) *Joint Response to CESR's November 2004 consultation on Draft Technical Advice on Possible Implementing Measures of the Directive 2004/39/EC on Markets in Financial Instruments* (MIFID, 1st Set of Mandates, 2nd consultation). <http://www.cesr-eu.org/> (accessed 8 April 2005).

LIBA *et al.* (March 2004) *Comments on CESR's call for evidence on the European Commission's draft mandates for implementing legislation under the Financial Instruments Markets Directive* (FIMD). <http://www.cesr-eu.org/> (accessed 13 April 2005).

—— (October 2004) *Second part of Response to CESR's June 2004 consultation paper (CESR/04–261b) on advice on possible implementing measures of the Directive 2004/39/EC on Markets in Financial Instruments ('MIFID')*. <http://www.cesr-eu.org/> (accessed 8 April 2005).

—— (April 2005) *Joint Response to CESR's March 2005 consultation on Draft Technical Advice on Possible Implementing Measures of the Directive 2004/39/EC on Markets in Financial Instruments (MIFID): Investment advice, best execution, market transparency, Second consultation paper*. <http://www.cesr-eu.org/> (accessed 6 April 2005).

Loayza, N. and Ranciere, R. (2002) 'Financial development, financial fragility and growth,' *CESifo Working Paper* No. 684(5) <http://www.cesifo-group.de/pls/guestci/download/ CESifo%20Working%20Papers%202002/CESifo%20Working%20Papers%20March% 202002/cesifo_wp684.pdf> (accessed 3 July 2006).

Lütz, S. (1998) 'The Revival of the Nation State? Stock exchange regulation in an era of globalized financial markets', *Journal of European Public Policy* 5(1):153–68.

—— (2000) 'From managed to market capitalism? German finance in transition', *German Politics* 9(2): 149–70.

Macartney, H. (2008) 'Articulating particularistic interests: the organic organisers of hegemony', *British Journal of Politics and International Relations* 10(3): 429–51.

—— (2009a) 'Variegated Neo-liberalism: transnationally oriented fractions of capital in EU financial market integration', *Review of International Studies* 35(2): 451–80.

—— (2009b) 'Disagreeing to agree: financial crisis management within the logic of no alternative', *Politics* 29(2): 111–20.

Macartney, H. and Moran, M. (2008) 'Banking supervision and financial market regulation under EMU', in Dyson, Kenneth (ed.) *The Euro at Ten: Europeanization, power and convergence* (2nd Edition), Oxford: Oxford University Press, pp. 325–40.

Marcussen, M. (2008) The Lisbon Process and economic reform: learning by benchmarking?, in Dyson, K. (ed.) *The Euro at 10 : Europeanization, power and convergence*, Oxford: Oxford University Press, pp. 87–107.

Marx, K. (1973 [1857]) *The Grundrisse*, Harmondsworth: Penguin.

—— (1978 [1885]) *Capital: A Critique of Political Economy* (Volume Three), translated by David Fernbach, London: Penguin.

—— (1990 [1867]) *Capital: A Critique of Political Economy* (Volume One), translated by David Fernbach, London: Penguin.

—— (1991 [1894]) *Capital: A Critique of Political Economy* (Volume Three), translated by David Fernbach, London: Penguin.

McCreevy, C. (2006) 'Recent regulatory and structural developments in the EU financial sector', *2 EU-China Dialogue on Macroeconomic and Financial Regulatory Issues Beijing*. <http://europa.eu.int/rapid/pressReleasesAction.do?reference=SPEECH/06/303andformat=HTMLandaged=0andlanguage=ENandguiLanguage=en> (accessed 17 May 2006).

McMichael, P. (1990) 'Incorporating comparison within a world-historical perspective: an alternative comparative method', *American Sociological Review* 55(3): 385–97.

Menz, G. (2005) *Varieties of Capitalism and Europeanization: National response strategies to the Single European Market*, Oxford: Oxford University Press.

Messerlin, P. (2002) *Niveau et Cout du Protectionnisme Européen. Économie internationale* 89–90, pp. 19–38. <http://www.cepii.fr/francgraph/ publications/ecointern/rev8990/rev8990messerlin.pdf> (accessed 7 February 2006).

Mittelman, J. and Chin, C. (2005) 'Conceptualising resistance to globalization', in Amoore, L. (ed.) *The Global Resistance Reader*, London: Routledge.

Moloney, N. (2003) 'The Lamfalussy Legislative Model: a new era for the EC securities and investment services regime,' *International and Comparative Law Quarterly* 52 (2): 509–20.

Montgomerie, J. and Williams, K. (2009) 'Financialised capitalism: after the crisis and beyond neoliberalism', *Competition and Change* 13(2): 99–107.

Moran, M. (1991) *The Politics of the Financial Services Revolution: The USA, UK and Japan*, Basingstoke: Macmillan.

—— (1994) 'The state and the financial services revolution: a comparative analysis', *West European Politics* 17(3):158–77.

—— (2002) 'Politics, banks and financial market governance in the Euro-zone', in Dyson, K. (ed) *European States and the Euro: Europeanization, variation, and convergence*, Oxford: Oxford University Press, pp. 257–77.

Moravscik, A. (1998) *The Choice for Europe: Social purpose and state power from Messina to Maastricht*. Ithaca, NY: Cornell University Press.

Morin, F. (2000) 'A transformation in the French model of shareholding and management', *Economy and Society* 29(1): 36–53.

Morton, A.D. (2003) 'The social function of Carlos Fuentes: a critical intellectual or in the "shadow of the state"?', *Bulletin of Latin American Research* 22(1): 27–51.

—— (2006) 'The grimly comic riddle of hegemony in IPE: where is class struggle?,' *Politics* 26(1): 62–72.

—— (2007) 'Unquestioned answers/unanswered questions in IPE: a rejoinder to "non-Marxist" historical materialism', Debate in *Politics* 27(2): 132–36.

Mügge, D. (2008) 'Private–public puzzles: inter-firm competition and transnational private regulation', *New Political Economy* 11(2): 177–200.

New York Times (5 March 2008) '*Filings for bankruptcy up 18% in February*'. <http://www.nytimes.com/2008/03/05/business/05bankruptcy.html> (accessed 11 November 2008).

NIESR (2004) *Annual Report* <http://www.niesr.ac.uk/pdf/AR–2004.pdf> (accessed 1 November 2005).

—— (2007) *NIESR website* (various links) <www.niesr.ac.uk/> (accessed 30 August 2005).

OECD (2000) *Economic Survey – France 2000, assessment and recommendations*, http://www.oecd.org/home/0,2987,en_2649_201185_1_1_1_1_1,00.html (accessed 2 October 2007).

—— (2009) *OECD national statistics* <http://www.oecd.org/statsportal/0,3352,en_2825_293564_1_1_1_1_1,00.html>(accessed 26 November 2008).

Offe (1985) Challenging the boundaries of traditional politics: the contemporary challenge of social movements', *Social Research* 52(4): 817–68.

Ohmae, K. (1990) *The Borderless World: Power and strategy in the interlinked economy*, New York: Harper.

Overbeek, H. (1980) 'Finance capital and the crisis in Britain,' *Capital and Class* 11: 99–120.

—— (1990) *Global Capitalism and National Decline: the Thatcher decade in perspective*, London: Unwin Hyman.

—— (2000) 'Transnational historical materialism', in Palan, R. (ed.) *Global Political Economy: Contemporary theories*, London: Routledge, pp. 168–83.

—— (2003) *The Political Economy of European Unemployment*, London: Routledge.

—— (2004) 'Transnational class formation and concepts of control: towards a genealogy of the Amsterdam Project in international political economy', *Journal of International Relations and Development* 7: 113–41.

Overbeek, H. and van der Pijl, K. (1993) 'Restructuring capital and restructuring hegemony: neo-liberalism and the unmaking of the post-war order', in Overbeek, H. (ed.) *Restructuring Hegemony in the Global Political Economy: The rise of transnational neo-liberalism in the 1980s*, London: Routledge, pp. 1–27.

Overbeek, H., van Apeldoorn, B. and Nölke, A. (2007) *The Transnational Politics of Corporate Governance Regulation*. London: Routledge.

Pain, N. (2002) Senior Research Fellow, NIESR: 'EMU, location and investment: some unresolved issues', speech at Conference on British Business and the Euro. 6 February 2002 <http://www.niesr.ac.uk/event/6feb02/Pain.pdf> (accessed 18 November 2005).

Pain, N. and van Welsum, D. (2002) *Financial Liberalisation, Alliance Capitalism and the Changing Structure of Financial Markets*, London: NIESR, pp. 1–25.

Parker, R. (1999) 'From national champions to small and medium-sized enterprises: changing policy emphasis in France, Germany and Sweden', *Journal of Public Policy* 19(1): 63–89.

Parsons, C. (2003) *A Certain Idea of Europe*, Ithaca, NY: Cornell University Press.

Peck, J. and Tickell, A. (2002) 'Neoliberalizing space,' *Antipode* 34(3): 380–404.

Phillips, N. (2009) 'The slow death of pluralism', *Review of International Political Economy* 16(1): 85–94.

Polanyi, K. (2001 [1944]) *The Great Transformation: The political and economic origins of our time* (Third edition), Boston: Beacon Press.

Polsby, N. (1983) *Consequences of Party Reform*, Oxford: Oxford University Press.

Popper, K. (1963) *Conjectures and Refutations: The growth of scientific knowledge*, London: Routledge.

Poulantzas, N. (1973) *Political Power and Social Classes*, London: Sheed & Ward.

—— (1978) *State, Power, Socialism*, translated by Patrick Camiller, London: Verso.

Quaglia, L. (2007) 'The politics of financial service regulation and supervision reform in the European Union', *European Journal of Political Research* 46(2): 269–90.

—— (2008) 'Setting the pace? Private financial interests and European financial market integration', *British Journal of Politics and International Relations* 10(1): 46–64.

RBS (2003) Response to CP189. Personal correspondence with Simon Hills (BBA, Director) (16 April).

—— (2004) *Annual Report* <http://www.shareholder.com/Shared/DynamicDoc/ rbs/813/RBS_Group_Accounts_2004.pdf> (accessed 12 January 2007).

—— (February 2004) *CESR's Call for Evidence: Provisional mandates financial instruments markets directive response of the Royal Bank of Scotland Group of companies.* <http://www.cesr-eu.org/> (accessed 15 April 2005).

Reberioux, A. (2002) 'European styles of corporate governance at the crossroads', *Journal of Common Market Studies* 40(1): 111–34.

Rees, R. (2009) Email correspondence (4 March) with Professor Ray Rees (Director, CESifo).

Richardson, J. (2000) 'Government, interest groups and policy change', *Political Studies* 48(5): 1006–25.

Robinson, W. (2004) *A Theory of Global Capitalism: Production, class, and. state in a transnational world*, Baltimore: Johns Hopkins University Press.

Robinson, W. and Harris, J. (2000) 'Towards a global ruling class? Globalization and the transnational capitalist class', *Science and Society* 64(1): 11–54.

Ruggie, J. (1982) 'International regimes, transactions, and change: embedded liberalism in the postwar economic order', *International Organization* 36(2): 379–415.

Scharpf, F. (2000) 'Economic changes, vulnerabilities and institutional capabilities', in Scharpf, F. and Schmidt, V. (eds) *Welfare and Work in the Open Economy*, Oxford: Oxford University Press, pp. 21–124.

Schmidt, V. (1996) *From State to Market? The transformation of French business and government*, Cambridge: Cambridge University Press.

—— (2002) *The Futures of European Capitalism*, Oxford: Oxford University Press.

Schularick, M. and Steger, T.M. (2006) 'Does financial integration spur economic growth? New evidence from the first era of financial globalization', *CESifo Working Paper No. 1691 Category 5: Fiscal Policy, Macroeconomics and Growth.* <http://www.cesifo-group.de/pls/guestci/download/CESifo%20Working%20Papers%202006/CESifo%20Working%20Papers%20March%202006/cesifo1_wp1691.pdf> (accessed 20 June 2006).

Seabrooke, L. (2007) 'Varieties of economic constructivism in political economy: Uncertain times call for disparate measures', *Review of International Political Economy* 14(2): 371–85.

Sharman, J.C. (2006) *Havens in a Storm*, Ithaca, NY: Cornell University Press.

Shields, S. (2001) 'Globalisation and Poland: transnational social forces and the Polish transition to a market economy', unpublished PhD thesis, University of Wales, Aberystwyth.

—— (2006) 'Historicizing transition: the Polish political economy in a period of global structural change – Eastern Central Europe's passive revolution?' *International Politics* 43(4): 474–99.

—— (2008) 'How the East was won: globalisation, transnational social forces and Poland's transition to a market economy', *Global Society* 22(4): 445–68.

—— (2011) *The International Political Economy of Transition: Transnational social forces and Eastern Central Europe's transformation*, London: Routledge.

Shonfield, A. (1965) *Modern Capitalism: The changing balance of public and private power*, London: Oxford University Press.

Sinn, H.W. (2006) *CESIfo Forum.* <http://www.cesifo-group.de/pls/ guestci/download/ CESifo%20Forum%202005/CESifo%20Forum%202/2005/forum2–05-introduction–3.pdf> (accessed 30th June 2006)

Sklair, L. (2001) *The Transnational Capitalist Class*, Oxford: Blackwell.

Smith, S. (1996) 'Positivism and beyond,' in Steve Smith, Ken Booth and Marysia Zalewski (eds) *International Theory: Positivism and beyond*, Cambridge: Cambridge University Press, pp. 11–38.

Société Générale (2005) *Annual Report* <http://www.socgen.com/sg/file/fichierig/documentIG_5197/ra2005-en.pdf> (accessed 17 January 2007).

Solow, Robert (1956) 'A contribution to the theory of economic growth', *Quarterly Journal of Economics* 70 (1): 65–94.

Steil, B. (1995) *Illusions of Liberalization: Securities regulation in Japan and the EC*, London: The Royal Institute of International Affairs (Chatham House).

Strange, S. (1996) *The Retreat of the State: The diffusion of power in the world economy*, Cambridge: Cambridge University Press.

Streeck, W. (1983) 'Between pluralism and corporatism: German business associations and the state', *Journal of Public Policy* 3(3): 265–84.

—— (1997) 'German capitalism: does it exist? Can it survive?', in Crouch, C. and Streeck, W. (eds) *Political Economy of Modern Capitalism: Mapping Convergence and Diversity*, London: Sage, pp. 33–54.

Streeck, W. and Thelen, K. (eds) (2005) *Beyond Continuity: Institutional change in advanced political economies*, Oxford: Oxford University Press.

Swyngedouw, E. (2004) 'Globalisation or "Glocalisation"? Networks, Territories and Rescaling', *Cambridge Review of International Affairs* 17(1): 25–48.

Teschke, B. (2003) *The Myth of 1648: Class, geopolitics and the making of modern international relations*, London: Verso.

Thunert, M. (2004) 'Think tanks in Germany', in Stone, D. and Denham, A. (eds) *Think Tank Traditions: Policy research and the politics of ideas*, Manchester: Manchester University Press, pp. 71–88.

Tornell, A. and Westermann, F. (2004) 'The positive link between financial liberalization, growth and crises', *CESIfo Working Paper No. 1164 Category 5: Fiscal Policy, Macroeconomics and Growth*. March 2004. <http://www.cesifo-group.de/pls/guestci/download/CESifo%20Working%20Papers%202004/CESifo%20Working%20Papers%20March%202004/cesifo1_wp1164.pdf> (accessed 20 June 2006), pp. 1–53.

UBS (2005) *Annual Report* <http://www.ubs.com/1/e/investors/annual_reporting2005/financial_report/0006.html> (accessed 12 January 2007).

Underhill, G. (1997) 'The making of the European Financial Area: global market integration and the EU Single Market for financial services', in Geoffrey Underhill (ed.) *The New World Order in International Finance*, Basingstoke: Macmillan, pp. 101–23.

Useem, M. (1984) *The Inner Circle: Large Corporations and the Rise of Business Political Activity*, New York: Oxford University Press.

Van Apeldoorn, B. (2002) *Transnational Capitalism and the Struggle Over European Integration*, London: Routledge.

Van Apeldoorn, B. and Horn, L. (2007) 'The transformation of corporate governance regulation in the European Union: from harmonization to marketization', in Overbeek, H., van Apeldoorn, B. and Nölke, A. (eds) *The Transnational Politics of Corporate Governance Regulation*, London: Routledge, pp. 76–97.

Van der Pijl, K. (1984) *The Making of an Atlantic Ruling Class*, London: Verso.

—— (1998) *Transnational Classes and International Relations*, London: Routledge.

—— (2004) 'Two faces of the transnational cadre under neo-liberalism', *Journal of International Relations and Development* 7: 177–207.

—— (2006) 'A Lockean Europe?', *New Left Review* (37): 9–37.

van Overtveldt, J. (2007) *The Chicago School: How the University of Chicago assembled the thinkers who revolutionised economics and business*, Evanston, IL: Agate.

Vogel, D. (1996) *Kindred Stranger: The uneasy relationship between politics and business in America*, Princeton, NJ: Princeton University Press.

Webb, M. (1994) 'Capital mobility and the possibilities for international policy coordination', *Policy Sciences* 27(4): 395–423.

Weber, C. (1994) 'Good girls, little girls, and bad girls: male paranoia in Robert Keohane's critique of feminist International Relations', *Millennium* 23(2): 337–49.

Weber, Manfred (2002) 'The German banking market: I. Structural change', in *Die Bank: Zeitschrift für Bankpolitik und Praxis.* http://www.die-bank.de/index.asp?issue= 062002&channel=121010&art=190 (accessed 23 August 2005).

Wendt, A. (1992) 'Anarchy is what states make of it: the social construction of power politics', *International Organization* 46(2): 391–425.

—— (2001) 'What is International Relations for? Notes towards a postcritical view', in Wyn Jones, R. (ed.) *Critical Theory and World Politics*, Boulder, CO: Lynne Rienner, pp. 205–24.

Wever, K. and Allen, C. (1993) 'The financial system and corporate governance in Germany: institutions and the diffusion of innovations', *Journal of Public Policy* 13(2): 183–202.

Wilson, F. (1983) 'French interest group politics: pluralist or neocorporatist?', *American Political Science Review* 77(4): 895–910.

Worth, O. (2008) *Hegemony, International Political Economy and Post-Communist Russia*, Aldershot: Ashgate.

Wyplosz, C. (1998) http://www.wyplosz.eu/fichier/fondad.pdf (accessed 9 February 2009).

—— (2007) *Professor Charles Wyplosz homepage* <http://hei.unige.ch/sections/ec/ faculty/profile/wyplosz.html> (accessed 8 August 2007).

Young, A. (2005) 'The single market: a new approach to policy,' in Wallace, H., Wallace, W. and Pollack, M. (eds) *Policy-making in the European Union*, (Fifth edition), Oxford: Oxford University Press, pp. 93–112.

ZKA (August 2005) *Comments of the Zentraler Kreditausschuss on Working Document ESC/20/2005-rev 1 on implementing measures for articles 22(2), 27 to 30, 40 and 44 to 45 of Directive 2004/39/EC of the European Parliament and of the Council.* <http://www.bankenverband.de/pic/artikelpic/082005 /sp0508_vw_zka-finanzinstr_ en.pdf> (accessed 2 September 2005).

Zysman, J. (1983) *Governments, Markets and Growth: Financial systems and the politics of industrial change*, Ithaca, NY: Cornell University Press.

Index

Lightning Source UK Ltd.
Milton Keynes UK
UKHW020147060321
379882UK00003B/1060